OUT OF THE FR

Chapter One.

The early morning sun slowly drifting through the half drawn curtains, settles on a gold tube of lipstick placed precariously on the mantelpiece, coupled with a bottle of ruby red cough mixture, a concoction of the two were soon to be consumed.

Awakening once again in a bedroom of my Aunt Hilda's council house situated in the heart of Wythenshawe, Manchester, I could familiarise myself with its surroundings even at the tender age of two, for it was a room I was slowly becoming accustomed. James my elder brother of six years and whose room I was sharing had vacated his bed long since and disappeared downstairs.

It was a warm August morning and all was quiet except for the gentle ticking sound of the clock. Standing in my cot quite close to the mantelpiece restless yet somewhat intrigued by the gleaming tube, I stretched a little further. Boredom had set in slightly and patience was wearing thin, waiting for mother to enter the room with some milk and biscuits to quench my thirst and take away the hunger. My tiny hand was stretched to its outer limit - almost there.

My mother (Winnifred) a battered wife victim was taking refuge yet again, at my Aunt's home. She had recently separated from my father (Jimmy) after eight years of domestic violence but decided to remain in the marital home for she was again heavily pregnant with their fourth child due at any time, but my father wouldn't leave her in peace, even though they were legally separated and after weekend bouts of heavy drinking he would return to the home, terrifying her time and again. Fearing for the safety of her unborn child she decided to move in with her eldest sister.

In my early twenties, I too would become a battered wife victim, for history was to repeat itself.

1

Hungry and thirsty yet fascinated by the gleaming tube of lipstick reflecting in the sun I grasped the shimmering object and with delight took off the top and hungrily ate the waxy contents. The sun warmed cough mixture was soon to follow and flowed down into my hungry unsuspecting stomach.

'Wake up Veronica!' The smiling doctor looked into my eyes, while shaking my arm gently.
'She'll live, but we'll keep her in for observation over night.' The tired doctor concentrated his attention on the dark navy blue eyes of my Aunt. 'Never leave medicine in the reach of children and the lipstick could have choked her! So be more careful in the future.' Aunt was getting agitated.
'I didn't know she could reach the mantelpiece from her cot!' The doctor looked somewhat annoyed.
'Please don't raise your voice to me you will alarm the child!' He continued to study the notes in his file without as much as a second glance in her direction and then quietly left the cubicle. Aunt rolled her eyes to the ceiling in annoyance as she appeared to be taking the wrath for the accident and was none too pleased.
'Who does he think he's talkin' to? He must think I've got eyes in the back of me bleedin' 'ed and it's no use cryin' Winnie, 'cos It's your fault the accident 'appened' in the first place, yer were stupid enough to leave your makeup and medicine in easy reach of the kid.' Mother continued to cry, which annoyed Aunt even more.
'Oh stop cryin' our Winnie. Come on we might as well go, there's nothing more we can do 'ere, today.'

Our James had been living with my Aunt Hilda and Uncle Bob, for two years. It was an arrangement that suited both sisters, for Aunt was childless, so it was nice having her nephew around to keep her company and to take care of, It was also a great help to mother, as her family had continued to increase over the years and she'd found it difficult to cope. Aunt's home was becoming quite cramped, with the added addition of, my mother, my elder sister Ann, and myself.

Early hours of the18th.of September 1949, my brother Geoffrey was born, leaving mother little option but to push the issue with the council to be re-housed quickly. Having put her name down on the council waiting list for the Wythenshawe area, in previous years, she was soon found suitable accommodation. Through the violent circumstances she had endured in the past she also wanted to move far away as possible and make a fresh new start.

We eventually moved into our new three bed-roomed house situated on Brookcot Road not far from Aunts home on Holly Hedge Road.

Mother had now separated from father for over six months, she was managing nicely and we finally settled down to our quiet, violent free way of life. Mother started a job as a child-minder in the area and with the extra money earned, enabled her to buy some new furniture on a weekly credit system, making our home nice and comfy for the first time.

Some month's later my father visited us, he was supposedly missing his family, the visits didn't last long though for he was uncertain of mother's feelings towards him through their long months of separation. We were quite young at that time and didn't know much about him so were not prepared for the sudden changes in our lives, which was about to occur in the very near future.

It was the early 1950s poverty was rife with rationing still in full force. My mother would buy all her rations every weekend and keep them all in the kitchen cupboard. I can remember quite vividly waking early one morning while everyone else slept in. I made my way down stairs and opened the sideboard cupboard for a biscuit. Seeing the flour, sugar and eggs, I decided to mix them in a bowl and make a cake, after watching Aunt baking cakes so often, of course there was a dreadful mess to say the least, as well as using up all mothers weekly rations. So engrossed in my new found activity, I got such a shock on hearing mother's shrieks of horror.

3

'O my god! What the hell have you done? My rations for the week are completely wasted. How on earth will I manage till the end of the week? Get up stairs! Hurry up, before I give you a damned good hiding'

Not understanding the reason for her sudden outburst of temper I quickly made my way towards the staircase. As she set about cleaning up the mess there was a knock on the front door she cleaned her tearstained face on her nightdress and answered it gingerly as she was not dressed for visitors at such an early hour. It just happened to be my father he was working in the area doing some painting and decorating, so decided to call in for a cuppa. Mother seemed reluctant to let him in at first but after a few moments she allowed him to step inside.

Feeling a little afraid for the trouble I'd caused, I gauged his response while peering through the staircase banister and quietly observed his nonchalant manner towards all the kerfuffle. Waiting for the right moment I ran down stairs to greet him, he appeared happy to see me as he picked me up and swung me round.

'What ave' yer been up to today lady?'' He asked, as he took a clean hanky from his paint stained overalls and cleaned my sticky hands. After putting me down, they set about cleaning and in no time at all they'd cleaned up the awful sticky mess. My father suddenly weighed up the situation around him for some moments, before talking to my mother.

'Don't worry Winnie! I'll get the food replaced today, and you little monkey, will have to be cleaned up.' Being given a wash in the kitchen sink then some fresh clothes to wear, I joined the rest of my siblings for breakfast. He then proceeded to comfort mother till she stopped crying. It was the first time I'd witnessed a display of affection between my parents and sadly, it was to be the last. Later that same day father called with the replaced rations as promised, so giving him the opportunity to get one foot in the door (so to speak).

4

Some months later a dreadful happening took place, which was to be a turning point in my life.

Mother had taken Geoffrey with her to the corner shop so leaving me asleep in the bed room. We had a pet Alsatian bitch named Judy and mother loved her and treated her like one of the family.

Judy was locked in the kitchen while mother went on her errand but somehow Judy managed to open the bedroom door with her paws, and must have been awaiting her chance to catch me alone. Leaping into the bedroom she savagely attacked me by grabbing my left arm, dragging me into the kitchen and mauling me, causing severe damage, as she tore the skin from under both my eyes and leaving my left arm, almost severed.

Mother never being a gossip, purchased a few items from the corner shop and came home immediately, but the sight that met her as she opened the door, was horrific. Blood streamed fro m my face and my left arm. As she started to scream for help, Judy looked on sheepishly then dived for cover under the kitchen table.

The next -door neighbour, on hearing the screams rushed in to help and called an ambulance and the police. They soon arrived but not before Aunt Hilda, who had decided to visit us that morning, before her committee meeting of the week. .

Wherever she lived total involvement on her committee, reached a significant scale for she always took a keen interest in the community and fighting for women's rights, was always top of her agenda.

It always amazed mother how Aunt managed to be elected, as she was quite rough and ready, her language left a lot to be desired too, although she was clever enough not to use it at a meeting.

'Where's that bleedin Judy? I'll kill the bleedin' bitch!'
Seeing Judy cowering under the table, she rushed after her waving a hammer she'd taken from the garden shed.

'Come 'ere yer bastard! Yer don't deserve to live after what you've just done!"

Mother was beside herself and tried to retrieve the hammer, but to no avail, as Aunt had lost her temper and the situation was getting out of control.

'I told yer Winnie! To get rid of Judy after Geoffrey was born didn't I! If you'd done as I said this would never 'ave come about. You've fussed over that Judy far too much in the past, for my likin'.'

The police soon intervened by trying their best to calm Aunt down and eventually retrieving the hammer from her grasp. Mother was in a state of shock after the horrific attack, but even more so, when her beloved Judy was finally taken away and put to sleep.

The injuries I sustained were quite serious, receiving thirty stitches in all and having to stay in hospital for days. Physically, the scars remain with me, today.

Aunt offered to look after me when I came home from hospital, as mother found it increasingly difficult to manage, she was suffering from traumatic postnatal depression after the birth of our Geoffrey, so causing her to have very little interest in her work and eventually losing her job.

I moved into my Aunt's home soon after, and found it to be a completely new experience, for she kept an orderly home with a different chore set out for each day of the week. It was also very comfortable, for it was well furnished and had wall, to wall, carpeting.

My first awareness of stepping into her home was the wonderful smell of lavender polish, combined with scented soap, for it was far more refreshing than stale cigarette smoke, which I'd become accustomed to at home. For as young as you are, pleasant fragrances are to be remembered captured forever, in that moment in time. Fresh flowers were also evident on top of a white- laced cloth, covering an oak dining table, in the front room. The sound of a radio could also be heard, making it feel even more homely and inviting.

I had my own bedroom which was also nicely furnished and an unusual table lamp in the form of the three bears which stood on the bedside table which I frequently switched on and off, being fascinated by the pink light. I was told off though for this extravagant amusement for wasting the electricity. The bed was unbelievably comfortable, with bedding of pure white linen and the cover was of a beautiful patchwork design.

Under the bed were kept a pair of fluffy slippers, and slipping my feet into them each morning felt great. The following day I was taken into town and bought a new wardrobe full of clothes.

Aunt was good to me, she cared and was always there to comfort and support me. I loved her with my whole being for over the years she became my surrogate mother. She was an attractive woman but dressed very matronly and a hint of lavender scent was always evident on her clothing. To this day, if I smell the scent I am assailed by memories. Sometimes I'd brush her brown curly hair, it smelt of shampoo, and when brushed, it would spring back into beautiful waves, she also had a generous smile and a good nature, but not to be crossed, which I was very soon to discover.

I lived there quite happily, for about a year until mother decided she wanted me to return home. Her and my father had reconciled much to Aunt's disapproval and was proven right yet again, regarding mother's inane decision. For it was a case of, out of the frying pan into the fire, so to speak.

'I can't believe you can be so stupid, Winnie! Tekin' Jimmy back after all you've been through. You've got a nice comfortable 'ome 'ere, and you'll lose it all if yer not careful, because he won't change for the better, that's for sure.'

Mother blew her cigarette smoke towards the yellow tarnished ceiling on answering.

'Mind your own business, our Hilda! I'm quite aware of the pitfalls, and can assure you they won't occur again and besides, I can take care of myself. Thank you very much!"

'Why yer ungrateful get! Who did you come runnin' to whenever he beats yer up? Me! That's who! You've never valued my opinion Winnie, and I'm just wasting my bleeedin' time as always, it's like talkin' to a brick wall these days.' She sighed heavily while standing up to put on her coat.

'Anyway, I'm goin' 'ome! I'm fed up with the lot of it.'

'Hilda! If you'll just listen to me and let me explain. Jimmy's changed for the better and besides, we've both got a new job. He's promised to give up drinking and gambling too. That's another reason for wanting our Veronica back, and he thinks we should start again, as one happy family.' Aunt tied a headscarf around her head, while making her way to the door.

' appy families- my arse!" Well don't say I didn't warn yer' and if yer won't let me tek' Veronica, back 'ome with me now, don't ask me to 'ave her back, in a few weeks, when you've decided yer can't cope.'

So I was returned to my parents. It seemed strange sharing a bedroom again and having siblings to play with, it also took a long time in getting to know my father.

A couple of weeks later while father was out working, mother busied herself tidying the back garden. Aunt was visiting and making a cup of tea in the kitchen. Ann and my-self were playing a game of ball in the garden, when suddenly the ball got out of hand and ended up in the neighbours back garden. Mother asked for it back politely, but the neighbour, hanging out her washing at the time, threw the ball back and leaving her language a lot to be desired also.

Aunt was quick to overhear the neighbour swearing and went outside and asked the neighbour to repeat it.

'Say that agen'?' The neighbour moved closer and bellowed down Aunt's ear. 'She should stop those bleedin' kids, of 'ers, lettin' the ball, come into our garden. They should keep the bleedin' ball, in their own, for ours is nice and tidy.' Aunt turned away then rapidly made her way from the kitchen and up the stairs, while mother chased after anxiously and followed her into the bedroom.

'I don't want any trouble Hilda! I've got to live round here and would like to enjoy some peace and quiet for a bloody change.' Aunt ignored her while changing into one of mother's old frocks hanging behind the bedroom door then neatly folded her smart tweed suit over the headboard and pushed passed mother. Ignoring all

8

pleas from mother for some peace and quiet, she then made her way downstairs and into the back garden.

We stopped playing our game of ball at that moment, for the commotion before us suddenly became more interesting. Aunt called the neighbour over to the privits, the neighbour being bold as brass strode towards her, when Aunt suddenly lunged forward and literally dragged her over the privits by the shoulders, then beat the living day lights out of her.

'Tek' that yer fuckin' bitch!' Punching her in the face several times, the frightened woman did her best to retaliate, but to no avail. We all started to scream with fright as mother did her best to intervene, but Aunt only stopped beating the neighbour when she finely pleaded.

'Don't ever swear at my sister agen'! Do 'yer 'ere me? Cos' next time, I'll fuckin' fleece yer, good and proper.' She finally let go of the neighbour's hair. 'Go on! Piss off back to your own garden and sharpish!' Aunt then walked away from the petrified neighbour, totally unruffled.

Making her way upstairs, she changed back into her tweed suit and carried on with the rest of her day as if the terrifying incident had never taken place.

The neighbour decided to take Aunt to court where she was charged with assault and battery and bound over for a year to keep the peace. She eventually lost her seat on the committee too, because of the offence.

It was the first time I'd witnessed Aunts violent temper and it wasn't to be the last, as she seemed to enjoy confrontation. Although she fought for women's rights, she also liked to fight them.

She moved away from Wythenshawe soon after the court case to a new area. Langley Estate, Middleton, which resulted in her visiting far less frequently.

Mother was epileptic. It started at the age of fourteen and just after she'd started her first job, in a steel foundry. Apparently, two apprentices were fooling around one lunch break when one picked up a piece of steel and threw it intending it to hit the other. Mother got

9

caught in the cross fire and was hit about the head. Days later, she had a black out which she'd never experienced in the past and a few weeks later had an epileptic fit, which was to occur every couple of months, for the rest of her life. She always blamed the accident at the factory for her epilepsy and would recognise the symptoms when a seizure was imminent for she would feel light- headed and make her way to a chair, the room would start spinning and she would scream out loud. The tremors would start and vomit would seep from her mouth, should father be out at work, I'd run next door for a neighbour's help, they would respond quickly by thrusting a spoon in her mouth, so as not to choke on her tongue. When she came out of the seizure she would repeat her last chore or do things the wrong way round for instance, put a match in her mouth and try to light a cigarette. One particular day she'd been to the corner shop, soon after a seizure and went out shopping yet again, so purchasing the same items.

A neighbour living nearby took it upon herself though to tell the other mothers in the area, concerning mother's epilepsy. The inevitable soon happened, causing her to lose her job as a child minder.

Father wasn't pleased at being the only breadwinner again and as the family income dwindled, returned to his old ways of drinking, gambling and beating mother, which terrified us all. All of which goes to show, a leopard never changes its spots.

'Jimmy stop it your ruining our home!' I was awoken yet again by the crashing sound of crockery, together with the pathetic screams of mother. I jumped quickly from my warm bed, into the front room, and watched in horror, as father wrapped her beautiful blonde hair around his fist and bash her face against the table- top. He threw her against other parts of the furniture while reigning blows down upon her face and head. Her merciful cries for help went unaided as she crumpled to the floor in excruciating pain.

10

He then proceeded to smash more pictures and ornaments. Some of which were new, for mother had bought them with some of extra money she'd earned while working.

'Jimmy you promised you wouldn't drink or gamble! You promised, you promised!' She screamed, as blood poured from her battered nose.

'You'd drive any man to drink, yer bitch. It's always left to me as usual the responsibility of this fuckin' lot.' I quickly rushed to mother's side at this stage as she slowly slid to the floor. Father looked to me then, still full of rage while pointing a finger.

'You lady, can piss off back to Hilda's? We can't afford to feed another mouth in 'ere, seein' yer mothers not workin any more.' He suddenly stepped forward with a gesture of his hand as if to slap my face, but suddenly had second thoughts of such an atrocious action.

Bewildered, I watched him turn and walk away, as the broken glass from a picture frame crunched beneath his highly polished shoes. He roughly grabbed his overcoat off an armchair and strode out of a room he'd left in mayhem and not even caring to close the front door behind him, so letting in the cold night air.

Ann could be heard whimpering from her bedroom, she would never have got out of bed as father's violent temper petrified her. She was six years old but being of a nervous disposition would retreat into her shell whenever there was a fight until all the trouble was over. Geoffrey…Miraculously slept through it all.

Putting a thumb in my mouth, I snuggled up to mother on the floor. The fire had burned out through lack of fuel long ago, leaving the room chilly and damp. Focusing my tired eyes on the blood stained floor, a photo of a happy couple on their wedding day stared up, but was now sadly lying amongst the debris, torn and unframed. Traumatized, I finally found solace in sleep.

Awaking suddenly and seemingly to have slept for hours, I looked up to mother and watched as the blood trickled from her battered nose on to my sleeveless nightdress. I shook her arm gently and waited for some response, but there was none for she had lapsed into a state of unconsciousness. Thinking she might have died, a wave of panic suddenly engulfed me.

Treading carefully a mist the shards of broken glass, I put on my shoes and ran outside the chill of the late night air suddenly taking my breath away. Looking round for the nearest house lit up, I ran down the path and urgently knocked on the front door.

Soon a couple of neighbours were helping mother into one of their homes. She eventually became conscious as they cleaned her up then making her comfortable and warm. I was given a hot drink of cocoa in front of a welcoming fire and a cardigan put around my cold shoulders. The neighbour suggested mother should call the police and make a complaint about father's vicious attack, but she wouldn't hear of it.

In those days it was practically unheard of, taking your spouse to court, for domestic violence was firmly kept behind closed doors. She had escaped the violence at one time in her life, but why she ever took him back, only she will never know. The neighbours helped to sweep up the mess in our home, and once mother was feeling better we eventually went to bed and thankful to be under the covers to leave the terror of the night behind, until the next time.

In the months ahead, mother persevered and accepted quietly, without a fight, a returned performance of father's old ways. Seemingly there was no escape from her violent way of life, for she couldn't tell my Aunt, as it would have been a case of. 'I told you so.'

Our standard of living gradually dropped below the poverty line and the electricity supply was soon cut off. Candles dotted around the house soon became a familiar scene. I thought it looked quite magical, as we watched the shadows dancing on the walls and played games, imitating animal figures with our hands and making hours of entertainment. Mother had different views on the matter of course, as she tried her best to fry food each night on a small gas ring, while the flicker of a candle- light hovered over.

Father would even fiddle the gas meter by cutting round a shilling piece with two pieces of thick cardboard then taping them

12

together. The exact weight would then serve its purpose in the meter.

When the gasman called to empty the meter and give the customer their quarterly rebate, mother's usually consisted of £2 of cardboard cut outs. She decided to keep some back for her own use for whenever she had no money, at least there was still use of the gas ring to cook on.

Inevitably the furniture was repossessed and we watched from the window as the furniture was carried out into the front garden for all to see then put into the awaiting furniture van. Mother sat down on the stairs after they'd gone and wept buckets. Our comfortable seating was soon reduced to orange boxes which were covered with old curtain material, to make them look more presentable, and comfortable to sit on.

Though father was working he gave very little money to mother to support us, for most of it dissipated on drink and gambling.

Deprived of shoes and clothes, but more importantly food, for very little was put on the table at that time, such circumstances resulted in us all becoming malnourished, and our way of life stayed pretty much the same throughout the following months.

Chapter Two.

Nine months on, and it was my 5th birthday. Crayon pencils and some books were given as a present, from my mother which I shared with Ann and Geoffrey. As we crayoned in the pictures mother listened to a play on the radio and as father was out at work for the day, all was nice and peaceful.

The peace was soon interrupted though by a knock at the front door, mother went to answer it and surprise, my Aunt followed her in. She came into the front room carrying some presents and as always wearing a lovely smile.

'Happy Birthday" Aunt gave me a peck on the cheek, and handed me a present, it was a baby doll so I named him (Rodney). He was to stay by my side for many years for he was taken everywhere. Hilda took the cup of tea, mother handed to her, while observing me carefully.

'Whatever is the matter with Veronica, Winnie? She looks so thin these days, like something out of a P.O.W. camp, and ave yer taken her to the doctors lately, to find out why she is so under weight?'

'Not to worry Hilda, she's fine! She always looks the same but nonetheless, I did take her and he prescribed a course of iron tablets, but they don't seem to have taken effect yet as her appetite still hasn't picked up.'

'I've been thinking Winnie. I wouldn't mind looking after her for a while if that's all right, just ask your Jimmy when he comes ome from work "

Within hours I was happily making the journey back to the home I loved. Father was also pleased as there'd be one less mouth to feed in the family.

Arriving at Aunts, my brother James opened the front door and was pleased to see me as we always got on fine together. He'd mend my toys if they were broken and would stand my corner, should I be in any trouble outside. But apart from that, we didn't mix, because of our age difference.

Life took on a regular routine, as I settled in my new school, St Mary's. The uniform was quite smart, consisting of two colours, navy blue and yellow. I made some nice school friends, and interest in my schoolwork progressed, and because of a healthy diet, I started to put on some weight.

My favourite subject was English, although one particular subject I disliked was maths and just couldn't get it right. Deciding one day to miss the dreadful subject, I told a white lie. Telling Aunt, it was a holy day so there would be no school for the day, she was Church of England and was not so well informed of such occasions. It was a lovely warm sunny day so I sat in the garden reading and enjoying the sunshine. Aunt was getting ready to go shopping alone which seemed unusual as she always took me along.

'I won't be to long luv! I'm just going to do some shopping! I'll be about an hour.'

While she was gone, writing my absentee note seemed a good idea and writing it time and again to make it look similar to her handwriting, but in no time at all she'd returned and looking not so pleased as she charged through the back garden gate. I quickly tried to shove the written absentee note under the deckchair, but to no avail.

'Wait till I get my bleedin' ands on yer, lieing to me about the school holyday and trying to forge my signature too. Put your uniform on, I'm tekin yer into school to see Mr Brogan, I had an idea you weren't telling the truth so I checked up on it.'

After a damned good hiding, I reluctantly went into school and had to apologise to the headmaster. I vowed never to play truant again for the incident taught me a lesson, but not quite enough.

Playing truant became a habit once again in my early teens, so resulting in no serious academics and no qualifications on leaving school at fifteen, and of course regretting every minute much later in life.

Summer holidays were soon upon us, I spent quite a lot of time with Kate, my friend from next door. She called round one morning suggesting we go swimming for the day.

'You only need two shillings and it will pay your bus fare too! I took my money out of my mum's purse.' She announced casually.

'Well I wouldn't dare! Aunt would do her nut if I even thought about it, I have two shillings and that's all, each week" Kate became more interested at this stage.

'Does your Aunt keep money anywhere else in the house?' I pondered for a moment.

'She keeps some in the sideboard but I'm not sure what it's for.' She looked thoughtful, for a moment.

'Borrow something out of that then and put it back when you get your spends at weekend, I bet your Aunt won't find out.'

And so it was, for each week of the summer holidays for a month, I borrowed two shillings out of the top draw.

The fourth week of borrowing the money, we were on our way to the swimming baths when I noticed the inside of my fingers turning blue. Kate thought I'd been near some blue paint and to ask my Aunt when we return home for some turpentine to remove it.

That evening sat around the dinner table when I was suddenly aware of being the focus of attention. Aunt looked across the table, her dark navy blue eyes piercing, making me feel more uncomfortable by the minute.

"There is something strange going on lately! Money is going missing out of the draw in the front room, then replaced at weekend.' We looked across the table from one to another as she continued.

'Our James wouldn't touch any money on me! Would yer luv, and as Its Uncle Bobs bus fares and dinner money to work- well need I say more. So all hands on the table, and whoever's got blue finger tips, is the culprit.' I suddenly realised, why my fingers were blue and shamefully put them on the table, as they suddenly clashed with my plum coloured face.

'I bleedin'knew it was you, she shouted loudly, while standing up quickly and giving me an almighty crack across the ears.

'Well I'll teach yer not to tek' any money on me agen'. I won't tolerate it. Do yer 'ere' me? Yer can go to your room for a week, and see if that'll make yer see some sense, and yer won't bother with that Kate agen' either, 'cos she's obviously the instigator in all this. I've a good mind to ave' a word with her mother too and get it all out in the open once and for all. She thinks her daughter is some sort of angel, all that butter wouldn't melt in her mouth, shite! The woman makes me bleedin' sick.'

Uncle Bob finally calmed her down that evening, trying to explain. It wasn't fair to go blaming Kate, for I had a mind of my own and should have known the difference between right and wrong.

Spending most of the week in my room, reading and painting, I decided to paint in the picture for the weekly competition in the local Advertiser, which was delivered each Wednesday. The following weekend, I found I'd won the competition, so receiving a postal order for 2/6. It made me feel better so spending it on some chocolates for Aunt and trying to make up for the wrong I'd done. Apparently the weeks building up to me being found out, Aunt had put some blue powdered dye in the draw that day, when she realised what I was up to, and making sure to nip it in the bud before it became too serious. It certainly gave me a scare and I never touched anything on her, again.

Three weeks into the school holidays and Aunt took me on my first holiday to Wales. We were all staying in a caravan on a holiday camp sight, and seeing the beach for the first time was a unique experience for me. We'd had two glorious days of sunshine and today we were going to the beach for a picnic. I was to have a ride on a donkey and taste my first Candy Floss.

We'd just finished our breakfast and Aunt noticed there was very little water left in the buckets, so deciding we'd go to the stop- tap first, before making our way to the beach.

'Bob were just going for some water.'

17

'Okay luv, I'll finish the washing up with the water that's left over then settle down and read the morning paper.'

'Veronica, pass us the buckets luv' and we'll get there early before the queue gets too long.' I skipped next to Aunt as we walked the distance, feeling really happy, as the world was for once a beautiful place to live.

As we approached the stop-tap, three ladies stood before us and we joined the queue. A lady arrived and stood in front of us, she started chatting to the lady next to her so Aunt waited a bit then expected her to move away but she made herself, comfortable in the queue. Aunt looked puzzled and tapped her on the shoulder.

'Excuse me! What do yer think yer doin,' standin' in front of me?' The woman turned around, looking a little perplexed.

'I'm sorry luv!' I forgot my purse, so I nipped back to the caravan for it. Our Doris minded my place for me and I'm back, as yer can see.'

'Well I've been standing 'ere ages! You've lost yer place, so get to the back of the queue.' The woman coloured slightly.

'I don't think yer quite 'erd me properly luv!'' I've already explained. I went for my purse because I forgot it. I'm back and I'm certainly, not movin.'' Aunt tapped her shoulder yet again.

'Well I don't think yer quite 'erd me, either. Get to the back of the queue, or else!'' The small plump woman standing next to her sister pointed a finger.

'Our Gladys won't be intimidated by the likes of you, or anyone else, for that matter. She's not afraid of anyone, are you are Gladys?'

'I'm certainly not!' Gladys stood her ground.

'We've been coming to this holiday camp, every two week, for twenty years. We've stood at this stop- tap twice a day and never a spot of bother, ave we our Doris?' Doris was looking decidedly uncomfortable at this stage under aunts piercing gaze.

'Never, in all our born days, we avn't' Aunt stared at Gladys with her dark navy blue eyes. 'Get to the back of the queue! I'm warnin yer.'

My heart was starting to sink as I looked at one angry woman to the other. Gone from my mind, two glorious happy sunshine days to be replaced with the fear of my knowing the extreme violence my Aunt was capable of, when losing her uncontrollable bad temper.

'Please Auntie? Let her go in front of us, I want to go to the beach, to make sand-pies and have my candyfloss.'… 'Shut up you and you, missus had better move now!" Gladys folded her arms tightly over her well endowed, breasts.

'I'm not bleedin' movin' cos' yer nothin' but a bitch, and a trouble maker!"

Soon a crowd had gathered round, clearly amused and intrigued by the argument, which was about to erupt at any moment, some even started to goad them on.

'Go on, let er' go first! Go on!' The inevitable was soon to happen and the fight was on.

Doris had filled her bucket with water and soon it was Aunt's turn. Her bucket was under the stop- tap, and filling up fast. Gladys started to pull at Aunts dress then the back of her hair, pulling it with all her strength, causing Aunt to scream out in excruciating pain. Soon the water was brimming over the top of Aunts bucket, as she suddenly retaliated, throwing the icy cold water over Gladys's head.

'Tek' that yer fuckin' bitch! I'll fuckin', kill yer.' All hell was let loose, it was mayhem. Women and children scattered in all directions, as icy cold water splashed everywhere. The empty bucket was finally plonked over the top of Gladys's head as she was mercilessly kicked and punched to the ground. By this time, Doris was running around the holiday camp like a headless chicken.

'Help somebody help! There's a mad woman in the camp and she's beating up our Gladys.' Horrified, I ran into Uncle Bob who was quietly minding his own business and filling in the daily crossword.

'Please come quickly! Aunts gone mad, she's beating up a woman at the stop- tap.' He paled slightly while putting on his shoes. When we arrived at the scene, two women were holding Aunt back and Gladys's bruised body was being helped off the slippery ground. It wasn't long before we were evicted from the holiday campsite, bringing our holiday to an abrupt end, which wasn't surprising. Needless to say, I never did get to taste that well awaited-candyfloss.

I was to recall much later in life, when I remembered Doris running round the holiday camp, screaming. 'Mad woman in the camp!' for never a truer word had been spoken. Aunt was indeed dangerously mentally ill with a dreadful dark secret looming, and I'd been living with her quite happily for years, totally oblivious to the fact.

Two weeks left of the summer holidays and a favourite pastime was spent playing on the golf course. A few of us would collect the stray golf balls then bag them up and return them to the golfers. They in turn would give us a shilling to buy sweets or some ice cream. As the evening grew late we all made our way home, feeling both tired and hungry and wanting something to eat.

I made my way to the back door of the house, it wasn't lit up which I found unusual for Aunt would normally be preparing the evening meal for Uncle Jim, who would be home from work at any time. On opening the door, there was no wonderful cooking smells to greet me, only the familiar smell of, Brasso. Thursday was polishing day and Aunt polished the brass until it shone. I looked into the front room and called out, but there was no reply. Wandering into the hall then the bathroom while calling out, there was still no reply. Noticing her bedroom door open I decided walked in.

Aunt was sitting on her bed, she looked dark everything about her, and the room looked dark. A strange feeling suddenly enveloped me as she looked up coldly.   'Get out of my sight, just get out!'

I hurried from the room, picking up my coat on the way, but once outside it started to rain heavy. I didn't know where to go or what to do, our James was out with his friends, and Uncle Bob was still on his way home from work.

I thought about Kate, I could call on her although I was forbidden to see her again after the trouble over the money incident. I felt upset as well as being uncomfortably wet, so regardless of the consequences I knocked on her door.

She was friendly and invited me in, and after taking my wet coat she gave me a glass of orange juice and a biscuit. Once feeling a little dryer and warmer, we went into the lounge for a game of Ludo with her younger brother, Jack.

Kate's mother came in soon after from work and popped her head round the door. 'Hi, my little sweethearts I'm back.' Her happy expression suddenly dropped on seeing me.

'What the `ell are yer doin' 'ere? After what your Aunt said about our Kate too, and tellin' all and sundry how she'd taken money from me, well none of its true. Your Aunts not right in the bleedin` 'ed and yer can tell her that from me and if she wants a fight, she knows where I bleedin' live!"

What was up with every one today?' It seemed I couldn't do a thing right. I soon left Kate's house feeling suddenly unwelcome and walked around the shops to kill another half-hour before returning home. Feeling hungry and hoping Aunt had calmed, I made my way through to the back door, cooking smells were now evident in the kitchen and she looked much better, and uncle Bob was home from work, but the look on Aunt's face when I returned home earlier was to remain firmly at the back of my mind.

As the years passed, everything started to fall into place like a jigsaw- puzzle and I was to find out the reason why Aunt looked so disturbed that dismal evening.

Only a couple of days left before starting back at school and the kids on our road kept themselves occupied by playing the popular game of hopscotch. It was my turn to play the game and throw my slate onto a number. The sun was shining directly on my face, so I couldn't quite make out the figure walking towards me in the distance until he was close up. It appeared to be my father as I recognised his walk, as he always wavered slightly when he'd been drinking. I suddenly stopped the game and rushed into Aunt screeching loudly.

'Auntie it's my father!' Looking puzzled she stopped washing the dishes and dried her hands on a tea towel nearby.

'What on earth can he be, wanting?' She answered the front door and was confronted by a man she disliked immensely but allowed him inside the hall nonetheless, out of earshot of the nosey neighbours.

'I've come to tek' our Veronica 'ome with me! Our Winnies having a baby in a couple of days, so she's got to come 'ome and 'elp tek' care of it.' He looked down for a second to avoid the familiar threatening look in his sister in law's eyes.

'I don't know! You've got some bleedin' nerve comin' 'ere. I've looked after her and given her the best in life which yer should be grateful, but all yer want her back for is to do yer skiving, well you can piss off, and don't come 'ere 'agen.' Hearing the raised voices Bob rushed out from the front room.

'What the hell is going on?'

'Tell him, Bob!" Veronica's, been 'appy with us and now he wants to tek' her back.' Father lunged forward and grabbed my arm.

'She's comin' 'ome, with me! She's my daughter and yer can't stop me.' Aunt released me from his grasp and ushered me into the kitchen, she'd paled considerably too, a sure sign she was losing her bad- temper.

'I know what you've come for, the family allowance book? I'll just get it.' She was back in minutes and threw the book at him.

'Tek' it and piss off! yer pissed anyway and yer not fit to look after anyone' He slowly picked it up while pointing a finger.

'I'll be back tomorror' with her mother, so 'ave everything packed.' Bob was seething and rushed forward, his fists clenched.

'Don't come here causing trouble you bastard or I'll sort you out once and for all.' Father clenched his fist as they squared each other up.

'Go on hit me?' Bob goaded. 'Or can you only hit women?' Father shrugged. 'I'm just warnin' yer that's all. Make sure

Veronica's case is packed or else I'll tell her all about Hilda's little secret.'

They both appeared uncomfortable under fathers threatening gaze and satisfied he'd got some form of reaction, turned on his heels and left the house, shutting the door behind him with a loud slam.

Father had obviously got Hilda over a barrel and she would have to give in to him reluctantly even though it would break her heart to do so. As she started to make the tea, I watched on somewhat intrigued as to father's last words before leaving.

'Aunt, have you got a secret? Because if you have, you can tell me and I promise I won't tell anyone.' 'Of course I 'aven't luv,' don't tek' any notice of your father, he'll say anything, to try and scare me into returning yer to them. Come on we'll 'ave some tea and then it's early to bed. It's been a traumatic afternoon to say the least, for us all.'

Sleep didn't come easy that night for I was still upset at seeing father's purple coloured face when he'd been drinking and coupled with the overpowering smell of cigarette smoke too, when he was close by. I really didn't like him and he knew it. Aunt said he wouldn't return as he only wanted the family allowance book, but she couldn't have been more wrong.

The following night father returned as promised with my mother by his side. I didn't recognise her on first sight as her face was much fuller and had taken on a different look. Looking so much like Aunt, I could hardly differentiate between them, but her belly was quite swollen and I couldn't understand why.

After they'd had a lengthy discussion in the kitchen Aunt walked into my bedroom looking none too pleased and looking tearful, while packing my suitcase. I helped by taking the remaining clothes off the hanger and putting them in the case. She suddenly took them out again.

'Yer can't tek' those beautiful clothes with yer cos yer mother will ruin 'em in the wash.' I tugged at them rebelliously.

'What do you care? Anyway they'll never be worn here again will they? She reluctantly handed them back.

'Oh Tek' them then, if that's what yer want! But you'd better wash them yer self or they'll be ruined.'

As the case was packed and put in the hall, I looked around my neat bedroom once more before picking up my Rodney doll and closing the door. I walked into the kitchen to say goodbye, but on seeing my parent's faces suddenly went to pieces, throwing myself onto the floor and protesting against their decision while kicking and screaming loudly. Aunt tried to pick me up, but to no avail.

'Well I've never seen her have a tantrum before, never in all my born days. Yer can both see she doesn't want to go with yer.' Mother tried picking me up from the floor and seemed really stressed out at this stage.

'Jimmy! We can't take her home carrying on like this! Someone will think we are trying to murder her!' Father pulled her away roughly

'Shut up yer stupid bitch and you lady can shut it or I'll murder yer meself. Any more of it and you'll get a crack around the ears good and proper.' I shut up instantly and in sheer fright as I'd never heard such a threatening tone before. My first tantrum was to be my last and was soon to learn that my father's word was god, in our household.

By this time a distraught Aunt and mother each held one of my arms and slipped them into the sleeves of my coat, mother eventually took hold of my hand and led me to the front door.

Glancing back, my Aunt and Uncle could be seen waving their goodbyes as Aunt put a handkerchief to her face to stop the droplets of tears running down her cheeks and I'm sure were thinking the same, would we ever see each other again in the distant future.

Chapter Three.

We were soon seated on the bus, taking us on our journey to my new home. Returning home to a place I had never known, a brother and sister, whom I would scarcely recognise and remembering the violent poverty- stricken way of life I experienced when younger. It filled me with dread. In the near future there would also be a baby to look after, my only knowledge of a baby was my Rodney doll, and held him closely to my chest.

Looking out of the bus window, it was now quite dark. Curtains had been drawn and all looked cosy from the outside. The curtains ranged in different colours red, green, yellow and purple. I counted the windows as we drove by and soon fell into a deep sleep so pushing the traumatic day's events to the back of my mind and to be stored away for future reference, in my later years.

I was suddenly disturbed, by a rough hand of my father.

'Come on lady, yer 'ome!' We vacated the bus and crossed over City Road, towards the most depressing dismal looking three storey flats I'd ever seen. He stopped to light a cigarette then ushered me on in front.

'This is where you are going to live from now on so you'd better get used to it.' We walked along the gravelled path and entered the passage of the flats and soon mother was unlocking the front door.

'Mummy.` It was the familiar sound of our Ann's voice as she came running down the stone steps from the second storey, our Geoffrey was soon to follow. A tall slim woman in her late forties followed with a cigarette hanging limply from the corner of her red painted lips, and a turban style headscarf adorned her head, with the odd roller protruding and resting idly on her low wrinkled forehead.

'Hi Winnie, your children are a credit to yer, and they've been so good, I would certainly mind them again.' Mother acknowledged her with a friendly smile.

'I can leave my children with anyone, Jessie! They always behave, and as they well know. She implied, while looking specifically in my direction. 'Tantrums and misbehaviour are not allowed.'

On entering the flat for the first time was a harrowing experience for I didn't know what to expect but it was extreme to say the least, to the home I had been accustomed for the last few years. The standard of living was appalling in comparison and the overpowering smell of stale cigarette smoke, combined with the strong smell of Izal disinfectant, quickly pervaded my sensitive nostrils. The unkempt smell was to eventually become part of my every- day life, clinging to my hair and clothes.

Looking up the long dark dismal hall, I wandered why it was so dark and noticed a light bulb missing from a yellow tarnished light shade above. To my right the bathroom, I looked in and was repulsed immediately by the sight of the bath still filled with dirty water, left in from the person who'd last used it and hadn't bothered to remove the plug. The toilet was clean but the seat was broken and the familiar newspaper squares hung on the wall beside it. The sink had a dark greasy rim around the edges with a bar of used slimy soap which stood on the side, and an old damp stripy towel hung on the back of the door. I continued through to the kitchen which was badly in need of repair and decorating. The cooker caked heavily in grease had a matching silver whistling kettle on the top. The draining board had dishes piled high waiting to be washed alongside chipped tea stained mugs that had seen better days. On the side of the draining board stood a used Heinz beans tin, obviously being used for cigarette butts.

The high ceiling held a clothes rack, it had clean clothes drying but the whites were now a yellowish colour from the fumes of the gas cooker. I continued exploring my new home then wandered into a bedroom I was to share with Ann and Geoffrey. A single bed sat on each side. I had to share our Geoffrey's bed and didn't relish the thoughts and the bedding consisted of a sheet underneath a blanket and an overcoat of my fathers, acting as an over cover. A dressing table stood on the opposite wall, brimming over with old un-ironed clothes. Unwashed socks together with some shoes cluttered the threadbare carpet. The bedroom next to ours was my parent's. A cot stood at the side of the bed, obviously awaiting the new arrival.

Situated down the hall was a spacious living room. An old fashioned sideboard was to the left, again doors unable to close properly and brimming with old newspapers. Two fireside chairs each positioned on either side of the large open fireplace had a large fireguard surrounding it with more clothes hanging over the side to air. I had noticed an orange box next to the front door on arriving and was later to discover our Geoffrey used it to make his rapid escapes, using it to stand on and open the door when father would violently attack his beloved mother.

In the centre of the room a large dining table stood and a table-cloth was not present, so making it look almost naked. Aunt always had fresh flowers or a bowl of fruit in the middle, of course being too young to realise my mother couldn't possibly afford such luxuries yet even at an early age because I'd become used to a more comfortable standard of living with all creature comforts at hand I had become materialistic minded, which in all, was quite sad really. The table did not stay naked for long though, as it would become cluttered at mealtimes with plates, food and family.

At the back of the room a pair of ill-fitting curtains donned a large size window and at the right side stood a balcony which I quickly learned to appreciate, for like Geoffrey I too could make a rap id escape from my father if need be.

After exploring every corner of my new home I stood in the centre of the room and suddenly became aware I was centre of attention. I shuffled my feet from side to side as I felt decidedly uncomfortable and being concerned for my new royal blue corduroy coat, didn't help any either, for any minute I could get some dust or grease on it. Ann looked a little shy as she walked towards me and touched the velvet collar of the coat, I felt sorry for her for she'd always been a little slow by nature. Intrigued, she bent down and touched the shiny buckle on my black patent shoes, as the light from the ceiling reflected on them. Looking at the shoes she was wearing it was obvious none had been bought her for quite some time. I suddenly stifled a yawn being exhausted by the traumatic upheaval of the day and said goodnight. Geoffrey soon followed, obviously happy to be reunited with his long lost sister.

Opening the suitcase onto the bed I took out a nightgown and undressed quickly. After putting on the nightgown I folded my lovely clean clothes up and put them over the side of the headboard so as not to get them creased. Ann looked at the pretty nightgown I was wearing and as she was only wearing old vest and knickers, I handed her one of the three nightgowns which Aunt had packed then watched as she slipped it on over her unwashed body, she then proceeded to dance and sing around the bedroom with an exuberant happiness. Not knowing what to expect next I quickly hung my coat up behind the door and jumped into bed quickly..

Geoffrey was already making him-self comfortable in bed and made some room for me. A rubber sheet was placed under the top sheet which was strange to lie on as well as being new to me, but I eventual succeeded in making myself fairly comfortable. Before going to sleep though, I looked to Geoffrey and threatened him.

'Don't you dare move over to my side of the bed, do you hear me? Don't you dare!' Geoffrey was puzzled at my sudden outburst of bad temper which suddenly caused him to dive under the bedclothes and remain there until early hours of the following morning.

I lay awake for a while unable to settle that night for my mind was in turmoil. While they slept I un-braided my plaits and brushed my hair with a plastic hairbrush lying idly on the side of the windowsill, and automatically transmitted head lice to the freshly washed hair without even realising.

The following morning, I found to my horror, Geoffrey had urinated over the back of my nightgown. It was to become a regular habit, of at least once a week for about a year, and it appeared not only had my standard of living dropped dramatically overnight, but I was pissed on too. Geoffrey couldn't help himself, as it was nerve related through the violent environment of which he lived, and of course suddenly realising why the rubber sheet was on our bed. Each time he wet my nightgown I'd make sure there was a fresh one to wear, by washing the urinated one immediately and drying it on the fire- guard.

Washed and dressed I made my way to the kitchen, mother was making breakfast and father had gone to work, she smiled as she filled the greasy silver kettle with water.

'Good morning, did you sleep okay last night? It must seem strange sharing a bed after having your own for so long, but you'll get you to it soon enough.'

'It was okay.' I fibbed, taking the unwanted slice of jam and toast from her and not mentioning Geoffrey wetting the bed, she interrupted my thoughts while explaining.

'They'll be a little baby brother or sister added to the family in a couple of days, all being well, which would you prefer?'

'I don't really mind although a little sister would be nice and I could brush her hair every day and she would be able to wear pretty dresses.' Mother just shrugged.

'Maybe, still, you are going to have a lot to do, whatever it is. I just hope the stork delivers it soon though, as I'm very tired.'

Stork indeed' I thought. Well I don't believe that for a moment. I know where a baby comes from. The midwife brings it in that big black bag she carries around with her, but never mind, I'll just pretend anyway. 'Yes mother.'

Nibbling at the jam and toast, I made my way to the balcony a key was in the door so I unlocked it and wandered outside.

A large croft of about an acre stood opposite. I didn't know at that moment in time but an abundance of life would take over each weekend.

All social and sports events took place. Football, cricket, garden fetes, and to my delight a fair made its home there, two weeks of every year. One week in the summer and one week before Christmas.

Some nights when the fair was in full swing our Ann, Geoffrey and myself, couldn't always go, but we could still watch from the balcony. On a rare occasion we would be treated off mother, so spending it on the dodgems and the big wheel. It was really exciting especially if it stopped at the top, enabling us to drink in the atmosphere and the excitement the fair provided, as well as being dazzled by the brightly coloured lights from the top of the big wheel. It had to be said -everything well and truly amazed us.

From an early age, the stark contrast of my father and his home were clearly evident. A crisp clean shirt, pressed trousers and shiny shoes were to be seen on a daily basis, and his thick dark hair, well groomed. I loved his hair and wished I'd taken his side of the family trait. But it was not to be, as mine was to stay fine, taking after my mother's side. He was a gunner in the Royal Navy, but later he trained as a signalman. He enjoyed football and his sporting activities included boxing, of which he became quite keen and entered into boxing championships, while in the Navy.

Sometimes I think it would have been better for all of us, if he'd never met mother and stayed at sea. Some people just aren't cut out for family life. He was very restless after the war and never settled properly after returning to land. I did here stories where he had lost some good friends in the war, mainly at sea. Sadly seeing some of them killed then eventually washed up on the beaches, of which some were decapitated.

Also being in the navy was a reason for him being so smart and fussy in his appearance, obviously all that discipline never left him, and neither did the boxing, which obviously spilled out into his married life.

Chapter Four.

There was a strange feeling, living in the flat. I couldn't quite put my finger on it but it was definitely there, maybe it was a feeling of being ill fated, which became obvious in the coming months.

John was born, a couple of days before I started my new school. He was a lovely baby with a head of dark hair and weighed in at 8lbs, not a small baby. He was also very contented and very rarely cried. Mother named him John Frances.

It was my first real contact with a new baby and his tiny hands and feet held a fascination for me, we bonded immediately, which was just as well for in the months ahead I become a second mother to him.

Mother started to rely on me from the moment I came home from school, to near bedtime. She had post- natal depression quite severely after the birth, resulting in her having a very limited interest relating to our home life. The chores inevitably piled up leaving precious little time to lead a normal child -hood and make any real friends in the neighbourhood.

I eventually manage to make one nice friend, Maureen. She loved being around a new baby and enjoyed pushing the pram. She lived in the next block of flats to us on the second floor, so we could wave to each other and could see each other and ask if the other wanted to go to the park, or the shops. It was my first real communication with anyone since moving to the flat and when I look back on those days she was my life saver.

One day she invited me into her home to meet her parents. Walking into the plush hallway and feeling the thick luxurious carpet beneath my feet suddenly brought back the way of life I'd once been accustomed to. The smell of scented soap, combined with the smell of roast meat cooking in the oven was also homely and inviting, causing me to ache even more for my beloved Aunt.

Maureen's parents were sat in the kitchen, they acknowledged me in a friendly manner, and were interested to know if I'd settled in my new home.

Mrs Newly was short and on the plump side and wore large rimmed spectacles and her hair was grey and very curly. She wore a welcoming smile, warming me to her immediately.

Mr Newly, was a tall hefty looking man, he spoke with an Irish ascent. His thick dark curly hair always seemed to have speckles of cement in it through working on the building site, and his clothes smelt of lime and clay, he too was nice and friendly. In all they were a hard working respectable family and I was always made welcome whenever I was in Maureen's home, making it the only time while I lived in the flat with my parents, feeling anywhere near comfortable, relaxed and happy.

I couldn't settle in my new school. St Lawrence's- It was R.C. and run by two nuns- Mother Dimpna and Sister Elizabeth. My teacher was called Mrs Hill she was the image of Maggie Thatcher. I didn't know it then of course, but when Maggie Thatcher first became prime minister, I thought Mrs Hill had been cloned.

Everyone at school was in fear of Sister Elizabeth, she was very beautiful to look at but it was a pity her temper didn't match. She was also very handy with the belt, or ruler. If anyone stepped out of line they would be thrashed mercilessly so all pupils did their best to be well behaved while in one of her lessons.

Ann went to the same school as me but as she was a little slow she soon became a target for the bullies. Standing her corner time and again resulted in my having countless scraps with the other kids, so being the brunt of Sister Elizabeth's merciless thrashings. I was to tell my father about the bulling incidents at school one evening hoping he might sort out the problem, only to be told to piss off, as he had to fight his own battles when he went to school.

I made a few friends at junior school but they were dressed very poor too. It seemed in those days children were categorized if shabbily dressed as I was soon to find.

My once beautiful corduroy coat was now stained, my shoes were very small and my whites were now a yellowish colour and permanently smelling of stale cigarettes. All the nicely dressed girls gave me a wide birth, obviously not wanting to catch nits.

Mother noticed I was scratching my head repeatedly, so decided to buy some nit lotion, it was applied to all of us but we had to leave it on for two days while it worked thoroughly. The smell left a lot to be desired too so we stayed home from school, being nit free Though was a fantastic feeling.

I awoke one particular morning it was no different to any other everything had fallen into a regular routine, preparing myself for school and then seeing to our John. Making sure he was washed and changed before giving him his bottle then putting him back into the cot next to mother. She was unable to get out of bed early because of her epilepsy, for to suddenly have one of her fits, on top of her post-natal depression, was an unbearable thought to say the least. Having to support her in those depressing months was no easy task, either.

After finishing my day at school and unforeseen at that time, I was to experience a beating from my father I would never forget.

Mother handed me a list ready for the shops for when I arrived home from school.

'Take our John with you as there's 6llbs of potatoes on the list and as their quite heavy you can put them in the bottom of the pram.' Making John comfortable, and putting his dummy in his mouth, we went on our way. Calling to the park first for a swing then carrying on to the shops. Craving, for the taste of some sweets I decided to buy tuppence worth of chews out of the shopping money, toying with the idea at first because it was dishonest. Should I, shouldn't I, should I, but the temptation was too much and as the devil himself looked on, I chose the latter. Having a sweet tooth and always used to having sweets bought me in the past, didn't help, either. I would have to work out the change first though, as it was always put on the table when I'd been shopping and checked under the scrutiny of father's eye. Deciding to buy only 5lbs of potatoes instead of 6lbs, I then put them in the bottom of the pram with the rest of the groceries and returned home.

Father worked on the private residential area in Urmston, as a refuse collector. People from the private houses would give him and his work friends, parcels of shoes, clothes and household brick a brac. Some of the parcels contained leather shoes and handbags and mother could choose whatever she wanted before the parcel was wrapped again and taken to Silverstones- a second hand shop. Although mother had expensive clothes and shoes from her pickings, she never wore any of them, as she hardly ventured outside of the home. Some of the parcels contained children's clothes and shoes, so we all wore second hand shoes, resulting in my feet not being a pretty sight, to this day.

Mother often wrote poetry and sometimes she would sing us songs relating to fathers new job and would sing the famous Lonny Donnigan song. My Old Man's A Dustman. She wouldn't have dared sing it in front of father though, as he wouldn't have seen the funny side. I thought it rather appropriately fitted his description. We'd all set about laughing and I found it rather amusing when mother would make a little fun of him for it made me feel a little secure in my knowing, she wasn't a 100% on his side. She could be quite fun sometimes but when father was around she was a different person, for he'd probably knocked most of the fun out of her, years ago.

On the way home from the shops, I ate one of the fruit chews and put the others down the side of my socks, just in case. Father was already seated at the table when I arrived home and must have finished work early. He glanced up and looking in a bad mood as he frequently did, and watched as I started to put the groceries on to the table, he then added each item up mentally.

34

'Where's the change then?' I handed him the change and he looked again at the groceries.

'There's not 6lbs of spuds in that bag! Winnie come 'ere a minute will yer? Is their 6lbs of spuds in that bag?' Mother looked over and could see the fear mounting in my eyes.

'Of course there's 6lbs, that's the amount I sent her for.'

'Are yer blind woman? as well as being fuckin' thick! I've seen and peeled enough spuds in my time, to know the fuckin' difference.' He stood up quickly his anger emanating from every pore as he fetched to the table a parcel wrapped up in string.

'Well, just luk' what I've been given today!' He opened it carefully and produced a pair of old fashioned weighing scales. Everyone looked on in awe, and mother took on a palid look, as father weighed the potatoes. I watched with baited breath as they topped the scales at just 5lbs.

'I bleedin' new it! Well I want the truth lady or else yer in trouble."

I looked to the floor while shuffling my feet from side to side, as he stood up and started to circle round me and talking loudly down each ear as he passed from one to the other.

'Well! What 'ave yer to say for yourself? If yav' nothing to hide, yer don't 'ave to be afraid of me do yer?' Mothers colour had returned slightly as she moved around the table to protect me.

'Jimmy, just leave her alone, it's only tuppence and after all it's hardly going to break the bank, is it?' Father threw my coat towards me while ignoring mother's pleas.

'Tek' the spuds back and ask for another 1lb. They've under weighed yer.' I stood looking at mother for some support, but she suddenly looked afraid again, as he suddenly gave me an almighty shove, causing me to land against the balcony door.

'Yer can't, because you've spent the tuppence 'aven't yer? On sweets, was it? I'll bet it was. Well give us the sweets then?'

After the initial shock of the fall, I looked to my socks to see if they were showing the shape of the sweets, as mother run over to help me up. 'Look this is going to far Jimmy, leave her alone!'

'You just don't get it do yer? Winnie! There's a principle involved 'ere. I go to work each day, I work hard to bring money 'ome, to put food on that fuckin' table. Only to find we've got a thief in our mist, tekin' my hard earned money. Not only is she a thief mind yer, but she's a fuckin' liar, as well.'

He walked away from me, confronting mother, and staring her in the face. 'Winnie, what 'ave you brought into this world?'

'What on earth do you mean Jimmy? Don't be taking it out on me, because of Veronica's wrong doings.'

'Well, I'll make it clear to yer shall I? She's certainly not got her thieving, cheating ways from me! So it must be your side of the family, and after all, that sister of yours doesn't help matters any does she? She's got a lot to answer for.' Mother defended her sister immediately.

'You leave our Hilda out of this! It's got nothing whatsoever to do with her. Veronica! Apologize to your father, and say how sorry you are for the wrong you've done today. Hurry up, because I'm sick and tired of the bloody lot of it.'

I was again looking to the floor, shuffling my feet from side to side, and wishing time and again I hadn't been tempted to steal the tuppence. Without looking directly at father, I whispered in a soft nervous voice 'Sorry I won't do it again!'

'I knew it!' He abruptly stood up from his chair and lunged towards me.

'My judgements never far wrong, well lady, I'm going to teach yer a lesson you'll never forget.'

By this time, I was thinking it was all over and would probably have to go to bed early, but couldn't have been more wrong.

He suddenly pulled my hair, causing excruciating pain. I was then dragged into the hall, and my head bashed several times against the wall, causing my nose to bleed, profusely.

I could hear Ann and Geoffrey screaming in the distance as everything started to go dark, as mother was screaming at father and trying to tear him away.

'Jimmy stop it, you'll hurt her, stop it!' He held my head back against the wall, as the blood ran down the back of my throat, causing me to splutter and choke. He started to slap my face on each side with the back of his hand. With every slap he spoke.

'Don't yer ever tek' money from me agen! Do yer 'ere me?' He pulled me by the hair then threw me into the bedroom on to the floor. The bedroom door suddenly slammed shut behind then all went quiet apart from his fading voice.

'Leave her Winnie! Let her stew in her own juice.'

Getting up slowly from the floor was unbearable, as my body ached all over, and trying to move my neck was just as bad. Having no such luxuries as tissues, or hankies, I tore at a piece of bed sheet and held it to the bleeding nose. Lying on the bed until the nose-bleed subsided, I looked up to the ceiling thoughtfully, and trying to comprehend, his vicious attack.

Thoughts turned to Aunt, was her secret so terrible she had no choice but to hand me back to my parents. I couldn't understand any of it, but wanting more than anything, someone to explain what had happened in the past and why it was so secretive.

Finally the nose stopped bleeding. Sitting up on the bed and taking the sweets from the over turned socks I quickly hid them under the pillow. If father was to see them his temper could easily flare up, yet again.

Sleep must have gradually taken over, as Ann and Geoffrey came to bed, unheard. I was awoken next morning by mother's enquiring voice.

"Wake up Veronica, why haven't you got our John is feed? He's been crying for ages.'

'I didn't hear him, and anyway my neck hurts and I can't lift my head up.' Mother took a closer look.

'I can see! You'll just have to stay away from school for a few days, as your face is marked on both sides too. I'll give our Geoffrey a note to take to school and say you have a bad cold, and for goodness sake, I hope you've learnt your lesson. Keep out of father's way and don't do anything else to upset him. I'll run you a hot bath as a good soak will relax your muscles then the pain will ease eventually, I should know it's happened to me enough in the past. I'll give you an aspirin and a cup of tea after your bath then you'll start to feel a little better.

I stayed in bed for the rest of the day, unable to move my neck. The following morning when I got up to see to our John, I seemed to ache from head to foot, but the way mother was acting towards father you'd think nothing had ever happened.

Later that day I went out onto the balcony, John was asleep in his pram so I watched the game of school football taking place on the croft. Mr Newly came out onto his balcony apparently it had been raining early morning, so he'd been rained off from his job on the building site. He looked over, to our balcony enquiringly.

'Veronica, are you not at school today, and what on earth have you done to your face?'

'I fell off a swing, yesterday in the park!' I lied.

"I don't know, you shouldn't swing so high, it's not safe! So be more careful in the future.' He disappeared for a moment, then came back and threw some sweets across to our balcony. 'Maybe they'll help take your mind off your bruises for a while!'
Mr Newly was really nice and I secretly wished my father could be of a similar nature.

The marks on my face finally subsided and the incident over the potatoes was never mentioned again. I returned to school a few days later and funnily enough, was looking forward to it.

A writing competition was taking place in school that week and all the classes were to participate. It gave me a chance to exercise my mind, so taking me away mentally, for a while, from the chaotic upheaval in my new life.

It had to be a very interesting story, involving a little intrigue and suspense.

The story was about a friend and myself, walking through the woods and taking a short cut to the shops. We were chatting away about something and nothing, when a few yards in front of us were three men. One had a briefcase holding it close to him, another was digging a large hole next to an old oak tree and the third was showing him how deep to dig.

We stood hiding behind another large tree, intrigued by the unusual activity, before us. Soon the digging stopped and the briefcase was lowered down into the hole very carefully. The soil was shovelled back over the case and trodden firmly down, and the three men hurriedly left the scene.

Out of sheer curiosity we decided take a look, we started to kick the soil away with our shoes and some heavy stones and eventually we reached the briefcase. It was muddy, quite heavy and locked, so thought it best at this stage to take it to the nearest police station.

The police were just as interested as we were to its contents, and a skeleton key was used to open the lock. Everyone was completely taken aback as beautiful sparkling diamonds suddenly shone before their very eyes.

It appeared to much of a coincidence that a robbery at the local jewellery shop had taken place that very morning, in the town centre by three men fitting the description we'd given the police. All three were soon arrested, and eventually sent to prison for a long time and needless to say, we were both rewarded.

Teacher was thrilled with my story and it was chosen to enter into the writing competition. A week later, I found out I'd won. I was presented with a prize of two books of my choice and a postal order for five shillings. It was presented on stage and teacher was really proud. It was the only time I can remember feeling good about being at school.

Returning home, I excitedly showed my parents the postal order and books. Mother was really pleased and said. 'Well done!'

I looked to the floor in disbelief, minutes later, to see Geoffrey, tearing one of the new books into little pieces. I retrieved what I could from his grasp quickly but alas all too late. 'Look mother what he's just done!' She looked to the floor and sighed.

'Oh stop moaning! He's only young he doesn't know what he's doing yet.'

'He does know, he's over five years of age, and should have more respect for other people's belongings.' I was so upset and because mother never took my side, disliked Geoffrey even more. Father never commented and only accompanied me to the post office. I felt discouraged by his lack of response to my achievement at school, and leaving me feeling, totally dejected.

I cashed my prize postal order then, father took 2/6 from me saying, he was a bit bleedin' skint, this week!' The rest I spent on chocolate bars to share with my siblings.

Saturdays in the flat were nothing like the Saturdays I remembered, when living with my Aunt. There was no hustle and bustle of every one rushing around preparing themselves for a shopping expedition in the town centre. It wasn't mothers fault, as money was scarce, so a shopping trip into town was certainly not on the agenda.

Ann seemed notably quiet, sitting on one of the orange boxes looking pensive while looking out of the window. Strange really but I never could quite take to her and had an uneasy feeling she resented me returning home. Lack of emotional connection towards me was also apparent. We weren't close like other sisters, giggling together and sharing little secrets.

I noticed our Geoffrey too, he also seemed different and he'd moved his orange box, nearer to the side of the wall. Ready to stand on it seemed, to open the front door.

The atmosphere seemed very tense, but unknown to myself trouble was brewing, but I just didn't see it coming. I'd been home for just over four months and the only trouble I'd experienced with father, was the potatoes incident, of which I'd engendered.

Mother told us father had lost his job and gone on a bender, although I didn't quite understand what a bender meant, so didn't pursue it any further. She was busy in the kitchen preparing the dinner. A large pan of potatoes which had just boiled, were standing on top of the cooker to cool. I was settling John in his pram for an afternoon in the park and decided to call for Maureen, as soon as dinner was over.

Father had recently made a new friend Sammy Holmes. He'd been spending a lot of time with him in his local beer house. Dollies it was called and it was situated on Stretford Road. It wasn't really close to where we lived so mother never understood why he called it his local.

I'd only met Sammy Holmes the once, when he called to the flat to see father, he only stayed a short length of time, and left soon after. He was a tall stout Irish man with a reddish face, his hair was sandy coloured and he wore a short white beard, but on seeing him for the first time, Father Christmas sprung to mind.

Mother would sing one of her little rhymes about him and repeated it a few times over, which would start us all off laughing. SAMMY, YOUR FACE IS JAMMY, GO AND TELL YOUR MAMMY TO WASH IT OFF. When seeing him again I couldn't help but giggle inwardly.

Mother had a low opinion of him as he was separated from his wife and family, so having plenty of spare time on his hands. She blamed him for keeping father out late too and spending money he couldn't afford, although he didn't need much encouragement in that department. Dinner was almost ready and mother was waiting for father to come home.

'If your fathers not home soon we'll just have to start without him. Knowing him he'll be with that Sammy Holmes and appear home some unearthly hour.'

Voices could be heard soon after, as the front door opened, father had arrived home on time. 'Speak of the devil and he shall appear." Mother commented." Father was accompanied by Sammy, an unwanted guest, as far as mother was concerned.

'Winnie! Put an extra plate out will yer? Me and me mate, are 'ome, and were starvin'' Mother stopped putting out the vegetables and called father to one side.

'Jimmy! We haven't enough food to go round as it is. I can't possibly feed another mouth.'

'Well make it go round, ok! Cos' when I bring me mate 'ome for somethin' to eat, he expects to feel welcome. So get back into the bleedin' kitchen and get it sorted.' Sammy could see mother pale slightly.

'Yer okay Jimmy! I'll get goin' me old mate. I can see your Winnies busy, as it is! So I'll see yer later, in Dollies.'

'I won't 'ere another word mate, yer stayin' for yer dinner!' Mother knew her place and slowly walked back to the kitchen to put out another plate, taking bits of food from each plate to make up Sammys meal. She then carried the meals to the front room, calling to father as she did.

'Can you and Sammy eat in the kitchen, Jimmy? There just isn't enough chairs to go round the table" Fathers face changed to ashen as he chased after her and grabbed her arm tightly.

'Always something with yer woman, Isn't the. If there's not enough fuckin' food theres not enough fuckin' chairs! Well I've had it up to 'ere with yer. I'll teach yer a lesson, showin' me up in front of me mate.' He squeezed her arm more tightly, throwing her against the kitchen wall and banging her head several times. He started punching her about the head and face, as blood squirted profusely from her nose.

I'd blocked out the early years of violence, but it all came flooding back as I shook from head to toe. I started to scream along with our Geoffrey, as he rushed to stand on his little orange box near the front door, to escape the sight and sound of his mother's merciful screams. Sammy Holmes then became embroiled in the violent attack.

'Jimmy, for Christ sake, yer can't treat her as such and the kids are frightened to death.'

'Keep out of it mate! She's my wife and she deserves a bleedin' good hidin.'' Father turned towards the cooker, lifting the cooled pan of water, drained off the potatoes. If it had been boiling hot, well it would have been just too bad, for he viciously threw it over her as she slid down the kitchen wall. Blood had splattered her lovely blonde hair, along with the potatoes water, and her face was beaten to a pulp.

'Nobody treats me mate like shit! Do yer 'ere' me? And don't ask me for any more fuckin' money, either.' He then turned on his heels and quickly left the flat with a distraught Sammy in tow.

Mother was such a frightful sight and I was in a state of shock at witnessing the violence she had suffered at the hands of my father.

Making John comfortable in his pram, I rushed out the front door to get some sort of help from one of the neighbours. Jessie Parker came rushing into the flat soon after though, with her usual fag on. Obviously hearing mother's screams, yet waiting for father to leave the bloody scene first.

'My god Winnie, I think I should call an ambulance. What a bleedin' mess!" Mother stirred slightly.

'Jessie! Don't do anything, it'll only cause more trouble when Jimmy comes home- Just leave it.' She managed to get up from the slippery floor as Jessie helped her out of the flat towards her own home, to help clean her up and make her a little more comfortable.

As the panic subsided, I made my way to the park, just to have some feel of normality around me, and looking in all directions at the same time for our Geoffrey. Where on earth could he be?

I finally reached my favourite swing, glad to see the park deserted, and just to be alone for a while, to collect my thoughts. The park was usually quiet on a Saturday, as most of the kids were out with their mothers, visiting or shopping for the day. Putting the brake on the pram and covering sleeping John. I started to swing to and fro, till I could swing no higher, so taking me into another world, and trying to blot out the nightmare of the last half hour.

Why did mother have to take father back? I could ask myself time and again. We were quite happy in Brook Cot Road without him and she was just getting herself straightened, and a little more comfortable.

Still swinging high yet physically exhausted, I could hear John crying in the distance, bringing me back to reality as I brought the swing to a halt. I sat for a moment then, thinking of my other life with my Aunt, only memories left, to remind me of better days.

Taking the brake off the pram and covering John with the blanket he'd kicked off, I made my way towards the dismal flat. John was hungry and thirsty which didn't help matters and I was hoping mother had returned from Mrs Parkers to mop up the potatoes water off the kitchen floor.

Mrs nosey Parker, mother called her when she was on better terms with father. She assumed Mrs Parker enjoyed hearing about the fights as it took her away from the hum -drum existence of the life she shared with her own boring husband. Mrs Parker would also tell all and sundry the cause of the fights, whenever she got the chance. Mother would still go running to her for help though whenever father beat her, regardless of her assumptions.

While pushing the pram I started to shuffle the gravel under my feet when something caught my eye on the ground, a stone was moving along slowly by itself. Intrigued, I observed a little closer, as a tiny ant moved a stone towards a hole in the ground it then disappeared into the hole, bringing the stone on top, no doubt it was going home and I expect it was to a much happier place than John and myself were returning.

Reaching the passage to the flat, mother could be heard weeping from upstairs, obviously still in Mrs Parkers. I pushed open the front door which was slightly ajar and called to Ann, but there was no response. Looking into the kitchen, it was still swimming with water, so I pushed the pram into the front room and noticed our Ann was still sitting in the same position, before the fight.

'Ann! I shouted, making her jump, change our John, while I make him a bottle?' She seemed to suddenly snap out of it and started to make John more comfortable as I did my best not to slip on the kitchen floor while making up his feed.

Putting clean water into the mop bucket I started to mop the floor, after mopping up most of the water the colour of the lino started to change from its usual dull grey colour into a pale blue. It looked quite nice, so cleaned it over it once more which eventually revealed a much brighter blue and making the kitchen look bigger and brighter once dried. It must have been the salt in the potato water along with the long soak which brought out the original colour.

Geoffrey came in soon after, looking to see if father was in or if mother had returned and looked desperately in need of a cuddle. A couple of moments later mother walked in, looking a little better and all patched up. Ann ran towards her, wrapping her arms around her waist tightly and Geoffrey did the same.

After the terrifying upheaval, everyone started to settle down to some form of normality. My brothers started playing together on the cold linoleum floor, as Ann sat with mother in front of the fire, engrossed in one of their cosy little chats, they had most evenings.

Looking round the dismal room I felt lost and uncomfortable. An alien to this family unit and knowing I would never fit in, when it suddenly dawned on me, father didn't really care, certainly not for me but for any of us.

Growing older, I realised we were just objects resulting from his nights of passion, only to be thrown to one side to fend for ourselves, in the best possible way we could later in life. The dislike for my father from that day forward grew, with a great intensity.

Mother was going through such a difficult patch with father, worry gradually worsened as debts piled high. He still hadn't found a new job and the money he was receiving from the N.A.B. to live on, was insufficient, so giving mother very little and spending the rest on himself.

The corner shop where she had a tick book, against father's wishes but having no choice, because of her financial difficulties refused her anymore credit, for the bill hadn't been paid for two weeks. Being evicted from the flat was also a major worry.

My Grandfather Richard Morton (my mother's father) lived on Chester road, in a hostel for the homeless. It was run by the Salvation Army and he'd lived there for many years. He lived with us for quite awhile, but the arguments between my parents grinded on his nerves to the extent of him packing his cases and leaving.

In his younger day he'd owned his own business as a French Polisher, but he eventually became bankrupt, so leaving him penniless.

Mother sent me on many occasions to borrow money from him, and so returning it when she received her weekly family allowance.

'Veronica run an errand for me love! Go and see your grandfather and ask if he can lend me five shillings till next week. It doesn't look like your fathers coming home again, and there's nothing left to eat. So hurry up, and don't dawdle!'

I put on my coat reluctantly, why was it always me who had to do the errands around here? Deciding not to hurry on this errand, I cut through the park to play on my favourite swing, and continued my journey later.

I arrived at the hostel and rang the doorbell several times. A stern looking old man, eventually answered.

'What do you want?'

'Please can I speak to Mr Morton, my grandfather?'

'I'll have to see if he's in his room first!' I waited impatiently, it was beginning to get dark and suddenly felt the need to return home quickly. I knew my grandfather was on his way though, for he had a permanent smokers cough and could be heard coughing and spluttering as he finally appeared at the hostel door, looking rather strange too, and much older without his cap, for it was the first time I'd seen him cap-less and decided long ago it was a permanent fixture.

'Ello luv!' What brings you 'ere? It's getting dark and its late evening!'

'Can mother borrow five shillings from you till next Tuesday, till she gets her family allowance? We've no food left and she can't afford to buy any.'

'I've only 2/6 to spare luv, but tell her she can keep it, I suppose that father of yours, is playing up again too, Well tell her from me, she wants to get shut of him, once and for all!'

Feeling more impatient than ever and shuffling my feet from side to side, while having to listen to him putting the world to rights, he eventually handed over the money. Thanking him, I ran like the clappers all the way home before the night closed in.

Mother was waiting impatiently, presuming I'd have the five shillings. The shops would be closing soon and she needed to buy some powdered milk for Johns feed, but she looked a bit miffed as I handed her the small amount of money.

'Is that all your grandfathers given to you? Well it's not enough. You'll just have to go to your Aunt Agnus and ask her if she can lend me 2/6. Go on then, hurry up! It's getting dark.'

Agnus was my father's younger sister. Mother met her for the first time in the steel foundry in Salford, when she was only fourteen, she would take mother to her house at lunch- times, only living streets away from the foundry. They soon became good friends and started to go out in the evenings, sometimes dancing, or going for a drink and usually in a group, which is how she met my father.

They started courting for a couple of years and father being the perfect gentleman, finally won her over. The happy couple eventually married much to the disapproval of her parents.

They were disappointed with her, for she'd had a good education. They'd done without themselves to pay for piano lessons, dancing lessons and she was a brilliant gymnast. Why she couldn't have put those talents to further use, to better her education - one will never know.

I often wonder how mother's life would have turned out, if she hadn't made a friend of Agnus, which destined her to meet father, for fate had certainly dealt its hand, in giving her a raw deal in life..

Aunt Agnus lived on the next avenue to us, in one of the ground floor flats. She had eight children and was due to have another baby anytime.

Harold her husband was a nice placid sort of a man, he worked very hard as a labourer on the building sites, but because of the cold wet weather, it had caused him to be rained off.

Feeling dammed fed up of running errands I called to their house and asked to borrow the money, but Agnus couldn't lend it as they had very little money to manage on, themselves.

Mother paced the floor. 'I don't know what I'm going to do? I can't buy much with 2/6, and I'm at my wits end with worry. I know I keep asking you to do errands Veronica, but this will definitely be the last.

Make your way to Dollies beer house on Stretford Road! Ask your father for some housekeeping money for me and tell him there's no food left in the cupboards.'

It was a long walk to Dollies. My feet were aching, and the cold chill, of the November evening, didn't help any. I felt sure father would give me some housekeeping for mother though and that thought alone kept me going.

Approaching Dollies on the corner of the street, I suddenly felt nervous and had serious doubts. What if father wasn't there? Or what if he wouldn't give me any money? It would be a wasted journey and mother would be back to square one.

The smell of the beer was over powering as I looked inside the dismal lobby. It seemed quite busy in the room ahead though and the sound of a piano playing loudly, drowned out the chatter of the beer-swilling customers. I waited a couple of moments, watching people talking in small groups when suddenly father walked from one room to another, I called out to him and on seeing me he wavered to the door, his face was a purple colour and he looked like thunder.

'What the 'ell, are yer doin' 'ere?'

'Mother sent me to ask, if she can have some house- keeping money to buy some food with, only she thought you would be home earlier and the money's needed before the shops close.'

'Tell 'er to piss off! And tell 'er from me, when I get 'ome later, she's in for a hiding of a lifetime.' He looked me up from head to toe before I felt his wrath. 'And you piss off as well! Yer cheeky little get comin' 'ere', showing me up. Go on get away with yer!'

Bewildered and upset, I made the long trek home and sick to the stomach at having to face mother with no money in hand. It was

48

well dark and cold so I started to hurry, passing the odd drunk or two on the way as they urinated in shop doorways. What I needed was a hot cup of tea and to sit in front of the fire, the feeling of hunger had long since gone.

Mother was ironing when I returned home. Two irons were in use, one heating up on the gas ring slowly, ready for using, for when the other went cool, an old sheet and a blanket served their purpose as an ironing board, covering the table- top.

A brown leather suitcase, was opened out on a nearby chair, she started to fold the ironed clothes up and pack them away.

'I knew your father wouldn't give me any housekeeping, so I'm leaving! I'm going to live with our Billy. I've just about had enough of the lot of it.' She quickly finished her ironing, as I looked on.

'Mother, please don't leave us? It'll be terrible living with father and when he comes home tonight he'll take it out on me for showing him up at Dollies.' She locked the packed suitcase, ready for leaving.

'Don't be silly! He won't hurt you, it's me he wants to hurt, and if my leaving doesn't shake him up a bit, I don't know what will, anyway, he won't want to look after you lot on his own, will he? If he can't cope then you'll all have to be taken into care, at least you'll all be fed and clothed.'

I looked around the dismal flat as the chaos started to unfold. Mother had let herself go, and her beautiful ash blonde hair was lank, she'd also lost a considerable amount of weight, obviously through all the worry.

The flat had become a tip, as cinders spilled out of the fireplace in the front room and the dishes piled high in the kitchen sink. Dirty washing lay on the floor of our bedrooms and the flat was also freezing, as the coal hadn't been delivered due to none payment of bills in the last two weeks.

'I'll make a cup of tea, mother!' She was putting the iron away and folding the blankets.

'You'll be lucky, there's no tea or milk!' I went to the kitchen sink to rinse out a dirty tea stained mug and filled it with water, just as John started to cry for his bottle. Trying to rock him back to sleep was hard work, as he was desperately hungry, but putting a dummy in his mouth I'd dunked in a half pot of jam, and rocking his pram, finally worked.

With all the dunked dummies, he'd been given in the past. It was a wander all his teeth hadn't fallen out, but miraculously, he had beautiful teeth as he grew older, as we all did, maybe it was due to the fact we had very few sweets to eat in our younger days.

Ann had retreated into the front room once again, unable to cope with the family crisis unfolding, so dealing it with it in her own way, by retreating into her shell. Geoffrey, awaiting the inevitable, stood close to the front door. The snot dripped onto his old unwashed jumper and his ill- fitting trousers hung around his thin dangly legs, as always inadequately clad, and now desperately wanting his mother to stay home. I noticed his little orange box nearby too, ready to make his escape from the violence, which was about to erupt, at any time. In his fear, where he ran or whom he went too, god only knows.

We were four frightened hungry children and if mother decided to leave, there'd be no one to care, or protect us.

Fathers key could be heard opening the front door, and we all froze in terror, as his loud voice could be heard shouting from down the hall.

'Where's that bitch of a woman?' He rushed into the kitchen as mother tried her best to quickly hide the packed suitcase.

'What's all this about then? Tryin' to fuckin' leave me, are yer. Well there's only one way out lady and that's in yer coffin.'

'All I want is some house- keeping! How can I manage without?'

'Yer don't deserve any money! Yer bitch, cos the place is a tip. Who the 'ell, wants to come 'ome to this pig sty, after workin' all day.'

'How can I think about cleaning up when there's no money to buy food or coal with.' Mother was both crying and screaming as he staggered forward in a drunken stupor only to grab hold of her hair

50

tightly then systematically bash her head hard against the wall, before punching and kicking her about the face and body.

'Don't yer ever send 'er to Dollies agen' for money! She's just a scruffy bit of a kid. Yer could 'ave least made her 'ave a wash before comin' out and showin' me up, in front of me mates."

After a fruitless and traumatic day, with a build up of fear and dread, and in shear desperation I opened my mouth to scream but only a mimic of that scream appeared on my lips as I stood helpless and in shock at witnessing yet another violent sickening attack on my terrified, defenceless mother. I ran towards him and pulled the back of his jacket, only to be pushed back which caused me to bang the back of my head on the opposite wall.

Kicking mother on the floor and leaving her flinching from pain, he proceeded to throw her clothes out of the suitcase, putting some of his own clean clothes in and mumbling under his breath something about being glad to be out of the shitty place. He stormed out of the flat in a hurry, leaving a trail of destruction and the responsibility of his wife and four hungry children, behind him.

Trying my best to help mother up from the floor, she then managed to make her way to the bathroom. She rinsed her battered face in cold water, then brushed her blood stained matted hair. Her face looked distorted as her bottom lip swollen and bleeding, hung down to rest on her chin, and both her eyes appeared like tiny slits, in her swollen face.

'Get your coats on! I'm going to phone Mr Jackson from the N.S.P.C.C. Hurry up! He might be going out for the evening, seeing it's a Saturday night.'

We made our way to the phone box and in minutes she was in touch with him, and explaining her desperate situation. Mr Jackson gave her his home address, so she could call immediately and he would help her out with some food to last the weekend.

He lived on the second floor of some high flats, on Stretford Road. Ann and Geoffrey stayed down stairs when we arrived, as John was in his pram. Mother and me, went up stairs to his flat.

He opened the front door, drying his hair with a towel. He must have been shaving, for he had bits of tissue stuck on his face something I noticed my father always did, when he'd cut himself.

He was a tall pleasant looking man, but flinched, on seeing mother's battered face. 'You only just caught me in time, Mrs Neill! I'm getting ready to go out for the evening, but I'll help all I can. First thing Monday morning, I will put your case forward at our meeting but you'll have to ask your husband to leave the matrimonial home, as you won't be able to claim N.A.B. otherwise. You will have to see a solicitor as soon as possible too, if you decide you want to go through with a legal separation. It will also help in the future, if you need an injunction to keep your husband away, should he proceed with any further violence toward you. In the meantime, I'll give you some food from my cupboard. It will keep you going till Monday.

Mr Jackson filled two carrier bags, with a box of cornflakes, milk, tea, sugar, biscuits, tin foods and a large fruit iced loaf. Mother was eternally grateful, and would return the food to him when she could afford it. He wouldn't hear of it of course, but nonetheless, she did eventually take me with her some months later, to return the food.

She felt embarrassed, and said a quick thank you, and apologised for any inconvenience she might have caused.

As we made our way back to the cold unwelcoming flat, mother started to get some strange looks from passers bye, looking in a somewhat sorry state, after her beating.

Once home, mother put the food in the middle of the table while she went to make some tea and some hot milk for John. We sat for a few moments, seated around the table, looking at the iced fruit loaf but we couldn't wait any longer as we were so hungry, so we started tearing the icing off the top in a frenzy then eating the unbuttered chunks of bread, with our hands.

When mother came in from the kitchen with the cups of tea and seeing the performance before her, she slowly sat down. Fatigued and in pain, she started weeping, uncontrollable tears, like a river damn that had burst its banks. "Something will have to be done, and quickly."

Monday morning arrived and no sign of father, so mother went out early, deciding not to send any of us to school that day, and leaving me in charge as she went ahead to make immediate plans for the future.

Her first visit was to the solicitor to make an appointment, regarding a legal separation. She then went to the N.A.B, as she was unable to work because of her disability and was eventually straightened out financially. We were bought much needed, clothes and shoes and eventually settled down to our violent free way of life. Mother put on some weight and started taking an interest in her appearance and the home, and at last we all had piece of mind, and could sleep peacefully in our beds at night.

Our peaceful way of life didn't last for long though, as father made his pathetic appearance and gave mother the usual sob story, of how sorry he was for mistreating her in the past. He told her, he'd been working for a while and earning good wages especially with over time, so once again coaxed her into believing, he was a reformed character. Showing no animosity towards him and gullible as she was, she took him back, much to our fear and disappointment.

Home life settled into a regular routine for a while, as my parents seemed to be getting along fine, and decent meals were once again, present on our table.

Sometimes father would come home from work early, especially when the nights, were drawing in. He didn't mind cooking and so would make the tea, if mother should happen to be busy. Credit where it's due, he was a great cook, and this particular night, he was making our favourite meal, of boiled ham, cabbage and potatoes.

There was a sudden loud knock at the front door, mother went to answer it, and was confronted by two tall hefty looking Bailiffs, they'd called unexpectedly to arrest my father for none payment of fines, relating to debts. He was escorted from our flat sharpish, with only enough time to put on his jacket, and was sentenced the next morning in court, to serve six weeks in prison.

Mother went into the kitchen to finish the tea when father had been arrested that same evening, but not being a brilliant cook, our favourite tea was ruined and tasted dreadful. Pity really that the Bailiffs didn't call for father, an hour later.

Life was bliss once again, for the six weeks. I still couldn't understand why mother needed father to live with us. I put it down to the fact she couldn't possibly cope on her own.

It seemed in no time at all, that father had served his sentence and was home again. His job was still safe and he returned to work immediately, much to mother's relief.

It was Barbara Jones eighth birthday party. I had been invited together, with my friend Maureen. Looking in the cheval mirror, my waif thin body looked too small, for the dress I was wearing and my dark grey eyes look too large, against my gaunt, delicate features.

Brushing my long greasy fine blonde hair, I happen to look down at the dirty socks riding down the backs of my shoes. It was silly I couldn't possibly go to the party dressed like this. Mother weighed me up as she made her way to the kitchen.

'Where do you think you are going?'

'I've been invited to a birthday party, but I've changed my mind.'

'You can't possibly go dressed like that! And anyway, you haven't got a party dress or a birthday gift.' We were suddenly interrupted by a gentle knock on mother's front bedroom window and looking up Maureen could be seen as she beckoned me out.

'Come on! Or we'll be late.'

'I'll leave it Maureen!' I told her, through the half opened window. 'I've decided to take our John to the park instead.' She looked disappointed as she waved, but not half as disappointed as myself. Everyone on the avenue would be at the party and I'd so wanted to participate in the late Saturday afternoon birthday activities.

Watching her walk away, her beautiful long shiny auburn hair in a ponytail, bounced from side to side. She wore a lovely blue chiffon party dress and dark blue patent shoes, and in her hand a birthday present, tied up with a beautiful silver bow.

I ached inside remembering the once beautiful clothes I once wore, when living with my Aunt, and how pretty she'd made me look whenever there was a birthday party to attend.

Well it was no use feeling sorry for myself, so I washed our John and took him to the park for the rest of the afternoon to play on my favourite swing. Arriving home later, I found Maureen had already called from the party with a bag of sweets for all, and some birthday cake, wrapped up in pretty birthday paper from Barbara Jones mother. So it wasn't such a bad ending to the day, after all.

Whit-week was soon upon us, and I was quite taken aback, when mother took us out shopping a few days earlier to a store in town. The store allowed credit facilities whereby she would pay three shillings a week, to an agent. We were told we could choose a new coat, clothes and some new shoes. My coat was a dusky pink with a dark dusky pink velvet collar and Ann chose a blue coat of a similar style. It was the first time I'd seen her looking nicely dressed, and Geoffrey looked ever so smart in his new grey trousers, white shirt and jumper, and a dark navy blue jacket.

Whit Sunday arrived and we all went to church, with mother. I was supposed to attend every Sunday, but because of my shabby clothing, in-comparison to the other kids, I felt conspicuous, so never attended. Everyone was clad in their Sunday best and sat with at least one of their parents. I'd go to church and peep through the door and take note of the priest's vestment, for that particular service, then quickly disappear to play down the valley for an hour, until the church service had ended.

Each Monday morning, mother Dympna would ask any one of us in class. What was the colour of the priest's vestment worn for the Sunday church service? If you couldn't describe it, she'd know you hadn't been to church and you'd get a good belt.

Attending church with mother was unusual as she hardly ever went, although she was religious and a firm believer in blessing each room in the home with holy water and was often heard to say.

'If you want to say a prayer, you can say it anywhere, for god is always watching and listening.' I felt a little concerned at this finding and wandered if god could see me in the bathroom, of which I looked around for quite some time afterwards.

I felt proud that Whit Sunday, as we sat in the church pew as one family unit. As well as blending in nicely with the rest of the congregation for once, I secretly wished it could be the same every week.

Playing on the avenue afterwards, with the other kids, my father seemed unusually observant. He would knock on the front bedroom window from time to time and beckon me over and warning us to keep our coats clean. It seemed even more unusual when it continued into Whit Monday.

Tuesday morning, father decided to take a day off work, I started to feel uneasy, for it seemed to fall into a familiar pattern. Knowing that a day off work would inevitably lead to another then he'd go on a bender. He quickly wrapped our new coats in a brown paper parcel, put on his jacket and left. I later discovered he'd taken them to the local pawnshop, whereby the money was spent on his favourite pastime of drinking and gambling. Our coats were never redeemed so we had to revert to wearing our old one's again, until he found some suitable from work, for each of us to wear. We were allowed to keep the rest of the clothes and shoes bought us for whit-week though, which was some consolation, I suppose. I could never understand why mother tolerated such a selfish act from father, for it wasn't as if she would benefit from the money from the pawnshop. She would also have to pay the agent when he called round each week, until the coats were paid for, so why she was so lenient with him? I'll never know. I could also question father's selfish attitude. How could a father see his children without a warm coat to wear? Mother once commented on this.

'There has to be something radically wrong with a father who can see his children without any decent clothes or shoes to wear.' And there must be something radically wrong with a woman who puts up with it.' I thought.

She also made it quite obvious, that concern was only for himself, as she continued. 'And I just hope you take heed young lady and never marry a man, of a similar nature.'

He came home that night, a bit worse for wear, but went into work the next day, much to mother's relief.

Returning home from school one afternoon and not relishing the thoughts of the usual chores awaiting me, I was stunned as mother opened the front door and was immediately taken aback by the beautiful woman before me. Her beautiful ash blonde hair had been styled, like the movie star Veronica Lake, and a touch of face powder and some red lipstick, completed her sophisticated look. Wearing one of the expensive brown tweed suits, a cream blouse and a pair of crocodile shoes, which she'd decided to keep, from one of the clothes parcels, father brought home from work. She looked every inch, the lady.

I gasped. 'Mother you look so different, like a fairy princess.' She smiled broadly at my approval. It was a nice change to see her dressed up for she was usually wearing an old pinafore and slippers while making the tea or sat in front of the cinder spilled fireplace smoking heavily, as well as looking depressed.

'Wait till father sees you tonight! He'll be so proud at the effort you've made for him.'

'Well actually, I'll be gone by the time he arrives home love! I'm off out with your uncle Billie tonight. (Uncle Billie being my mother's younger brother.) I met him while out shopping this morning. Which reminds me, you don't have to do any shopping today, it's all been done. It'll also make a nice change to go out for the evening, as I hardly ever venture out these days and I'm sick and tired of looking at these four walls, day in and day out.'

Thinking of mother, usually dressed in her old gabardine and flat shoes and not wearing a trace of makeup, she still turned heads and got a few wolf whistles, being of a natural beauty. Seeing her dressed up for the first time and wearing some make-up only enhanced that beauty. Whenever she went shopping, to the butcher or the fishmonger they would make a beeline for her, chatting away and telling the odd joke or two, it seemed the only time I was to see her laugh heartily.

Billie the butcher seemed quite fond of her and while chatting he would give me some ham or corned beef to eat and I'd thoroughly enjoy it. A mug of tea usually stood at the side of his counter, with the odd blue bottle or two, floating on top. He would take a gulp every now and again along with the dead blue bottles and laugh at the repulsed look on my face. 'Clean your inside out lass, clean your inside out!' He'd repeat cheerfully.

'Tell your father, the potatoes have boiled and there's bacon and eggs in the larder? It won't do him any harm to cook his own tea for once.' I responded half heartedly while talking to our John in the front room, yet at the same time feeling troubled. When she was ready to leave, I lifted him out of his pram and carried him into the kitchen.

'Don't go out? They'll only be trouble when you come home tonight, and father will be really angry at your not being here when he comes home from work.' She slammed the larder door shut with an abrupt force.

'You just listen to me lady! I'm entitled to go out sometimes on my own, your fathers out every weekend. What's good for the goose is good for the gander, so you can just shut up. Anyway, I'm sure you'll all manage quite nicely for once, without me.'

I was too young to realise she was of course right and only trying to prove a point. Why should she stay home, just to keep peace, for it was enough to drive any one mad in this dreary flat, day after day and after all, it was hardly Buckingham Palace. Father should have been less selfish and shared her views on the matter, so creating a nicer atmosphere, in which we could have all benefited from.

Ann and Geoffrey came in from school soon after, and both looking amazed, at mothers transformation, as they made their way to the kitchen, to make some bread and jam to eat, before tea. I hoped mother would always look nice, from now on, for it brightened the flat, and she looked so much better in herself. At this point father's key could be heard in the latch, he was home much early than she'd anticipated. She paled slightly as her red lipstick suddenly clashed, with her palid look. He strolled in, looking dusty and hungry.

'What the 'ell's goin' on 'ere then? Looking stunned for a split second at the beautiful woman before him.

'What are yer doin' then, all dressed up to the fuckin' nines? Will someone tell me? or else!' He slammed his fist hard onto the kitchen table, causing mother to flinch.

'I met our Billie today, while out shopping, if you must know.' She spoke nervously, but nonetheless stood her ground, as her colour slowly started to return.

'I'm going out this evening with him and our Maggie for a drink! It'll make a nice change for me.'

'What! Dressed like that?' Father weighed her up and down for a moment, questioningly. 'You've not seen your Billie for bleedin' years, so where's he suddenly sprouted from?'

'I'm only telling you what happened today.'

'Well, yer can tek' that suit off, and wear your old gabardine for a start? After all, you'll only be goin' for a drink in a scruffy pub, knowin' your Billie, and yer can tek' that red lipstick off as well. Yer look like a fuckin' tart.' She threw her head back defiantly, as her Veronica Lake hairstyle fell back into place.

'You should be pleased I've made the effort, to look nice! I've never had a chance to wear any of the clothes, you brought home from work. And anyway, you go out every weekend with your friends, so I'm going out tonight and its too bad if you don't approve.' He banged his fists, repeatedly on the table.

'I 'ave to go out at weekends, I've got to luk' at your miserable face every bleedin' night of the week, aven't I? And anyway, I need me mates to cheer me up a bit, or I'd go bleedin' mad. He went quite for a moment and looked at her thoughtfully.

'Anyway, yer never dress up for me! Never once 'av' yer wore any of those beautiful suits. They just hang behind the bedroom door, gatherin' bleedin' dust.'

'That's because you never take me anywhere!' She chimed. He paced around, after her.

'Just tek' a good luk' at yerself, woman! Prancin' around like Veronica fuckin' Lake! Well the only prancin' about your doin' tonight, is in that kitchen. So get in there and get me tea sorted, I've worked 'ard all day, and I'm fuckin' starvin'.'

Mother took no heed and carried on walking, down the dark hall towards the front door, collecting her beautiful matching crocodile handbag, from the bedroom door handle, as she did so.

'Don't turn yer back on me yer bitch, when I'm talkin' to yer?' The front door was already slightly ajar, as Geoffrey had hurriedly climbed up on his box and left the flat, and John started to cry, obviously alarmed at his parents raised voices. Father grabbed her arm tightly then, and swung her round to face him.

'Let go of my arm Jimmy? or I'll scream the place down. I mean it! Leave go?' She screamed.

'I'll give yer somethin' to scream about yer bitch. I'll tear yer fuckin' 'ed' off!' With those words, he beat her systematically. Leaving her battered and crumpled on the floor. One of her shoes had fallen off, so he picked it up, and through it hard against the kitchen door, leaving a huge dent, in the process. Neighbours ignored her plea for help, as they gave up long ago trying to help, for she always made friends with him later, regardless, of the consequences.

As always, he put on his coat and left the flat for a few days after beating her. I don't think he ever realised, just how hard he punched her, and I don't think he cared, once losing his temper. She could have died, for all he knew and as always it was left to me to pick up the pieces and clean up the flat afterwards.

'Should I go to Mrs Kershaws mother? She's got a phone. I could call an ambulance as you've lost a lot of blood.'

'Sod Mrs Kershaw! Just help me to my bed all I want is to die. I don't want to live a life like this anymore."

Helping to take off her jacket, she curled up in a ball on the bed. I went to the bathroom to rinse out an old piece of cloth, so as to bathe her battered face. She just wept then, till sleep finally overcome her.

A feeling of disquiet swept over me later. What if father went on a bender? Any excuse would do and we'd be back to square one. No two ways about it. No decent food, no electric, no fuel. If mother hadn't dressed up, looking like Veronica Lake. None of this would have happened.

I needn't have worried, as father didn't give up his job, although he did stay away for a couple of nights. When he eventually returned, the dreadful night of violence was never again mentioned.

Father was raged that night though, and had undoubtedly become jealous, jealous of his wife's beauty, anyone could see for it was registered on his face. He'd got quite a shock on arriving home to see her dressed up, for she looked so different, not like the usual drab wife he was use to seeing each evening, although he had to admit to himself, as drab as she was in her dress she couldn't look plain.

Being dressed up and wearing make-up, only reminded him of the woman, he'd fallen in love with all those years ago and didn't like what he saw, one bit. After all, she wasn't dressed up for him now, was she? Well, he'd sorted her out good and proper and no one would be lookin' at her for a good few weeks-that was for sure.

Over the weeks, mother slowly retreated back into her shell. The smart outfits hung behind the bedroom door and the expensive shoes alongside the matching handbags were left in a corner to gather dust, as they were never worn again.

I was once again, having to do the shopping at weekends and Billie butcher enquired after mother on several occasions, as to why she hadn't called into his shop. I gave some excuse and left it at that, and never mentioned him asking after her. After all, some things were best left, unsaid.

Mother knew her place and father kept her there, or so he thought, but something happened after that last savage beating and she started to change, only gradual, but nonetheless, the worm was about to turn.

Chapter Five.

November 1955, I was eight years old, and been living with my parents for just over a year. The winter nights were drawing in, as Christmas was approaching, and would soon be upon us. Father was bringing home even more parcels of clothing, as the wealthy residents on his patch, were giving away plenty of the old, to make room for the new. One evening while eating his tea, he looked across the dinner table towards me, looking thoughtful.

'I think you are old enough to go to Silverstones, the second hand shop. He threw my coat towards me, after we'd had our tea.

'Come on! I'll tek' yer there, I'll show yer where it is and then you'll know in future, should I bring a parcel 'ome where to tek' it. If it's heavy, yer can tek' our John with yer, and put the parcel in the bottom of the pram.' Mother shouted from the kitchen on hearing his suggestion and appeared concerned.

'It's getting late Jimmy! Siverstones will be closing soon can't you leave it till tomorrow?'

'It's okay, I might as well show her now then, I won't 'ave to go tomorror` as I've got a lot on.'

Silverstones, was a long trek down Stretford Road, but we finally arrived and father took me into the shop to meet Mrs Silverstone. I was introduced.

'This is my daughter Veronica! She'll be comin' 'ere in future with parcels of clothes.' Mrs Silverstone gave me a friendly smile, warming me to her immediately. She was a tiny slim Jewess, with a mop of black curly hair.

'Hello, my lovely child, I expect I'll be seeing quiet a lot of you, in the future?' Cupping my face in her warm hands, she then looked to father. Her expression changed quickly, to a scowl.

'What have you brought for me today then?' He showed her the leather shoes and handbags.

'I was thinkin' of 6/6 or even 7/6! As there dead expensive kid leather these are.' She looked at them closely, feeling the excellent

63

quality of the goods. 'Not a chance! I'll give you 5/6, that being my one and only offer, take it or leave it!' She offered him the money coldly as he thought for a moment, then snatching the 5/6 from her nastily, we quickly left the shop.

'Tight bastard, that's all she is! Well I'm warnin' yer' don't let her shout yer' down If I ask for a price make sure she gives it yer. Do yer 'ere me?'

I nodded, not quite understanding what-shout you down entailed, but I was soon to learn a little more about wheeling and dealing in the months ahead and was to benefit quite nicely.

We were soon approaching Dollies, on the corner of Stretford Road. Father went inside the pub to spend his 5/6 on the usual beer and cigarettes, and so leaving me to walk the rest of the way home, on my own.

Twice a week was the usual journey to Silverstones. Most of the time I took our John in his pram, as it seemed less boring, having someone to talk with on the monotonous journey. Walking in ill-fitting shoes didn't help any either, at first I'd get blisters on my heels, they would eventually pop and the skin would grow over. The skin eventually grew over quite hard, so I was able to wear any type of shoe afterwards without any discomfort.

Sometimes Maureen would come along, for she enjoyed pushing the pram, as well as Siverstone's holding a fascination for her, with its clutter and interesting brick a brack. Her mother never frequented such a shop so it seemed all the more intriguing to her.

One lunchtime father called home early, a friend had given him a lift, and he was going back to work to do some overtime. He handed me a parcel containing a new pair of men's black patent leather shoes.

'Go to Mrs Siverstone and ask for 9/6?' He paused for a second while scratching his dusty hair before replacing his cap. 'No, you'd better ask for 7/6? She's a tight bastard as yer well know, but I bet she'll sell them for three pounds at least, seeing it's nearly Christmas.'

Giving me food for thought, I decided to ask for the 9/6, toying with the idea for a few moments, on suddenly remembering the dreadful performance, regarding the potatoes and scales incident. But decided to ask Mrs Silverstone, for the 9/6, nonetheless, after all there could be no harm done, and father would hardly check up on me. I was handed the 9/6, as she was really pleased with the shoes, and they would obviously bring in a good price for her, especially at Christmas time. I gave father 7/6, which made him quite happy, and I kept the 2/- extra, which was saved in an old tobacco tin and kept hidden under the bed. Mother had never moved the beds to sweep under, the whole time I'd lived in the flat, so I was sure the money would be of safe keeping.

It became a regular habit, asking for 2/- more for the parcels. I'd sometimes buy John and myself a bar of chocolate, but was always careful to clean off any chocolate from our mouths with the cuff of my coat sleeve, for father would soon latch on and there'd be trouble. The money started to mount up and I wanted more than anything, to spend some on Christmas presents, but didn't want to arouse any suspicion, but I'd certainly think of a way nearer the time.

Preparing herself for school, on a frosty December morning, Ann stood in front of the cheval mirror. It was a beautiful mirror trimmed with a gilt scrolled pattern around the edges and so finishing off its expensive design. Father had brought it home from work one evening, for it had been given to him by one of the residents on his patch. Mother had liked it instantly and kept it, together with a beautiful figurine of a Victorian lady. The two were her most treasured possessions and wouldn't allow father to take them to Silverstones, to sell for extra money, to feed his habit of cigarettes and beer.

I was washing and changing our John, before giving him his feed, but time was running late, and Ann was still preparing herself in front of the mirror. Geoffrey had already gone to school, after washing and having his breakfast of tea and toast, which my father had made. He was always up at 5 30am each morning, building up a roaring fire and making a large plate of buttered toast, with a pot of steaming hot tea for us. Credit where it was due, when he was working, he always thought about us in the morning before leaving for his work and it was always appreciated, especially on frosty mornings.

Mother was still sleeping at such an early hour, and as the cheval mirror was in her bedroom, we did our best not to disturb her while getting ready. John was now sat up in his cot, playing contently, with a cuddly toy and watched with a growing interest, the commotion before him.

Ann, and myself started to push and shove one another in front of the mirror, for I was losing my patience while trying to tidy up quickly, otherwise I'd be late for school. I gave her an almighty shove which landed her on mother's bed, she started crying, this in turn woke mother, and startled her. She sat up angrily and leapt out of bed, but her hair being long and fine was stuck up all over the place, and as she was wearing one of her long flowing nightdresses, it made her look really wild. She rushed towards the dressing table and swearing at the same time. We were totally shocked as mother had never used such bad language, before.

'I'm not putting up with this first thing in a morning, I'll fucking kill the pair of you!' At the same time she picked up her most treasured figurine and smashed the cheval mirror, shattering its glass into smithereens.

Stunned, we rushed out of the bedroom towards the balcony door, but both getting stuck in the kitchen doorway, as mother came running after. At this stage, she was screaming like a lunatic.

'I'll fucking kill the pair of you, when I get my hands on you, mark my words!' I unlocked the door sharpish as we both leaped over the balcony wall and making a rapid escape, just in time. As I mentioned earlier in my book, I really appreciated living on the ground floor for it was easier to escape, if need be, but this particular morning if I'd lived on the third floor, I would still have jumped over, for mother terrified me.

I glanced back over my shoulder and couldn't believe my eyes. Oh no, mother had jumped over the balcony too and chasing after us, with an undying rage. With her long flowing nightdress and long wild hair, holding the figurine high above her head, she looked forever like the Statue of Liberty come to life, it almost looked surreal. She was getting some strange looks at this stage too, and I was really worried, for mother had lost it and it was my fault, I shouldn't have shoved our Ann on to the bed and disturbed her. Ann could be seen running into the school play-ground, well it was one place I wasn't running. It was bad enough being shabbily dressed for school, but this, I'd never live it down. I kept running and looking round from time to time, until mother finally disappeared out of sight.

Turning into a side ginnel, I stopped for a moment, trying to catch my breath, but feeling disorientated then physically sick, I stood against the wall for some support but suddenly threw up, and watched, as my breakfast slowly mingled with the rest of the debris on the ginnel floor. Cleaning my mouth with my coat sleeve, I tried to tidy myself up, but still managed to look disheveled. Eventually looking around and seeing no sign of mother, I quickly made my way into the school classroom.

'Veronica! Your 15minuts late! What on earth have you been doing?' The medicine I'd been taking for an irritable cough, suddenly sprung to mind and would be a good enough excuse.

'Sorry Miss! I'm taking medicine for a bad cough but I'd forgotten to take some this morning, so I had to return home.'

'Well you do look a bit peaky! Go and be seated at your desk, and you could have at least combed your hair this morning, you look ever so untidy.'

Glad to be seated, but my mind in a state of confusion, my imagination started to run wild. Our John might manage to climb out of his cot as he was over a year old, he would get splinters of glass in his hands and feet, he'd cut himself, and mother would be in no state to care for him. What if she had one of her epileptic fits, caused by rushing out of her bed, suddenly?

67

I had visions of her charging into the classroom, with her hand raised, and still holding the figurine, then suddenly reigning blows down on my skull, my body's warm blood, splattering the classroom walls.

'Veronica Neill! You are not concentrating! All you've done since coming into class is daydream. Well I won't tolerate it any longer, come to the front of the class where I can keep an eye on you immediately!" Being of an impulsive nature and in my sheer desperation, I rushed from the classroom, into the school playground and out of the school gates. My heart pounding, I found myself running across the croft towards the flats, and suddenly engulfed by a gripping fear, of the unknown. Eventually reaching the back of the living room window which was situated next to the balcony, I crouched down.

No sound of music could be heard playing from the radio, and all was quite. I stood up cagily and peeped through the window. To my relief mother was dressed, her hair tied in a ponytail and looking quite presentable our John was sat on her knee, he too was dressed and thankfully, wearing shoes and socks. She sat in front of the fire, smoking and staring into the dying embers, totally oblivious to the world around her. John was sleeping with a dummy in his mouth and looked quite contented.

What should I do? I could play down the valley until after lunch then make my way into school for the rest of the afternoon, and hope everything might return to a form of normality, for when I come back to the flat later, or I could face the consequences now, and get it over with.

Eventually I opted for the latter and knocked on the window gently. Mother looked towards the window, wearing a strange blank expression as I looked towards her sheepishly.

'Sorry mother for what I've done! Promise I won't do it again.' No answer, although she did stand up and put sleeping John in his pram. I watched as she disappeared out of the living room and into the dark hall and re-appeared into the kitchen to unlock the balcony door. She unlocked it, not even glancing in my direction, while still looking really strange.

'Sorry mother for what I've done! I promise I won't do it again.' Trying to appease her yet again, as I nervously climbed over the balcony wall.

On entering the kitchen, the usual stale smell of cigarette smoke pervaded my sensitive nostrils. I scanned the surfaces for the figurine, but it was nowhere to be seen and the last glimpse of mother was seen disappearing into the dark hall.

The place was a mess, with dirty plates piled high on top of the draining board from last night's supper along with the morning's breakfast dishes. The familiar Heinz beans tin still stood on the side of the window ledge, brimming over with days of cigarette dimps.

'Sorry mother for what I've done! I promise I won't do it again.' I heard myself repeating, like some demented family pet parrot, but still there was no response.

Walking into the hall and looking round nervously, she was nowhere to be seen. Noticing her bedroom door shut, I opened it gently and shoved it open wider with my foot, still looking for the figurine, but noticed it was still absent from its usual position. The shattered glass from the mirror now covered every nook and cranny, for it still hadn't been swept up.

Closing the door quietly, I suddenly felt the presence of her standing behind me, turning to face her she looked straight through me while holding the figurine high above her head. Fearing the worst, I suddenly felt the urgent need to pass water as I protected my head in my hands and awaited the inevitable blows. She brought the figurine down slowly, putting it to the side of her waist, and staring as if in a trance, then slowly turning and walking down the hall, to place it on top of the old fashioned sideboard, in the front room.

Sweating and hands clammy, I stood up. Someone must have been looking after me up there, as I well and truly thought my number was up.

Trying my best to sound normal after such a frightening ordeal I called out nervously.

'I'll clean the glass up from the bedroom for you! So our John won't get splinters in his hands and feet.'

Filling the mop bucket up with fresh hot soapy water, I carried it to the room then fetched the rest of the cleaning equipment.

The scroll mirror frame, looked odd and abandoned, standing in the corner of the room without its mirror, and would never again reflect our daily lives. Thank god.

Feeling totally disheartened, I set about sweeping then sweeping more vigorously, as all pent up feelings of fear and frustration were vented out on the brush head. Something was terribly wrong in this flat, the atmosphere was one of fear and dread, it was almost like treading on egg- shells and there had to be something wrong with mother too, for she'd never have broken her most treasured mirror and treated the figurine so carelessly.

Life was becoming intolerable. Talking to mother concerning any problems seemed nigh on impossible, with her seemingly on another planet, and father just seemed to shout most of the time. It wasn't so bad for my siblings for they knew no different, for they were used to their environment. I'd had a taste, of a better quality of life, through living with my Aunt, although the violence erupted from time to time in her home too, but somehow it didn't seem to affect me in the same way. Trust of mother was also dwindling, as she became more unpredictable in her mood swings. We were becoming terrified of her rages, and even more so, of her subsequent withdrawn silences. Since father stopped her going out that last evening on her own, then beating her, it had definitely caused a recognizable change in her.

No doubt father would hear about today's terrifying ordeal, causing Ann and myself, to be in for a hiding of a lifetime.

Life wasn't always unhappy in the flat for there were some good times to remember. Sometimes mother would take us to the lyceum picture house. It was situated on City Road, not far from where we lived, and would take us in turn, as she couldn't afford to take us all together, she would also spoil us a little, buying us sweets and ice cream.

Father would look after the rest of the family, so making it a nice change for her, to have some free time. He didn't mind her going out at night, as long as she took one of us with her. Heads still turned though, at the beautiful woman, wearing her old gabardine and flat shoes, whenever she ventured out. She loved to watch the old John Wayne films, and always made a point of going to the pictures, should he be showing.

When it wasn't my turn to go to the pictures, I'd make myself scarce, especially in the winter and asking father if it was okay to stay at Maureen's house for a few hours, for on dark nights he couldn't order me to take John to the park.

Walking into Maureen's home, made me feel happy as the feel of the luxurious thick carpet beneath my feet, always brought to mind the memory of the comfortable life I was once accustomed. Her parents would usually be listening to a play on the radio, and they'd always make me feel at home, and would give me pop and ice cream.

Sometimes, Maureen and few of us off the avenue would go to the pictures. I had some money saved from Siverstones, so was able to pay in along with a couple of the other girls. The rest that couldn't afford to pay would wait outside the back window of the ladies toilets. Soon after, one of us would go to the ladies, open the toilet window and let them clamber through. There was always a puzzled look on the usherettes face, as more kids seemed to be coming out of the ladies, than first went in. We were soon sussed, and bars were eventually put up to the toilet windows.

Every couple of weeks, mother would send me to St. Lawrence's church, to fill an empty bottle with holy water she would then bless each room while saying the Lords Prayer. A few of us were going to the pictures one evening, when mother handed me a bottle, not wanting to miss out on any of the fun with the other girls though, all thoughts of the holy water were pushed to the back of my mind.

The film was coming to an end, when I felt the bottle in my coat pocket and panicked. I looked over at the large clock, on the lyceum wall and realised, it was too late to go for the holy water. Mother would go ballistic, so there was no alternative but to fill the bottle from the tap in the ladies toilets. I felt really worried and thought god would be watching my every move. Making an exit from the lyceum, I quickly made my way home to find mother quite agitated.

'Where have you been? It's getting late, and I've been waiting ages.' She took the bottle and proceeded to take the top off, then in turn, blessed each room in the flat with the Lyceum toilet water. I followed her round and feeling somewhat afraid, as she continued her religious ritual of sprinkling the water and praying- In the name of the Father, and of the Son, and of the Holy Ghost Amen. `

I was afraid to sleep that night, worried that god might decide to punish me, and half expecting the ceiling to cave in at any time. Needless to say, I went to confession the following Saturday evening to repent, for thinking I might have committed a cardinal sin. Father Sheeran, was very disappointed in me, so I had to kneel down for half an hour to serve my penance of, ten our Father's, and four Hail Mary's.

Christmas Eve had arrived. It was 2pm. in the afternoon, and mother was waiting impatiently for father to arrive home from work. The shops would be closing early and she hadn't any money, to buy food or presents for Christmas. We all had our coats on waiting and John was wrapped up warmly, in his pram.

Every Christmas father and his work friends collected tips. They would start a few months early and it amounted to quite a large sum of money, which would be equally divided amongst them all, on Christmas Eve. Mother relied on the extra money, as it provided a decent Christmas for us.

I'd been waiting for a good excuse, to spend some of the money, from the trips to Mrs Silverstones, but crawling under the bed, without anyone noticing and taking some of the money out of the tobacco tin, was done with great difficulty.

Crawling from under the bed, an engine of a van could be heard outside the window, purring softly, so looking out of the bedroom window, father could be seen talking to one of his work friends he'd obviously been given a lift home.

'It's okay mother! I shouted excitedly, fathers outside.'
Soon afterwards he came in and went straight to the dinner table, where the money was tipped out of an old dusty carrier bag. We all looked astonished at such a huge amount of money, as he started to share the tips between him and mother. Her share would be for the family, his share for himself. I suppose we should have counted ourselves lucky really, for he could have gone straight to Dollies and then the bookies from work, and we'd have ended up with nothing.

It was bitterly cold outside and the December wind cut through our old coats. It was a long walk to Stretford Road, and mother was taking us to a caravan, selling Christmas toys, which was situated on a large croft, set back off the main road.

I'd never experienced anything like this, for Christmas spent with aunt, was so different. There'd be a large decorated Christmas tree, with presents stacked high beneath it, a stocking hung at the foot of the bed, and balloons and decorations adorned the ceiling. Aunt would take me to see Father Christmas a few days before to hand him my list to read, and he'd know what I wanted for a present. The build up to Christmas, was magical.

I felt sorry for my siblings, knowing they'd never experience a Christmas like mine, in a million years, especially while father was around.

We finally approached the caravan, and could see the end of the day was near, for few people were about. We were all feeling quite excited, knowing we were about to have a new toy to play with, so the bitter cold was soon forgotten. Most of the toys had been sold, and mother stood looking sadly, at what was left. The salesman winked at her. 'Not much left darlin'! Only a few dolls, some cuddly toys, two jigsaws, two books and a train set.' She shrugged her shoulders.

'What do you want Ann?'
'I'll have the doll with auburn hair, dressed in white and the jig saw puzzle.'

'Geoffrey! Will you have the last train set and a jig saw?' He nodded excitedly, while shuffling his cold feet from side to side and trying his best to keep warm. The snot dripped from his cold red nose, as he hurriedly wiped it on his coat sleeve, and held out his purple coloured hands, to receive his Christmas presents.

'Veronica! What will you have?'
'I'll have some books and the doll with the blonde hair, dressed in blue.' I named her Suzy. Mother chose some cuddly toys for our John then we made our way to the butchers shop.

'Go in the butchers, for me love! Ask for a small turkey, while I carry on to the green grocers.'

At last I had a chance, to spend some of the money, and bought a turkey twice the size, knowing there would be plenty to eat for everyone, over Christmas.

'Good god! Mother remarked. 'The butcher must be getting rid of his left over stock. That turkey will last till next Easter. I just hope it fits in the oven.'

Next stop was the sweet shop. 'You call in love,' while I go in the bread shop, and buy 4 lb bags of assorted sweets.' She handed me the money so giving me another chance, to spend some more money on the family, by buying extra sweets. Finally the shopping trip was over, John's pram was laden down with food, and it tilted slightly, because of the heavy turkey.

When we arrived home, it suddenly looked dismal, in comparison to the other brightly coloured homes we'd passed, for we didn't have a Christmas tree or decorations. Mother didn't seem to have any Christmas spirit in her, and probably had no incentive anyway, as she never new from one day to the next what was happening, as far as father was concerned, especially regarding his work. While she put away the shopping we put our presents at the side of our beds and after tea, it was early bath and bed. All the food preparations for the following day had to be sorted and it was much quieter, once we were from under her feet.

Late on that evening, mother put a large bag of mixed sweets, at the side of our beds, for Christmas day. Ann and Geoffrey must have been used to this tradition, for no sooner had she gone out of the room, the rustling of paper bags could be heard, as they took some of the sweets and munched away till early hours, resulting in them being physically sick next morning, obviously through having very few sweets all year round.

Christmas day was noisy and quite enjoyable, then later in the day we played on the balcony, with our new toys. Mr newly came out onto his balcony, giving us a wave.

'Had a nice Christmas Veronica?'

'Yes thanks!' I held up my Suzy doll, showing off my present.

'Do you want to spend the rest of the afternoon with our Maureen? If you do, she'll call then you can come up here and have some Christmas pudding with us.' I asked mother who was nodding off in the chair, after such a hectic day. It was okay to go, but not to be late home. I tucked Suzy doll under my arm as Maureen called, taking me into another world, for the rest of Christmas day.

Maureen's parents were quite merry, and were looking full of good cheer. Mrs Newly looked so much nicer too, than my last recollection of her.

The wonderful cooking smells combined with scented soap, were heavenly, and as always, I enjoyed sinking into the luxury carpet in the hall. Shoes had to be removed, on entering their home, so making the carpet feel even more comfortable to walk on, under my bare feet.

Silver decorations and coloured balloons, adorned the ceiling, in the sitting room, and in the far corner stood a large tree, crammed with opened presents, beneath. It was also tastefully decorated, with unusual white lights, which danced before my eyes. An ache for my beloved aunt went as quickly as it came, as Mr Newly interrupted my thoughts.

'I luv' your Suzy doll, lets place her carefully on a chair nearby and you can sit next to Maureen.' Once seated at the carefully prepared Christmas table, I looked across at Maureen who obviously took her luxury home life for granted, after all, she knew no different, yet remarkably refreshing to be around, so unspoilt and selfless, and never judging or making comparisons, regarding the extreme contrast of our daily lives.

One day she called to our flat, with some dresses she'd out grown. Being smaller than her, they fitted perfectly and some fit our Ann too. Her mother had sent them, and hoped my mother wouldn't be offended. We both ended up with plenty of wear out of them for many a month after.

Mrs Newly, was very strict with her family and there were set times allowing them to play out with the kids on the avenue. She was also prone to having a bad temper. A couple of weeks before Christmas, a commotion appeared to be going on outside our bedroom window. I looked at the clock and it was well after midnight.

Looking through the bedroom curtains, I was shocked to see Mr Newly crouching below the windowsill. I stood watching in horror, as he tried to protect himself from Mrs Newly, as she reined blows down on his defenceless body, with her offensive umbrella and leaving her language a lot to be desired, also.

'Yer won't fuckin' luk' at other women 'agen, when yer out with me, yer bastard! Cos' next time I'll kill yer!' He moved away as best he could then while fending off the blows. Soon lights could be seen dotted around the avenue, as he staggered into the passage of the flats. How could she treat him as such? He was the nicest man in the whole world. I felt upset after, as it was to play on my mind, for days. My thoughts were quickly interrupted by the voice of Mrs Newly.

'I hope you've room for some of this lot luv'.' Mrs Newly came out of the kitchen carrying a holly decorated Christmas pudding, seated on a large silver tray. A broad grin spread across her face, as she placed it in the middle of the table then a small amount of brandy was poured over the top before setting it alight. Everyone cheered then, as it flew up into brightly coloured flames.

'Be careful when you eat your puddin' angel? There three magical sixpences inside and you might be lucky enough to find one of them.'

Feeling the first sixpence grate on my teeth, I cleaned it with my napkin.

Soon after, the other two sixpences found their way on to my spoon, and everyone cheered. Mr Newly looked across the table, as he cleaned away some stray pudding, from his moustache.

'It must be your lucky day angel! Keep that money in a safe place. It's yours, no one else's.' I knew what he meant, and I would add the magical sixpences to the rest of my savings when I returned home. Later we all sat round the table playing lots of different board games. It was a perfect ending, to a perfect Christmas day. Just before bedtime I slid under the bed and surreptitiously put the magical sixpences in the tobacco tin, adding them to the rest of my savings which would obviously come in handy, for a rainy day.

This is how yer clean a floor properly, Winnie!' The front door was ajar, which was unusual and a bag of rubbish, was on the doorstep. I pushed the pram into the hall and lifted John out. He was able to walk quite steady, and on hearing father's voice from our bedroom he toddled in, while mother stood leaning against the wall with her arms folded tightly and looking positively bored.

'Hello my little wanderer!' She smiled, happy to divert her attentions elsewhere, so hopefully escaping a fate worse than death. She picked John up and swung him round, kissing him on his forehead, and looking very beautiful, as she did so.

I suddenly felt dumb struck. Father was actually cleaning under Ann's bed, and it wouldn't be long before he'd start on my side of the room. All colour drained, realising at any moment, my savings of £4-6/- would finally be discovered. A performance of the potatoes

77

and scales incident suddenly sprung to mind, turning my legs to jelly, at the very thought and what on earth could be done now? I hadn't thought so far ahead, as to anyone finding them.

'Yer move the bed away from the wall Winnie, sweep the dust up then mop the floor after.' Father was obviously being sarcastic towards mother, for she'd never have won` cleaner of the year award`, never in a month of Sundays. She rolled her eyes to the ceiling and tutted as she carried John from the bedroom.

"Hi, little fellow we'll get you some milk and biscuits for you, then I'll start the tea, it's getting late." Sunday tea was a little special, with sandwiches made from meat left over from lunch, and for afters, they'd be pudding and chocolate biscuits. These days, father was in work and behaving himself, and life again, seemed on a level footing. Food was also plentiful on the dinner table and mother seemed financially better off.

'I'll clean our side of the room, father!' Suddenly feeling a spring- cleaning mood take over, for it was imperative I reached the tobacco tin, first.

'Your okay, go and 'ave a bath before yer tea.' My hands were feeling clammy, as well as my heart thumping madly against my chest.

'It's okay really! I don't mind, as there's nothing else to do at the moment.' Father was getting irritable at this stage.

'I said, go and ave' a bath!' He moved my bed away from the wall, then taking the brush and shovel, started to sweep. I continued to watch with baited breath, as his eyes finally focused, on the dusty tobacco tin.

'Winnie! I've found my tobacco tin, I've been luckin' for it for ages, it's bigger than my other tin and I can put more dimps and rizla papers in it!' She chose to ignore him, being busy in the kitchen and continued preparing the tea. He rattled the tin to his ear as he picked it up from the floor. "The kids 'ave been keepin' their marbles in it!" He shouted, while keeping the one -sided conversation going. He then threw the unopened tin onto the bed, and with the other hand continued to sweep the floor but the impact of the throw caused the lid to burst open, scattering its contents all over the bed covers.

'What the fuckin' 'ell, is this lot? Winnie, come 'ere! 'ave yer been savin' money up, behind my back?'

Mother walked in the bedroom while opening a packet of biscuits and looking surprised at the amount of money scattered around the bed. She laughed scornfully.

'You must be joking! In all the years I've known you, I've never managed to save a penny. I just manage nicely, with the house- keeping, you provide.' He glanced up from the floor and noticed my change of colour.

"Well, well! Need I luk' any further. I think I've found the culprit. Lady! Is this your money? Come on, I want the truth, if it is, yer better be able to explain it away, and it better be good, cos' I've got all night to listen."

My hands were really clammy, for I couldn't think of a good enough reason, for having so much money. All I could do was think of my Aunt and happier times, for it would see me through the frightening ordeal ahead. She would never have allowed him to hit me, and would have made mince meat out of him, that's for sure. When I suddenly remembered, she'd always given me spends, it wasn't very much money, but I would just have to exaggerate. A lie is a survival tool, and it was necessary at that moment in time.

'Well! What excuse 'ave yer got? My patience is warin' a little thin.' He continued to count the money and became a little flustered, in the process.

'Aunt gave me 2/- pocket money each week, so I managed to save most of it. I had it in my suitcase the night you brought me home, so I put it under the bed for safe- keeping as I didn't know at the time what else to do with it.' I looked to mother for some support and noticed the packet of biscuits she held in her hands had long since been opened and crushed, causing crumbs to spill onto fathers spotlessly clean floor.

'It's feasible I suppose!' She answered a little nervously, while at the same time stealthily shuffling the crumbs with her foot until they disappeared underneath Ann's bed.

'There's £4-6/- 'ere! Can yer believe it, Winnie?' He strode towards me, holding the money in his hands.

'Yer mean to tell me, you hid all this money and you've seen me, 'aving to stay in some nights, without a penny. Not able to afford a pint of beer or a woodbine even, yet yer never thought to treat me.' Smacking me hard across the face, with the back of his hand, I fell backward, with mother catching me in time, and saving me from falling against the bedroom wall.

'Yer nothin' but a selfish little bitch, yer own father and you'd see me without. Well it speaks volumes in my book. What do yer say, to that Winnie?'

'For Christ sake Jimmy, don't hit her? You should be pleased someone's able to save money, in the family, and after all it might come in handy one day.'

'Well it's come in 'andy alright! I'm off to Dollies for the rest of the fuckin' night.'

Mr Newly was proven right. The sixpences were magical after all inside the Christmas pudding for I witnessed them swiftly disappear from my tobacco tin into father's jacket pocket.

Striding towards the door, on his way out he shoved the wet mop at mother. "Ere, finish yer own bleedin' moppin' up woman, I've had enough of the lot of yer."

Those weeks of visiting Mrs Silverstones were apparently for nothing, as the money would be frittered away in the next couple of hours, on beer and cigarettes. The situation could easily have flared too, but the money obviously put father in a good mood and the subject was never mentioned again.

The errands to Silverstones suddenly stopped, which suited me anyway, as father went himself one day, only to find he got a few extra shillings more for his parcels than when he'd sent me, which he found rather odd.

Chapter Six.

Only two days left in school before the Easter holidays, and on my way out of the classroom, Mother Dympna, handed me a letter. It was addressed to my parents and she wanted some form of acknowledgment for the following day, but on opening the letter, my mother appeared upset.

'The nerve of the woman, I'll show it your father when he comes home.' The letter was handed over immediately, on his arrival.

'Cheeky bastard, cause for concern, she writes 'ere. Well yer can go to school first thing, tomorror' Winnie. Yer tell her, theres plenty to eat 'ere, and it's not our bleedin' fault, if our Veronica doesn't eat much.' He threw the letter onto the table in disgust and went to wash his hands before tea. Mother picked it up again, and read on.

'Mother Dympna's implying, our Veronica's malnourished, and wants to discuss it with us both. Jimmy!'

'I've got to work all day tomorror woman! So go yer self, and see the bleedin' penguin.' She folded the letter then and sat down at the dinner table next to me.

'What am I going to do about you? What sort of food do you enjoy, for instance? Because it obvious, you don't enjoy my cooking.'

True.' I thought. But that wasn't the problem. I'd never settled in the flat, and had fretted for my aunt since leaving her, almost two years since. Food was also the last thing on my mind, even though it was plentiful now, but I couldn't possibly explain my feelings, for they'd never understand. Remembering a taste of food I had enjoyed, but quite a while since, was on one of our shopping trips to Billie the butcher.

'I quite liked the taste of ham and corned beef, when Billie the butcher used to give me, in his shop, do you remember? I'd eat it with tomatoes, bread and butter, every day.' She looked to father for a moment, not being sure if he'd agree to extra money being spent on one person, for a special diet.

'What do you think Jimmy?'

'I think she's just bein' bleedin' awkward! She should want to eat rabbit pie and stew, like the rest of us, but under the circumstances, I suppose we can stretch the budget that far. Although we can't afford to buy it for the rest of 'em, so they'd better not bleedin' ask, and the last thing we want is her getting malnutrition, cos' I'll be in real trouble, for I don't want the law on me back agen'. I've already served six bleedin' weeks for her majesty, and that's enough for any man, in my book.

Following morning, mother went to school to see Mother Dympna, and after a lengthy discussion, a decision was made. After the Easter holidays, if there was no improvement regarding my weight, she would be in touch with the welfare and arrangements would be made to have me stay in a convalescent home.

But after a week of eating my favourite food from Billie the butcher, a few pounds had been gained in weight, much to my parents delight.

Only a week left of the holidays. Mother was treating me to the swimming baths and thankfully, an afternoon free of our John.

Standing on our balcony and wrapping my swimsuit in a towel, while waiting for Maureen to call, I glanced across to City Road. It was the main bus route from Piccadilly, to Old Trafford and Manchester United football ground, and the bus stop was in clear view, of the passengers alighting, the buses. My aunt used the number 47 bus, when she'd visited in the past, so I'd often watch the buses driving past, half- heartedly hoping, she would visit. But it was a thing of the past, for she would never call again, especially after the last performance with my parents.

Feeling pensive, I looked over once again before going indoors, when the number 47 bus drove past, and when stopping, people started to alight it. I was just about to move away from the balcony, when I had to look twice. It was definitely aunt, she was unmistakable, wearing her best tweed suit, silk headscarf, and carrying the same brown leather shopping bag, as she always did.

'It's Aunt!' I screeched, excitedly. Mother quickly deserted her armchair and looked across the balcony, towards the main road.

'Well! I can't believe it! It's been such a long time! Maybe she's forgiven us for upsetting her, after all!' I was so happy to see her, I quickly ran to Maureen and explained I wouldn't be able to go swimming, then rushed outside and ran across the gravelled croft to meet my Aunt. . Throwing my arms round her waist tightly, and drinking in the familiar smell of lavender scent, a feeling of being safe and secure, once more enveloped me.

'Aunt, are you taking me home with you to live? Please say yes!'

'We'll 'ave to see luv, but don't build yer hopes up, for its yer father that's the problem, himself, being the funny one.'

Two sisters were soon in harmony once again, after burying their grievances, both sitting in front of the fire, smoking, drinking tea and generally putting the world to rights.

Feeling optimistic, yet my stomach full of butterflies, I washed the dinner plates in the kitchen, for whenever a member of the family visited, children had to make themselves scarce.

When father arrived home, he was surprised, yet unhappy, at seeing his sister in law, seated at the dinner table.

'What the the 'ell are yer doin' 'ere?'

'I'm not 'ere to cause any trouble Jimmy, for a confrontation is the last thing on my mind, so let's call the past, water under the bridge, shall we? and 'ave done with. All I want to know is, can I tek' Veronica 'ome with me for a while? I might be able to build her up a bit, and before yer say anythin' more, I don't want the family allowance book either. Yer can keep it.'

This brought music to father's ears, as he considered for a moment. I just looked on hopefully, and willing him to say yes.

'Aye, yer can tek' her! Were 'avin a few problems with her not eatin', so maybe you'll be able to coax her.'

'Well, that's sorted then!' Aunt handed me a parcel of new clothes to change into, and telling me to have a nice bath first.

The feel of the new cotton underwear next to my skin, felt heavenly. When completely dressed, I walked into the front room like a bright new pin, but suddenly felt a pang of guilt, as Ann watched on, in her old clothes. I tried to ease my conscience slightly though, by having a sneaky suspicion, she was pleased to see me leaving. Later she would sit happily with mother in front of the fire, having one of their many cosy chats, of which, I was always excluded.

I felt sorry, having to say goodbye to my brothers, especially John. For I knew he wouldn't be playing on his favourite amusements in the park, anywhere near as often, and probably end up playing on the balcony, most of the time.

Aunt left her chair and put on her coat and headscarf. 'Come 'ere luv', while I plait yer hair? Then we'll make our way 'ome.'

As I stepped outside onto the avenue, some of the kids made fun.

'Luk' at Neill, Neill orange peel, all poshed up! Who does she think she is?' I chose to ignore them, as I skipped happily at the side of aunt, who was taking me once again, into a different kind of world.

Seated on the bus at last, and happy to be returning home, I relaxed and started to count the windows and assorted coloured curtains, which in turn, caused me to remember that unforgettable journey into the unknown, when my parents brought me to the flat, that dreadful evening, two years ago.

Aunt looked thoughtful, as she lit up a cigarette and breathed in the smoke with gusto.

'I need to explain something of importance, before we reach 'ome'! I'm no longer with your uncle Bob, for we divorced a while ago, but I've been livin' with Jim for quite some time. Uncle Jim to you, so don't forget. We've decided to get married, in a couple of days and your invited to the wedding, although our James won't be comin', for he's at that funny age of fourteen, and doesn't want to go anywhere, except with his friends. Not to worry though, we'll still have a nice time and I'm sure you'll like Uncle Jim, he's Scottish too, but his ascent, is practically none existent. I've another surprise, waitin' for yer, when yer get 'ome, but you'll never guess.' I played the guessing game for the rest of the journey, but couldn't get her to spill the beans.

Setting foot into my old home seemed really strange. Maybe it was the absent sound of an echo, which I'd grown used to, when walking into the flat, or maybe I was simply missing, the patter of tiny feet.

Wandering into my plush bedroom and noticing nothing had changed. A sudden pang of loneliness and guilt ran through my veins. How could I possibly enjoy all this, when my brothers and sister, were living almost below the poverty line, and without a luxury in sight, even though father was working regular.

Maybe it was being a few years older and experiencing life, on extreme scales, which was thrust upon me suddenly, and all within a couple of years. It had changed my views somewhat, by putting value on life in perspective, and materialistic things, paling into insignificance.

Life had also changed dramatically, when our John was born, and becoming a mother figure at such an early age, was a traumatic experience. Yet I found we bonded remarkably quickly. But because of my move here, the bond would inevitably be broken. Whatever. Things could never be quite the same, again.

'Hello there! Daydreaming are we?' My hair was ruffled in a friendly gesture. 'I'm Jim, pleased to meet you.'

I responded sullenly, while observing his tall stature, fair hair and friendly outlook. He also wore thick- rimmed spectacles, which added an air of intellect, to his obvious good looks. He suddenly appeared uncomfortable under my fixed gaze, as he beckoned me into the hall.

'There's a surprise, in the sitting room for you, if you want to look`

Not knowing what to expect, I followed him in and was thrilled to find a Television set, standing in the corner. He switched it on, as children's viewing had just started, then seemingly a little more relaxed in my company proceeded to pick up the evening newspaper, and sit down, so leaving me sitting in front of the TV set, totally mesmerised. Our James came in soon after. He said a quick hello, grabbed a sandwich and disappeared again, till late evening. The whole time I lived at aunts, the amount of times I was to see him were few and far between.

The wedding took placed as planned, without any qualms. Aunt looked stunning. Dressed in a light grey suit, pale pink accessories and holding a spray of flowers.

There was also a buffet at her friend's home, planned later for that evening, and Uncle Jim bought her a piano she had always dreamed of, as a special wedding present.

Although we had a TV set, many of our evenings were spent around the piano, while Aunt played her favourite tunes. Tchaikovsky's Concerto Number One.' It being one of our favourites!

Unable to settle, through worry over John and thinking he'd never venture any further than the balcony for some fresh air. Aunt decided to take me home to visit, hopefully for some piece of mind but there was no reply when calling to the flat, so on a whim, we went to the park.

Mother was seated on a bench, chatting away happily to another lady, and our John was playing on his favourite seesaw amusement, with another child. Mother looked a little surprise to see us, and introduced us to her friend, it was also very obvious mother was heavily pregnant, with her sixth child, something I hadn't been aware of before leaving the flat, a month earlier. She wasn't showing, at that particular time, or maybe I just hadn't noticed, due to the fact, she'd let her figure get out of shape, after her last pregnancy. The baby was to be born end of June and I secretly hoped, she'd be able to cope on her own.

Apparently, she'd been taking John to the park every day. Weather permitting, of course, and so making a new friend.' Saying she was feeling much better and happier in her-self for venturing out more often. I returned home that day, comfortable in the knowledge, everyone was coping quite nicely, so able to live a guilt free life, with some added home comforts.

After living at Aunts for a period of time, it had to be said, there was a noticeable change in her and she definitely treated Uncle Jim differently, in comparison to uncle Bob. Jim seemed a little afraid of her and couldn't cope with her increasing mood swings. It was also obvious to all. She ruled the roosts. She'd pick on him for trivial things, for instance. Not putting the plates or pans back in their rightful place, after he'd dried up after tea, and he would never, ever start a row with her.

Seated round the dinner table one evening, aunt handed Jim a letter from the taxman.

'When are yer' goin' to open that letter from the taxman, Jim? Yer never know it might be a tax rebate.' He glanced at the letter at his side thoughtfully.

'It's okay Hilda it'll be of no importance or of interest to anyone, so it can wait till later!'

'Well, I'm interested! So how do yer know, it's of no interest to anyone, if yer don't open it?' Reluctantly, Jim opened the letter and suddenly turned an ashen colour, whilst reading on.

'What's to do luv'? Do yer owe them some money like?'

'No Hilda, it's nothing really! It's just the usual boring tax form that needs filling in, so I'll see to it at weekend.'

'Well yer luk' like you've seen a ghost, and if I can be of any help?' Just as Jims about to fold the letter, another letter falls onto the table, which he'd obviously tried to hide and quickly retrieve, but to no avail.

'Let's tek' a luk' at that letter! Aunt reached across the table, but he folded it quickly, to replace it in the envelope.

'Leave it will you, it's none of your business.' He snapped.

'This is my bleedin' 'ome, Jim! So don't tell me what to do in it.' She reached across again, ignoring his pleas and snatched the letters from his hand, but as she read on, all colour drained from her face.

'I can't believe I'm reading this!' By this time, Jim had his head resting in his hands, and scarcely able to look up and face her, as he took on a palid look. Aunt stood up, throwing the letters onto the table in a fury, whilst pushing her chair to one side.

'Yer bastard, you'v got a wife and six kids in Scotland to support, and yer only married me recently. Are yer all listenin' to this, everyone? I think I'm avin' a fuckin' nightmare. I've only gone and married a bigamist.' Our James looked across the dinner table and shrugged his shoulders, not quite understanding, what it all entailed. Until she rushed from the table, into the sitting room and back again, yielding a large poker. Holding the offensive weapon, she pointed it threateningly towards Uncle Jim.

'I'll teach yer, yer fuckin' bigamist! I'll kill yer, so I will!' James and myself, moved swiftly from the table, realising it was really serious, as she proceeded to hit Jim full force with the poker, causing his forehead, to split open. He screamed out in pain, as the blood suddenly oozed profusely from his gaping wound and spilled over, onto his unfinished Shepherds -pie. I stood rooted to the spot in fear, as James ran out to the nearest neighbour for help, and arriving back just in time, and saving Jim, from yet another frenzied attack.

He couldn't defend himself of course, as hard as he tried, for she'd suddenly taken on, the strength of four women.

'I'm goin' to report yer, to the local authorities, first thing tomorror mornin'! Just see if I don't!' Still screaming, she tried to hit him yet again, until a neighbour forcibly took the poker from her tight grasp. I looked at Aunt that moment in time, and as much as I loved her, I couldn't help but think, if she could carry out such a vicious attack, on another person, she had to be well and truly insane.

The neighbour took Jim to hospital, where he received quite a few stitches, to his forehead, and I can vaguely remember him staying away for a few days, until aunt had calmed down.

She never did report him to the local authorities, regarding her finding that night, as she was to live with him for quiet some years, later.

We received a letter from my mother some weeks later, letting us know of the good news, for a baby sister had been added to the family unit. They named her Jane. Mother must have been coping okay, for there was no mention in her letter suggesting otherwise, much to my relief. She did mention our Geoffrey though, for he was at present staying in Style convalescent home, because of being underweight, through lack of a poor appetite, but would be home in the summer holidays, all being well.

Nearing home after a day at school, a police car could be seen, parked outside our house. It was an unusual sight within our neighbourhood, so causing a stir within my circle of friends. On approaching our front window, they tried to have a sneaky look inside, by stretching over the privets.

Walking in the back door and feeling concerned, I put my satchel down on the kitchen chair, a strangers voice could be heard chatting in the sitting room, so pouring a glass of milk, I sat quietly and stayed put. Walking into a room uninvited, when there was a visitor, was a hanging offence, in my day.

Concern for Aunt was growing and I was hoping she hadn't caused Uncle Jim another serious injury, as lately her temper seem to flare for no apparent reason, especially since her finding not so long ago of marrying a bigamist, which seemed to have tipped her over the edge.

Voices could be heard as the sitting room door opened. A police officer left the room, and acknowledged me with a friendly smile, as he made his way to the front door.

'Don't you be worrying Mrs Mc Kennas! We'll soon find the culprit, sending the poison pen letters, and when we do, we'll be in touch immediately.'

Scare mongering had been happening quite frequently in the quiet neighbourhood and it seemed there was no end, to its soul destruction. Later that same evening a couple of neighbours called round.

'Were so upset Hilda! Whatever would we do without your help? Receiving such frightening letters, just doesn't bare thinking about, and the insinuations…Well, were just too afraid to go out alone at night.' Aunt was secretly in her element, as they looked to her trustingly, for her strength and support.

'I know how yer feel ladies! Why, I only received one meself, this very mornin' in the post, it was so upsettin' and insultin.' That's the reason I called in the police, and whoever it is, must be sick in the 'ed, that's all I can say. Not to worry though, yer can trust me, for I've contacts, being on the committee, so I'll soon get the matter sorted, one way or another.' The women nodded their approval simultaneously.

"Too right Hilda, your concern is much appreciated, and whoever it is, the sooner their caught, the better for all concerned."

'It's no use, we'll 'ave to move! We can't live 'ere any longer!' Aunt exclaimed, as she rushed into the sitting room, after one of her regular afternoon walks, with her pet mongrel- Mac.

'What on earths brought all this about? Uncle Jim stopped reading his afternoon paper, while looking somewhat confused, at such a rash statement. I was watching the television, but seemingly went unnoticed, with all the kerfuffle.

'Your never going to believe it! Yer know that tall slim woman, who's just moved into the house opposite? Well! She recognised me, she knows who I am. After all those years of livin' next door to her, who would ever believe she'd end up livin' opposite me, and around 'ere of all places.` Jim looked on, even more puzzled, as he folded his newspaper, while Aunt paused for breath. 'She's just passed me on the road, and luked' twice. I just know she recognised me, Jim… well! There's no alternative, we'll just 'ave to move away. I just know she'll tell all and sundry, what took place all those years ago, especially when she finds out I'm on the local committee too, and elpin' people in the community. She'll 'ave a field day, mark my words… life won't be worth livin'.' Jim scratched his head, for he was still none the wiser and was glad when he could finally get a word in.

'Let's start again Hilda! You took the dog for a walk, a woman looks at you twice and suddenly we've all got to move on! It's a bit rash to say the least, and if what I'm thinking is right. It must be near on, twenty- five years, since it happened. You forget, people have short memories and are far too busy getting on with their own lives, to be interested in yours…and remember, you've changed your surname since then!'

'I'm still called Hilda though. Aren't I? So she's bound to remember, eventually! I'm just tryin' to think of her name, and I'm bound to remember soon, erm… just let me think for a moment, Beatrice, somethin' or other.' Aunt suddenly snapped her fingers. 'Beatrice Charlsworth… That's it.' Jim couldn't help but laugh.

'Blimey! That's a name and a half, if ever I heard one.'

'Don't make light of it Jim! It's not funny my sanity's at stake 'ere…believe me.' Jim couldn't help but laugh again.

'Your sanity's at stake, all our sanity's at stake! With Beatrice bloody Charlsworth's, lurking in the background, so let's forget about her shall we? And if you mention her name once more today- I'm going down the pub.' Aunt was upset at this stage and Jim could see the problem was really getting to her.

'Sorry Hilda! I shouldn't make light of it, and I am trying my best to understand. The woman probably looked at you twice, simply because you were looking at her, that's all there is to it, so try to calm down. What happened, all those years ago, protrudes in your own mind, that's the reason, you recognised her in the first place. And I do understand how you feel love, you must know that?' Aunt clipped a few strands of hair back from her forehead, while pacing from one side of the room, to the other.

'Understand how I feel! Yer don't 'ave a notion. Yer make me bleedin' sick. I'll tell yer how I feel, shall I? I live it day in and day out. I eat it, sleep it, taste it, it's a nightmare. In fact, I don't think I can carry the guilt any longer, I really don't. Even my own brother-in- law, has me over a barrel and threatenin' me, whenever it suits him.'

The conversation was suddenly interrupted, by the door –bell, aunt went to answer it, becoming cool calm and collective, as she did so. It was as usual, the one and only, Mrs Nosey Parker.

'Hello Hilda! I hope I'm not calling at an inconvenient time, as you appear a little upset? Are you okay?'

'I'm okay Lily! What can I do for yer?'

'I just wanted to know if you've heard anything, concerning, the poison pen letters? Only I'll feel a whole lot safer, when I find out something positive is being done. I'm a little worried you see, as I might receive another. Only it's starting to play on my nerves, as well as our Jacks.'

'Call back later Lily! We'll 'ave a chat about it then, only I'm a little pushed at present, as I've got a few things to sort out. So I'll see yer later then, ta-ta, luv. Aunt returned appearing even more worried than ever.

'That's all I need! She's a right bitch…that one is! I can well do without the Lilies of this world, believe me. And that poison pen letter she received, is the most excitement, she's had in five years, since her torrid affair, with Fred Dunthorpe, from next door. If this comes to light, she'll tear me to shreds Jim, I just know she will, for her kind thrive on gossip. She was even jealous of me being elected for the committee, did yer know that Jim? She'd do anythin' to see me kicked out!' Aunt went quiet for a moment, before deciding.

'Well! Her callin' rounds, definitely clinched it! I've made my mind up I'm leavin', while I can still hold my head up high.'

'You can't Hilda? You can't run away from the past forever. Sooner or later, it'll catch you up! Think again please! Were settled here, and my works close by. Just see what happens next time you see her, and if you feel in anyway intimidated, we'll consider moving. So try pushing it to the back of your mind, for the time being. And besides everything else, I'm worried, as I don't know

92

what's wrong with you lately? You seem to be on a short fuse these days, maybe it's something to do with your hormones.`

It was the first time Aunt had noticed me in the room, watching the television, since she'd arrived home and suddenly appeared concerned.

'Will yer go out with yer friends, for a while luv'? And you'd better forget anything you've heard in this room today. Do yer 'ere me?'

Unable to settle, Aunt decided to tumble across the woman purposely, and get it over with. She wanted to know above all else, if there would be some sign of recognition on the woman's face, when confronting her.

Aunt watched the woman's house from our window the following morning, and waited for her to venture out. Once the opportunity arose, I reluctantly walked to the shops with her. Then felt somewhat embarrassed, as she amateurishly bumped into the unsuspecting woman.

'I'm so sorry luv'! I should watch where I'm walkin, I'll be needin` some new spectacles next.' Aunt waited for the dreaded recognition. But none came, as the woman just smiled and went about her business. Still not convinced though, aunt continued to follow.

'Exuse me, but do I know yer from somewhere? It could be as far back as a couple of years, as yer luk vaguely familiar.' Aunt was pushing it, but curiosity was eating away, for she had to know there and then. After all, the woman's answer would be crucial, so causing a dramatic change in her life - to the point of no return.

The woman turned and walked towards us, while studying aunt thoughtfully, then pausing for a moment.

'I have to say! Mrs 'er?'

'Mrs Mc Kennas! It is luv''

'Mrs Mc Kennas! I've got a terrible memory for faces, but it's excellent, regardin' names. So if yer can tell me yer first name? That's if I'm not soundin' too impertinent! I'll most probably remember.'

'Hilda, it is luv?` Aunt paled a little, while lighting up a cigarette and drawing the smoke, deep into her lungs.

'Hilda! … Let me think? No! I'm rackin' my brains, erm…but no, I definitely can't recollect yer! Not at the moment, anyway but I'll think on a while and let yer know, should I 'appen to see yer out shoppin' again… Perhaps?` We started towards home, when the woman stopped, and called after us.

'Oh! Mrs M cKennas! I just thought of something.' Aunt froze in her tracks and almost afraid to turn around.

'What area was it? cos' that might narrow it down somewhat?' Aunt turned, while putting on a friendly face.

'Funny yer should mention it! Only I thought you might be able to enlighten me. Should yer 'appen to remember, where we've met before. Not to worry though. Mrs erm…'

'Charlsworth!' Aunt took on an palid look, as she shakily put out her cigarette dimp with the heel of her shoe.

'It's not that important Mrs Charlsworth, but do feel free to call in for a cuppa, when yer 'ave some spare time? As I only live opposite, at number six. And by the way, I make a lovely Victoria sponge.'

'That's very friendly of yer Mrs Mc Kennas. 'Appen I'll remember by then, if our paths have ever crossed.'

Aunt was furious, for she was still none the wiser, and had only made matters worse, for herself. She should have let sleepin' dogs lie, for indeed without doubt, a ghost from the past, had finally reared its ugly head.

Tension was building up in the home, as she paced the bedroom floor till early hours, and planning her next step to end the nagging doubts, engulfing every nerve in her body almost to-screaming point.

'I'll make sure I see her tomorror and get it over with, once and for all. I've just got to know Jim, as it's driving me to distraction.'

'Will you come back to bed and try to get some sleep woman? As your becoming obsessed, with the whole situation! You've brought it all on yourself, so you've no one else to blame, and now you've pushed the issue way too far, causing yourself, to dig your own grave. Beatrice would never have remembered you, in a million years, now all you've done is given her food for thought. Well! I'm fed up with the bloody lot of it. I'm tired, so if you don't mind, I'll try to get some sleep. I've got to work all day, or have you forgotten? And I still haven't had a wink of sleep. Where would we be if I lose my job, through being tired and not able to concentrate? You'd be pacing the room then, wouldn't you?'

Watching from the widow, a couple of days later, Aunt once again seized her opportunity and dragging me along too, as she made a beeline for Mrs Charlsworth.

'Hello! I'm pleased to see yer agen' Mrs Mc Kennas. I'm just on my way to the butchers, as my Eric likes a bit of steak, for his tea.'

'It's my Jims favourite too…and by the way, please, call me Hilda.` She wasn't really interested in what Eric liked for his tea, and waited in anticipation to see if Beatrice's memory was still in good working order, and as quick on the mark, as she had so boastfully pointed out. 'Oh by the way Hilda, regardin' our recent conversation! I'm afraid I 'ave to disappoint yer, as I've no recollection of yer, from the past, or maybe my memories just fadin, with old age. But I will tek' yer up on that cuppa, yer offered, as its quiet and very boring round 'ere. Maybe yer can fill me in on the local gossip too. That's if there's anything to report, and I doubt it, around these parts.'

Mrs Charlsworth, became a regular visitor, calling two days a week, while enjoying tea and cakes and catching up with the local gossip. Although one particular Tuesday, came and went, and there was no sign of Beatrice.

'That's strange, isn't it Jim? Beatrice not callin' for a chat! Maybe she's poorly? Yer never know. Anyway! I'll call later, as there's a light on in her front window. So she must be 'ome.'

She left Jim to wash up the dishes after tea, that night, and as always he'd put the pots and pans in all the wrong places. But tonight for one reason, or another, it was the last thing on Aunts mind. We called to Beatrice's house later and knocked several times, but there was no reply.

'That's strange isn't it, as her Erics work vans outside, so they must be ` ome, never mind, we'll call back tomorror. Come on luv', we might as well go 'ome!'

We started on our way, when Aunt happened to glance back, only to see Beatrice's lace curtain fall quickly into place.

'She's definitely at 'ome, and I've a sneaky suspicion she doesn't want to speak to me. I can't think what I've done to upset her, but I'll get to the bottom of it, one way or another.' Aunt crossed back over the road and knocked hard on the front door.

I hesitated for a moment. 'Aunt, you won't shout, or hit her will you?' As a wave of panic enveloped me, suddenly remembering, the stop- tap incident, in Wales, `of course not, yer silly sausage I can't stand violence, meself.'

Curtains started to twitch, from all angles, but she gave them one of her frightening stares, and the curtains soon fell back into place. A few neighbours were unperturbed though, and standing blatantly on their doorstep with arms folded, and hoping for the prospects of a good fight, to brighten up their monotonous day.

'Come on Beatrice open the door? I know your there! Faffin' about with yer bloody lace. I want to know what's appening? Come on open the door! I'm not bloody movin, till yer do!'

The neighbours drew a little closer, as the front door finally opened. Beatrice stood in the doorway, wearing a dead- pan expression, and as she spoke, she came across all frosty and impolite.

'I'm sorry Hilda!' Hilda guessed, by her expression, so coming face to face, with her own worst nightmare.

'How long have yer known, Beatrice?'

'I tumbled over it quite by accident, as I was talking to a friend of yours, while comin' 'ome from shoppin,' yesterday. She 'appened to mention yer married, recently, but she couldn't remember your newly married name, so associating yer with yer previous name, being Scunthorpe. I put two and two together, and suddenly realised why yer bumped into me that first day and why yer should be so interested in where we'd met before? How could I ever forget that name from the past- Hilda Scunthorpe!'

Aunt answered shakily, while lighting up yet another of her many cigarettes she would smoke in a day.

'I see! So where does that leave me? Are yer goin' to tell all and sundry, what I've done? Which will no doubt, make my life a misery, until I move from the area.'

'I'm not goin' to say anythin' to anyone Hilda, but yer will never know for sure, will yer? The ball is in your court now, and all I can say is, I'll never darken' your door agen.' It's sad in one way, because I really liked yer and I know we could 'ave been good friends, but how can I associate, with yer, after my finding.` I could see my Aunt was struggling to find the right words, before answering.

'Your so self-righteous, Beatrice, aren't yer? Only too ready to judge other people, well, let him without sin, cast the first stone. Yer know there's nothing I can do to make things right, so I'll say goodbye, and start makin' plans for an exchange from around here, as quickly as possible.' Beatrice looked decidedly uncomfortable, as a cloud of sadness spread across her face.

'Goodbye Hilda, and good luk' in the future.` She closed her front door slowly, while leaving Aunt on the outside, looking somewhat lost and bewildered, as to what the future would hold there on.

That same night, there was a terrible row, for Jim was at the end of his tether.

'I'm not moving from here, Hilda! I've already told you, I'm settled in my work! If we move from here, I might not find another job so easily, so were staying put, and that's my final word!'

He slammed the sitting room door behind him, just as Aunt threw something heavy towards it, which in turn echoed round the house, as it came crashing to the floor.

'I'm the one who's committed the crime, Jim! And I'm already payin', for the rest of my life.' She screamed. 'And what's goin' to 'appen, if we stay? 'Cos I know, Beatrice will tell everyone, and

I'm the one who's to go out shopping and face everyone each day. It won't be yourself will it, yer selfish bastard.'

James came in soon after and tried to calm her down, then made her a cup of tea, and proceeded to clean up, whatever it was she'd broken. He went to bed later, but she could still be heard moving around restlessly, in the sitting room.

Confused, yet a little afraid, of hearing her screaming about the crime she'd committed. I tried hard to push all questioning thoughts, to the back of my mind, as I tried to catch up on some sleep. But in the early hours, I was awoken, by a terrible wailing sound, coming from aunt's bedroom.

James, and myself rushed from our bedrooms and into theirs, only to be confronted by Jim, sitting on the bed crying and holding some handkerchiefs against a large gash, at the front of his head. Apparently while sleeping, Aunt had hit him viciously over the head with a garden spade. Aunt was still holding the garden spade, as Jim stood up from their bed.

Taking a suitcase down from the wardrobe with one hand, and trying to stop the flow of blood with the other, he started to pack, while our James took the offending shovel very slowly from aunts shaking hands, and helped her into bed.

Jim was aware of my presence in the room as he started to pack, and looked thoughtful for a moment.

'Get your clothes packed Veronica! I can't possibly leave you here, especially after this happening! Your aunts not a well woman as you can see, so she won't be able to look after you, for quite some time.' I looked to her and hoping for some response, but James was covering her with a blanket, as she was shivering and looking really strange.

Once packed, I waited in the hall for Jim, and wandered what would become of her and our James, in the distant future.

'Come on love, we'll get a taxi to you parents, for it's way too early in the morning, to be waiting for buses!' Jim was concerned for our James too, but he insisted on staying with his Aunt, for he

98

was old enough at the age of sixteen, and quite capable, of looking after them both.

Chapter Seven.

I said goodbye to Aunt and kissed her on the forehead just before the taxi arrived, but she didn't seem to notice, and never said goodbye. I didn't really want to leave, especially as she was ill, but obviously had no choice in the matter.

On the journey home, Jim and myself were seated in the taxi, and both feeling emotionally upset. He was still holding a hanky up to his wound, although it appeared to have stopped bleeding.

He was never to win the fight,' I thought, and had to uproot after all, whereby leaving his home and his work and having to return to Scotland- so he'd told our James, before leaving. He would keep in touch regardless, and still showed great concern for Aunt, even after her vicious attack on him. I suppose he still cared for her, but in no doubt afraid, and obviously fearing for his own safety.

I was feeling apprehensive, on my journey home to the flat, but on the other hand, partly relieved. For the first time, I was beginning to feel insecure living with Aunt, as she was becoming quite a complex person to be around, yet was having mixed feelings, for having left her. The crime she had committed, must have deeply saddened her and whatever Beatrice knew of it, it must have been quite horrific. But I couldn't imagine Aunt hurting anyone, least of all myself.

The opportunity arose in the taxi and I could have questioned Jim, concerning my fears, but suddenly felt uncertain of his response to such question.

We were nearing the end of our journey, for we were approaching City Road, it could be seen as we looked out of the rainy window. I expect father would be surprised too, at us turning up at some unearthly hour.

Thinking about it, I didn't relish the thoughts of living there again- either, in fact I wasn't sure where it was safe to live anymore. The thoughts of mother and the cheval mirror sprung to mind, sending a shiver down my spine, and it wasn't long before the penny dropped and realising, I was being raised, by two mentally unstable women. Where was it all leading to? I expect god, knew the answer to that one.

But there was a new baby sister, which I hadn't seen yet, and would be just a year old, so that alone, would be something to look forward too, as well as seeing our John again.

As we abandoned the taxi, I could once again feel the familiar gravel beneath my feet, as we walked towards, the dismal looking flats. The white lace curtains adorning Mrs Newly's front windows stood out like a sore thumb, compared with the rest of the yellowish, precariously hung lace of the other residents.

The flat next door had been vacant for some time, before I'd left to live with Aunt, but it obviously had new tenants, for the windows were smeared with windolene to keep out prying eyes until they eventually moved in. I would hear all about my new neighbours in due course, but there was much more to be concerned about at the present moment, as Jim knocked hard on the front door, to awaken my father, and there'd be no doubt in my mind he'd be none too pleased to see us.

'What the 'ell!' Fathers face was like thunder, as Jim introduced himself

'Sorry, I've had to call at such an early hour! I'm Jim, Hilda's husband. I've brought your Veronica home, as Hilda's not well enough to take care of her.' Father looked nonplussed, as he widened the door to let us through.

'I see! Well come in and sit yer selves down, as yer both luk' like yer could do with a cuppa, and what the 'ell's 'appened to your face, mate? It luk's quite nasty, that gash does. Yer best tek' yerself down to the Royal later, you'll probably need a few stitches in it, by all accounts.'

'It's nothing serious Jimmy, I expect it'll heal up, in a few days.' Father handed us our cups of tea, as he eyed Jim suspiciously. Jim welcomed his tea and sipped it gratefully, as he continued to explain.

'Hilda's been having a few problems recently! Regarding... well you know? What she did all those years ago. Someone moved onto the estate recently and recognised her, so she's decided to move away from the area. It didn't help matters either, when the police discovered she'd been writing threatening letters, to the women on the estate. I still don't know the reason why she did it, but someday she might decide to explain. I expect she'll be in touch, in the near future though, to let your Winnie know, which area she's moved too.' Father looked a little closer at Jims wound.

'I expect she's done that to your face though? So if yer decide to go back with her mate, yer want to sleep with one eye open! I'm only tellin' yer, as nothin' surprises me with her. Just listen to some sound advice, comin' from a man that knows? Give 'em a gud' clip around the ears every once in a while, for it'll do 'em the world of gud, believe me, otherwise they'll lead yer a dog's life. Run rings round yer, they will, life just wouldn't be worth livin.'

Our Winnie knows her place. She'd never dare answer me back, she's a gud'n really, and wouldn't think of hurtin' me. Not like your Hilda. Bleedin' violent, that one is, and that's puttin' it mildly.'
Jim stood up to leave.

'She's been a good wife to me, Jimmy, and good to your kids! So I won't here you say a word against her! Anyway, I'd better be on my way, so thanks for the tea. I'll take your advice about having some stitches at the Royal. But that's about it, mate."

Jim pecked me on the cheek. 'See you soon love, and take care! I'll be in touch soon to see how your, keeping.'

I felt sad watching Jim leave, as we got on quite well, and just hoped he would return to Aunt soon, as she would be very lonely, without him.

The door gently closed and all went quiet, for quite a few moments. Father threw his dimp into the fire, and started getting ready for work.

'Well don't stand there gawpin'! Get yer coat off, and start unpackin.' Winnie! Get out of that bed! Yer daughters back 'ome!'

Mother walked into the front room, wearing her usual old long nightdress, and was looking heavily pregnant yet again, with her seventh child. She was still a beauty though, even first thing in the morning, with her tussled blonde hair, which she'd grown quite long hanging loosely around her shoulders She was carrying Jane in her arms and she looked a sweet little thing, with shiny dark brown hair, but she suddenly shied away, while burying herself into mother's chest.

John came out of his room soon after. He'd grown incredibly tall since I'd last seen him. I thought he might be the tallest of the family, unlike me who was never to grow any taller, than five foot.

He was so pleased to see me, and threw his arms around my neck, then wanting to know when we'd be going to the park. I told him as soon as he was dressed and had eaten all his breakfast.

Mother watched on, looking thoughtful. 'You look really well, and it's lovely to see you. It'll be nice to have you back, as you can help a little around the home. As you well know Ann's not much help really, and our Geoffrey's still away, convalescing.'

Father was still working to my relief, and put on his donkey jacket and hobnail boots.

'Oh by the way, I forgot to mention Winnie, your Hildas gone off her fruit and nut agen, so that makes two of yer. I'll be makin' my way to work then, and I'll see yer all later- ta-ra.'

Mother ignored his sarcasm and made her way to the kitchen, to start breakfast, which gave me a chance to nosy around the flat.

There was very little change, although a couple of new items of furniture were dotted around the rooms, making it look a little less sparse. It still carried the same stale cigarettes smell, but looked a lot cleaner. It seemed my parents were on friendly terms too, making me feel a little less insecure, as I started to unpack.

The new neighbours were called Bennett. They had three sons, ranging from the ages of one, eight and eleven years. Tony was the eldest, and soon joined our friendly group, on the avenue.

His parents seemed financially better off, than most of the families around, apart from Maureen's parents. Their father was part owner with, Bennett's Scrap Metal Merchants, situated on Chester Road.

Mother never took to Mrs Bennett, as she thought her a little bit above her station, and couldn't understand why she'd want to live in our area. Although I had a feeling, mother was a little envious of all her finery.

Tony's mother also made it quite obvious she didn't like him mixing with the other kids on the avenue, including myself. If a game of football kicked off, on the croft, he would join in nonetheless, and return home filthy and muddy, much to her disapproval.

He soon became my childhood sweetheart, and soon thought him the best thing since chocolate biscuits. He had thick dark wavy hair, his shirts were whiter than Persil white, and his clumpy shoes shone. We'd escape upstairs, to the third floor of the flats, some evenings, whenever I was free, of looking after our John, and drank lemonade, and eat crisps, which Tony pinched from his mother's larder. We'd sing our favourite songs, from the radio such as, Jezebel and Perry Como's. Magic- Moments, It was all much needed fun, which had been so lacking in my earlier years.

Mother received a letter from Aunt a few weeks later. She was pleased to be moving to her new home in Widnes. Uncle Jim had decided to return home, and she was so much better in herself.

There was mention of our James though, as she was experiencing a few problems regarding his recently changed way of life. He'd become a Teddy- Boy and joined a gang, much to her disapproval, and if he didn't alter his ways soon, there'd be no alternative, but to ask him to leave. So mother wasn't to be too surprised if he turned up on her doorstep in the very near future.

The end of that very same week, after mother receiving her letter, our James arrived, with his suitcase in hand. I opened the front door to him and was immediately taken aback, by his transformation.

He was clad in a, Teddy- Boys suit and wearing lime green socks, inside his beetle crushers, as well as sporting long sideburns, to match his D.A. hairstyle, which was held in place, with half a jar of Brylecream

'Our James is here, with his suitcase and I think he wants to live with us.'

It was soon after breakfast, on a Saturday morning, and the flat was a tip. James's face was a picture to say the least, after he'd made his way through the dark hall, and into the front room. At the same time, mother could be seen through the reflection of the mirror hung on the wall, tidying her long hair, before sitting down in her favourite chair, to light up yet another cigarette.

'Well what brings you here? Have you had cross words with our Hilda?' Putting his suitcase down, he ran his hand nervously, through his greasy hair.

`I have decided to move away and make a fresh start, for there are more jobs available in this neck of the woods, so I hear. He stopped talking for a moment as his eyes strayed towards the clutter, before him.

A newspaper acting as a table cloth covered the cluttered table, with its used breakfast dishes, half opened cornflakes packet, a half filled bottle of milk- minus the top, and a packet of margarine, with a used knife full of toast crumbs stabbed in the centre. It was an eye sore, to say the least.

I watched for a moment, somewhat bemused at his expression of distaste, as the odd fly dived into the sugar bowl to taste its last grain, before meeting its fate and joining the rest of its dead friends, swinging from the tempting sticky flypaper trap, on the ceiling above. James looked decidedly uncomfortable, and you could see, he was having none of it, as he looked round a room generally lacking in home comforts, and cleanliness, something at home he'd obviously been used to and now, took for granted.

He finished his tea quickly out of his chipped stained teacup, while looking thoughtfully at his heavily pregnant mother, probably wandering which best way to put it, without hurting her feelings that he wasn't staying after all, but didn't quite manage the softly, softly touch, somehow.

'I've decided to move on!' He announced, nonchalantly. 'I can see there's not much room 'ere, so I'll see if I can stay at my grandmothers. (Being my father's mother) so I'll be seein' yer all then, ta-ra!'

'Stay where you are?' Mother jumped out of her chair before confronting him angrily, causing us all to sit up quickly, and listen in the process.

'How dare you! Who do you think you are? Coming here and upsetting me, is it not good enough for you then, living here with your mother? He stood up abruptly, while picking up his suitcase and moving toward the door.

'You, my mother, that's an understatement, if ever I heard one! Hilda was like a mother to me, no one else. Anyway, she should 'ave let me be myself, all I wanted was to be a Teddy –Boy so what's wrong with that? She should 'ave let me alone and none of this would 'ave 'appened. I wasn't goin' to live in Widnes, either, just to suit her. I've all my mates to think about and I'm old enough to tek' care of myself, so if I choose to live at my grandmothers, I will`

Mother blew her cigarette smoke, towards the dull yellow tarnished ceiling, before answering.

'You'll break Hilda's heart you must know that? She's never liked your father's side of the family, either, and soon, you'll be handing over your wage packet, to your grandmother. You should be paying our Hilda some wage's, she's the one who brought you up, after all, for all those years.'

James wasn't listening anymore, as he turned on his heels and stormed out, so leaving his mother, due to have her seventh child within weeks, alone with her thoughts. Finishing her cup of tea, she sat down in front of the fire, obviously full of regrets, as she tearfully stared into the cinder- filled fireplace.

It was to be four years later, when I would see our James again, and under very sad circumstances, having to break the news, of Aunt Hilda's, tragic suicide.

A couple of weeks later, mother took to her bed. Unknown to us then, she was slowly dying of Pernicious Anaemia, in its worst state. She hadn't carried well, and never blossomed like she had in her other pregnancies. Father didn't send out for the doctor, as he said she was just under the weather, and suffering from a cold.

Father came home from work and on seeing mother ill in bed, sent me to do her usual heavy chore, of buying bags of coal slack, from the hardware shop, a job she had been doing for some time.

The thoughts of pushing a pram along the avenue, filled with coal bags, filled me with dread, for at the age of ten, I was starting to feel quite conscious of myself, and knew the kids on the avenue would make fun. Father threw my coat towards me.

'Yer can go, in future, as yer mothers not well! It's not too far to walk, and you've got the pram, so yer won't have any weight to carry.'

Our Geoffrey had recently returned from convalescing and growing twice his usual size and seemingly fit and strong. It was annoying though, as father never asked him to do anything, and after all, he was eight years old, and quite capable of helping around the flat, or going the odd errand or two. I threw my coat back, and stood in the hall, defiantly.

'Why should I have to go? Let that Geoffrey go instead! It's always me who has to do the errands around here.' Father rushed forward then giving me an almighty crack across the fac, which sent me flying across the hall floor.

'You'll do as I say! When I want an errand doin,' you'll bleedin' do it, do yer 'ere me?' He then proceeded to push the pram outside the door and me, after it.

Mother could be heard shouting, from her bed, but her voice sounded rather weak. 'Will you be a bit quieter? It's bad enough being ill, without having to listen to you lot arguing, so just shut up, while I try to get some rest.' I carried on to the shop, unable to take my mind off her, for she looked quite ill. Maybe, father would call in the doctor, if she were no better, by the following morning.

Nearing the hardware shop, a gang of youths could be seen, standing on the corner and looking like they had nothing but time on their hands. They spotted me pushing the empty pram towards them, and not being in my neck of the woods, suddenly felt uneasy. I walked past and continued into the shop to purchase the bags of coal slack, the assistant was helpful, by putting them in the pram. On leaving the shop, one of the youths noticed the bags and started to make fun.

'Neill, Neill orange peel, your supposed to push a baby in a pram, not bags of slack. It's stupid, that is!' He then proceeded to pick up one of the bags out of the pram then tip its contents onto the street. I screamed at him, but he just laughed, as he made an attempt to pick up the second bag, a passer- by, saw the commotion, and hurriedly came over to help. The youths then ran off, laughing and making fun as they did. The passer- by helped to pick up the slack, it was made easier for it was made into shapes of coal eggs, so making it quicker, to return to the paper bag.

Returning to the flat, I suddenly felt relieved that father hadn't sent Geoffrey, for the gang would more than likely have beaten him, and taken the money from him too, being a younger boy.
There was no sympathy from father, whatsoever, after telling him of my threatening ordeal.

'Tek no bleedin' notice, they'll more than likely never stand there agen, as kids usually move on!' Of course he was wrong, as they stood in the same place again and happily called me names, although they made no attempts to approach the pram, again.

Well! Something had to be done. Having to make the journey four times a week was bad enough, without having to persevere with them, making life a misery. So I decided to alter the time for the errand, to 8.30am when the shop opened. The youths would hopefully still be at home, getting ready for school and at weekends, they'd probably stay in bed later, so that solved that problem. Just as well, for a much serious one was just about to happen.

Mother was slowly dying of Pernicious Anaemia in its final stages, and father still hadn't phoned the doctor, but decided to take a day off work to clean the flat thoroughly, and do a much needed clothes wash. He also made a large pan of stew for our tea, which we all enjoyed immensely for it was the first decent meal we'd had in days since mother had taken to her sick bed. Concerned I asked if he'd phone for the doctor again, but he dismissed the idea, presuming it was probably a touch of flue, and she'd be better in a few days. He missed work the following day, then the next, until finally losing his job.

It was nearing the end of November, and Christmas would soon be upon usually he'd be working really hard, for he and his work friend's would be collecting the much needed Christmas tips, from the wealthy residents, he also knew it was the only extra money mother had, to make our Christmas worthwhile.

He then signed on the N.A.B, and gave little money to mother for housekeeping. Not that she noticed, being so ill in bed, for over a week, with her baby due, at any time.

She was now seriously ill, with only enough strength, to make her way, to the bathroom, and father still hadn't thought it serious enough, to call in the family doctor. He'd been coming home late at night, sleeping on the sofa then getting spruced up in the mornings, and leaving early, so ignoring all, and being totally unconcerned as to mothers, critical condition.

I'd been absent from school while mother was ill, having to look after John and Jane. A letter had been handed in, to cover for my absence, stating I had a bad cold. Mother thought it would suffice, but she was wrong, for just after Ann and Geoffrey had gone to school, there was a loud knocking on the front door. An abrupt voice shouted through the letterbox, carrying its way through to the hall, but only to fall on deaf ears.

I recognised it to be Mr Hall, the school board, so shushed our John up best I could, and at the same time put my hand over Jane's mouth, so as not to make any noises, while we hid behind the sofa in the front room.

'Open the door Mrs Neill! I know your, in there! Why aren't you sending your Veronica to school? Come on will you open the door at once?'

John, and myself, started giggling as we thought it quite funny hiding behind the sofa while listening to his persistent demands, but wasn't going to open the door, anyway, no matter how much he threatened. A letter was finally shoved through the letterbox, as he eventually gave up. On rushing to the door, John picked up the letter and took it to his sick mother. I followed him in, as she slowly took the letter with her weak hands and read on.

Her old nightdress was stuck to her sweaty body, and her usually lovely hair, hung limp around her head. Her hand fell to the side of the bed as she asked for a cup of water, for it was all she'd been taking for the last couple of days.

'Pass me my handbag love?' As I passed her handbag and went for the water, she sat up weakly, taking the cup of water and drinking it thirstily. She looked on at her two young children playing happily on the bedroom floor, and was totally unaware of the traumatic upheaval, which was about to affect their daily lives in the next couple of hours. In her close delirious state of confusion, and fearing for her unborn child, prompted her into to a desperate form of action.

'Take my medical card with you to the phone box, on City Road, and phone doctor Coleman's number, and take a few pennies, to make sure you get through? Ask the receptionist if the doctor will make a home visit, after surgery? You must stress the fact that I'm unable to visit the surgery, as I'm too ill! Tell her it's urgent, as I think I'm losing my baby.'

Jane was already washed and changed, so I put her in the cot close to her mother, then hurriedly made my way across the gravelled path with our John in tow, to make the urgent phone call.

Luckily the phone box was vacant, but making the call to the receptionist, was near impossible as John found the phone box quite entertaining, while clambering up and trying his best, to press button A & B.

The receptionist went on to explain. The doctor would visit within half an hour of closing his surgery!

'Tidy the place up a bit, will you love?' I feel so ashamed of anyone calling, as it's such an untidy mess. Can you pack some clothes for me too, in the little suitcase? As I feel sure doctor Coleman will have me admitted into hospital, and here put this away in a safe place, and don't let your father see it!'

She'd handed me a five pounds note, folded tightly into little squares, as she did with all her notes, to keep them safely hidden in the back of her handbag, away from the scrutiny of father's eye. It will buy you some food and coal slack, for the rest of the week. I know Mrs Kershaw won't give me any food on tick, as I still owe her from last week.'

The two young ones were kept reasonably quiet, with a plate of bread and jam and a cup of milk each, whilst I swept the floors and dusted round, making it a little bit tidier. Washing clothes, in the bath wasn't too bad, but the wringing out of each article, seemed an impossible task. Eventually, the wet clothes hung from the clothes rack on the ceiling, and dripped themselves dry, onto the kitchen floor, which seemed an ever ending mopping up session.

Doctor Coleman visited much earlier than expected knowing it was an urgent call, and his patient could be in danger of losing her baby. A tall man of slim stature came charging into the hall, with thick greyish white hair, falling into heavy waves about his forehead. And forever resembling, Sir John Barber Ollie, who I'd seen at the Free Trade Hall, a few months earlier, on an educational, school trip out for the day.

'Which is your mother,s room?' I pointed towards the inadequately ventilated bedroom, but on seeing the state of his patient, the doctor took off his heavy black coat, throwing it over the nearby chair then rolling his sleeves up to examine her more thoroughly. He came out of the room soon after, putting on his coat, and rushing to the bathroom to wash his hands. He proceeded to dry them on a freshly ironed handkerchief from his jacket pocket, for his face was twisted with disgust, at the state of the bathroom towels.

111

'I'm going to make an urgent phone call for an ambulance, and I'll be returning immediately, for I want a word with you!' He returned in no time and charging once more, into the hall.

'Where does your father work?' Catching me unawares, I wasn't sure of a convincing answer.

'He's not working! But he's gone out looking for work, and he'll be home, before tea.'

'It's absolutely disgraceful! I should have been called out days ago, your mother's seriously ill! I'll give you a note to pass on to him, and it'll explain which hospital, and the ward, where she's going to be admitted. You can also tell him, I'll be calling tomorrow morning first thing, and if there's no changes in your circumstances, regarding school, and the younger ones being looked after. I'm calling in the welfare!'

I was much later to find, my mother was slowly dying of pernicious anaemia. Threatening her baby's life, and even more so, her own. But with much needed, special care and attention, a baby sister, (Catherine) was safely delivered, and added to the family unit.

It seemed really strange in the flat, once mother had been taken into hospital, and was also feeling afraid of what father's reaction would be, when learning of the day's events. There didn't seem much point in staying at home though, so I took us all off to the park, for the rest of the afternoon. I would have to wait till Ann and Geoffrey came home from school, before going for the teas.

When they came home from school, and finding mother gone, Ann especially, seemed beside herself, our John started to play up, as he was missing her too, and there was no doubt in my mind, there'd be problems, at bedtime.

It was teatime, and everyone had decided what to eat. Geoffrey liked bananas for he'd acquired a taste for them, being given lots of fruit while convalescing, and Ann wanted Carnation cream poured, over. John and Jane wanted a large bar of chocolate, we all wanted a large bar of chocolate, and so the menu was set, but all thoughts of buying coal slack for the next day, went out the window.

I took John along to Mrs Kershaw's, being so boisterous he couldn't be left with anyone, then we hurriedly ran across the gravelled path to escape the cold dark, November evening.

On entering the shop, we were hit by the warmth and homely cooking smells, of roast meat wafting in the air, but Mrs Kershaw stood behind her counter, looking sullen, with her arms folded across her, well- endowed breasts.

'Before yer start ordering any food on tick, think agen, cos yer can't 'ave any! Yer mothers not paid me for last weeks, as yet.'

I strolled towards her, unfolding the five pounds note which mother had given me earlier and plonked it arrogantly on top of the counter.

'I've got five pounds, and can buy anything I like.'

'Don't be so cheeky, yer little monkey! I'll be 'avin' a word with yer mother, when I see her next time. What do yer want, anyway?'

'I want 2lbs of bananas, a tin of Carnation cream and five large bars of Cadbury's chocolate...Please?' Mrs Kershaw eyed me suspiciously.

'Where've yer got all that money from? That's what I'd like to know!' I went on to explain, but not quite understanding myself as to what it all entailed, and wandered where mothers baby would go if she should lose it.

'Mother gave it to me this morning, to buy some food with! She's been taken into hospital, for she might be losing her baby. Mrs Kershaw suddenly looked sympathetic.

'That's dreadful news, I'm so sorry to 'ere it, I really am! Tell yer mother next time yer see her, I hope she gets better soon. Poor woman, it's a cryin' shame, it really is...that'll be 6/6 please.'

I handed her the money, but while handing me the change, which included a sweet, for each of us, she started to quiz me.

'Where's yer father then? or need I ask, Is he workin' these days, or is he in the pub?' I wander why she should be so interested in his whereabouts and answered cautiously.

'He's looking for work today, and he'll be back later.'

'More like midnight, if yer ask me! Well, I don't like the sound of any of it, believe me. So go straight 'ome and lock yer front door, and don't let anyone in, do yer 'ere me? Except me, I'll be along later, with the N.S.P.C.C. in tow.'

Dear me, what had I let myself, in for? I should have kept my mouth shut, for she'd have been none the wiser, and they'll be murders tonight when father returns, to find I've let strangers into the flat. I tried to push the last hour to the back of my mind as we enjoyed our tea, and the younger ones their chocolate bar, for dessert, but the rich food proved too much for John and Jane and they became violently sick on the living room floor. I was in the middle of changing Jane, when Mrs Kershaw could be heard, calling through the letterbox.

'It's only me! Yer can open the door luv' Its okay?'

'I won't be long!' I answered, as a feeling of panic overwhelmed me, while grabbing hold of a mop, to clean the chocolate sick, off the slippery linoleum floor.

I braced myself on opening the front door and wasn't surprised to see her accompanied by two police officers, one being a policewoman. The familiar face of Mr Jackson, of which I remembered from three years since, from the N.S.P.C.C. acknowledged me, and smiled broadly.

'Hello Veronica! Do you remember me? I'm Mr Jackson!' I nodded shyly, as Jane rushed towards me for protection.

'I have no alternative under the circumstances, but to take you all into care, until your mother is well enough to take care of you. The two younger ones will be looked after by foster parents, and you Ann and Geoffrey, will go into a children's home. It's in the Altrincham area, so it's not too far away from here, and don't be concerned about your father, I'll be calling first thing tomorrow morning, to explain.'

Ann and Geoffrey looked completely bewildered at the strangers before them, but did as they were told and put on their coats. John was having none of it though, and threw himself to the floor in a tantrum and started screaming for his mother. The

114

policewoman handled him remarkably well, and managed to change his soiled clothes, before taking him away into the awaiting police car. Jane was inconsolable as well as looking pathetically sad, and in desperate need of a cuddle, from her absent mother.

At this stage, I was feeling devastated, as my younger siblings were being taken away, and Mr Jackson could see my great concern.

'It's not for you to worry love! Your father will be able to visit, every weekend, so you'll still have regular contact with him.'

I'd have felt a whole lot better, if he hadn't mentioned father at that moment in time, for I was feeling very angry and hoped I would never have to set eyes on him again, and blamed him totally.

Mrs Kershaw smiled sadly, as windows were closed, curtains drawn and lights put out. Putting on my coat, I slammed the front door shut behind, and wasn't to know when I'd be back, or when I'd see my younger siblings again.

What would become of us, god only knew, for the future was looking quite bleak ahead. A few kids off the avenue hovered outside the flat, obviously intrigued with all the commotion, alongside my friends, Tony and Maureen, as they watched us being driven away, in separate police cars.

Chapter Eight.

We settled in the children's home fairly quickly, for it was clean warm and comfortable. Ann and me, shared a dormitory with eight other girls of similar age, and made friends fairly quickly, so adding a nice general feel to the place. The school we were to attend was a stone's throw away from the home, which was quite convenient. We each had a wardrobe next to our bed, with a variety of clothes, some for school and some for casual wear. Our uniform consisted of a colourful print dress and a black blazer, and our long blonde hair was plaited, so we always looked quite smart.

Life eventually fell into a regular routine, and in the evenings, before bedtime, we'd have supper consisting of sandwiches and some fruit, and sometimes the menu varied a little, so making it more interesting. A roster was pinned to the kitchen wall, so we'd take it turns to do the washing up and generally keep the kitchen clean and tidy. We'd then take a bath, and once in bed would read for half an hour, as lights were usually out by nine thirty.

Father didn't visit for a few weeks, and I was hoping he never would. I expect he was still smarting, from the visit from Mr Jackson, and knowing the neighbours knew all about his business, from Mrs Kershaw.

Christmas Eve was soon upon us, and as it was cold and frosty, we wrapped up warm, while taking a long walk in the private grounds, surrounding the home. Some of the children's relatives walked through the gates, and the children ran to greet them excitedly, for they'd been given presents, to put under the Christmas tree which was situated in the lounge next to the bay window, where we'd all had great fun in decorating, the previous week.

Not far behind the group of visitors, was the familiar figure of my father, and could see he'd been drinking, for his face had the usual purple tinge added. He didn't stay long either, for there wasn't much to talk about, but I enquired as to mothers well being, and was told she was doing fine in hospital, along with our new baby sister. When

116

he was about to leave, he handed us a bar of chocolate and 2/6 each to spend.

'I'll be seein' yer all next week then! Ta-ra.' No mention of Christmas' I thought.

I handed over the 7/6 to matron, not being sure of the rules for keeping money and such like, then she went on to explain.

'I'll save any money given to you for safe keeping, and when you leave, you'll each have some savings to take home.'

Eight months on, I was called into matron's office, to be told my father would be calling the following Saturday morning to take us home. So we had to be ready and waiting near the entrance door, for 9.30am.

Saturday morning arrived and we were waiting for father in the entrance hall, it was only 9.30am, and matron called in to say goodbye, while handing us our savings, in a brown envelope. When opening our envelopes, they only contained 2/6 each.

'This can't be right! Father gave us 2/6, each week, so it should be a least £3 each. I'm going to see matron before he arrives, so I shan't be long!'

Knocking on the office door, she called me to enter. 'How can I help you?' She asked in a condescending manner.
I felt a little intimidated, but nonetheless I would stand my ground, and enquire, as to the rest of our savings.

'We saved up about £3 each, over the eight months we've been staying here, but you've only given us 2/6 each.'

Standing up quickly from her chair, whilst staring with her dark piercing brown eyes, she swiftly moved around her desk, and towered over me, whilst pointing to the door.

'How dare you be so impertinent child, as to ask me concerning your savings, get out of my office at once! Do you hear me?

I left her office feeling defeated, for there was no one else who could help, relating to my query. Maybe father would have a word with her, or on second thoughts, maybe not.

From a distance, father, Ann and Geoffrey could be seen. Father looked impatient, as he walked from one side of the entrance door to the other, and on seeing me, beckoned me to hurry up. I could see he was sober and in a fowl mood too, which didn't help the situation any.

'What the bleedin' 'ell 'ave yer' been doin?' I've been 'ere over ten minutes, waitin for yer.' The welfare people will be bringin' the others 'ome at anytime.' I tried to explain why I'd been to see matron, but he just dragged my coat sleeve, towards the bus stop.

'Yer cheeky little get! You've no right to question matron about anythin'. Yer should 'ave a bit of respect towards yer elders, yer ought to be ashamed of your-self! Don't mention another word about it today, or you'll be in for a hidin' lady, I'm warnin' yer. Come on! We've only got a couple of minutes left and the bus is due, if we miss that we'll 'ave to wait another bleedin' hour and it'll be all, your fault.'

I knew father wouldn't stand my corner, for he wouldn't have had the nerve to confront matron, on such a matter for he'd always disliked anyone in authority, so would have given her a wide birth, anyway.

I gazed through the bus window, on our return to the flat and day dreamed a little. I don't know why I bothered to complain to matron, as father would have taken our savings from us anyway once we'd boarded the bus, and kept it for his own use. It was just the principle of the matter, as we'd been looking forward to buying something nice for the others, on our return home.

Remembering the last time I'd seen my mother, being carried from her bed, into an awaiting ambulance, suddenly filled me with sadness, and hoped she was now better in herself. Thinking of our new baby sister, I just hoped she would be the last and mother wouldn't have any more additions, to the family.

Finally arriving at our destination, we clamoured off the bus excitedly and ran across the familiar gravelled croft, towards the flat.

Geoffrey and Ann knocked on the door impatiently, to see their beloved mother. She answered quickly, giving us all a hug, and obviously pleased to see us.

John had grown even taller and so had Jane. They'd put on a considerable amount of weight too, and seemed happy and well adjusted, as well as being nicely dressed. It had obviously done them a power of good, living in a stable and violent free environment.

We took a peek at Catherine, who was asleep in her pram. She was long legged with short blond hair and looked ever so pretty. It also looked like she'd be another tall one, added to the family.

There was a sudden screech of excitement, from the others in the front- room, and walking in, a television could be seen in the corner of the freshly decorated room. Father switched it on, and the floor was suddenly cluttered with four children as they sat mesmerised at the new 14inch box, which was to open a whole new world for them, in their very own front room.

Looking round the freshly decorated flat, I picked up my belongings and unpacked, putting them away in a new chest of draws which had been added to our room, as well as new beds and bedding. Someone did get a good talking to after all, I thought, as there was a great home improvement all round, whilst we'd been in care.

We never did get around to discussing our adventures, or misgivings, whilst in the children's home. Not with our parents or each other. Looking like a family unit on the outside, but obviously not within.

Mother had some bad news some months later, for her father passed away peacefully in his sleep.

I attended the funeral, so meeting up with a few relatives and friends, and mother put on a buffet for them afterwards. It was a sad occasion for her, as she was quite close to him, being the baby of the family. He also left some money in his will for her, which was quite surprising, for she had always thought him, penniless.

Of course the money helped a little, so enabling her to buy some new furniture and an outfit of clothing, for each of us.

Chapter Nine.

Just as our lives started to fall into a regular routine, mother announced, we were moving to a new home in Peel Hall Wythenshawe. Explaining, it was a really nice house, situated at the end of an avenue, next to a catholic school (All Hallows.) which was convenient for us all to attend. The house also had a nice garden, at the front and back, where the younger ones could safely play.

Knowing father, I wandered if he would ever find the time to keep the garden looking presentable, and if such time should happen to fall into his hands, I expect he would happily do a rain dance.

Moving was a traumatic experience to say the least, as father hired an old van, to save money, so having to make three trips, before the move was completed. He took Geoffrey and John with him, and the rest of us accompanied mother, on the bus.

Finely arriving at our new home, it was found to be delightfully fresh and airy, and with lots of space, in comparison to the dreary flat. Each large room was tastefully decorated, and the bedrooms each had fitted carpets. In the front room, an unvarnished square of wooden floor was displayed, where the carpet had been laid. Father put down our old piece of carpet, which didn't quite fit, much to mother's disapproval. Well, she would just have to wait for a new one to be fitted, but when, one will never know.

Mother didn't look at all well either, at having to get up early for the move and rushing around, could easily set off one of her seizures. She had taken her daily Phenobarbitone tablet, but had an idea it wasn't going to work, for she looked quite insipid and had to stop quite frequently, to hold onto a chair.

'Ello luv'!' A woman's friendly voice could be heard shouting up the hallway. Do yer all want a cuppa? Only the kettles on the boil, and I know yer must be parched!'

On hearing the stranger's voice, mother walked from the kitchen, to be confronted by an obese woman with a round cheerful friendly face. Even though mother was feeling a little wobbly on her feet, she quickly put on a cheerful expression for her new neighbour.

'Hello! I'm Winnie, pleased to meet you! I'd welcome a cuppa and thanks a lot, as we haven't had time to unpack the kitchen essentials yet.'

'Great! I'll be back in a jiffy! By the way, I'm Madge! I only live at the back of yer, so if yer should want anythin', just give us a shout.' The woman turned and waddled down the garden path, as mother sat down shakily.

'I don't feel very well and I think I'm going to have a fall!' At that moment she went into one of her seizures, shaking and screaming, as she fell to the floor, with a thud.

Father was on his second trip to the flat, and wouldn't be back for ages, so without a second thought, as I could never cope alone with the frightening situation before me, called after Madge, before she faded out of sight. We managed to pick her up between us, and make her as comfortable as possible on the couch. After putting a spoon into her mouth, Madge asked if any tissues were on hand to clean the vomit from her mouth. The only ones were in mother's handbag, so Madge took the bag and rummaged through, taking out, the much needed tissues.

Later, when mother was feeling better, the two women enjoyed their cups of tea and a lengthy chat. While I was feeling forever grateful, that Madge was on hand at the time, and seemingly might prove to be a good neighbour, in the future.

Father returned soon after, with his removal journey completed, and was to learn of mother's incident, but wasn't too happy to find, we'd had a new neighbour in to help. That evening, when beds had been assembled, we all retired early, thoroughly exhausted, and thankful that the day was over.

Early hours of the morning, I was awoken by voices whispering, downstairs, and presumed the worse. I went to my parent's room, but they were asleep. Waking father gently, I told him of my fears.

'Well I can't 'ear anthin', so go back to bed! Your imagining things, cos' your in a strange room!'

122

Suddenly, there was a clatter downstairs, causing father to leap out of bed, dress quickly then run down stairs, only to frighten the thieves away, and find them clamouring through the back kitchen window.

Mother's handbag had been stolen and her personal belongings alongside her empty purse were strewn across the back garden. The police were soon called and said they would do everything possible to help, but were surprised to learn that the only neighbour mother had made friends with that day, was Madge.

'If only someone could have warned you, never to mix with the likes of Madge, or her family! For her sons are well known around these parts, for burglary, and are forever, in and out of Borstal!'

Mother was beside herself, for it was the only money she had left to last the week, and with her being new to the area, the local shopkeepers, would be reluctant to give her any groceries on tick, so father ended up, having to get a sub from his work.

There was no proof of course, that Madges sons were anyway involved, but when mother found out that Madge had been rummaging in her handbag, while she was semi conscious after her fall, decided to give her a wide birth, after all, she would have known the handbag was kept underneath the television table. Mother felt a little uncomfortable afterwards, regarding her decision to keep away from Madge, as Madge had helped when most needed, the previous day.

The other neighbours on either side of us were quite friendly with each other, and invited mother along to join the catalogue and coffee brigade, being a new comer to the estate. It was a ritual, organised by women, to find out all about your business and if you didn't join in, you were soon classed as an outsider.

Mother was having none of it, but while out shopping one day, and quite by chance, she coincidently bumped into an old work friend, Joanie, who was found to be residing, on the next avenue to us. So they made arrangements to meet up each week, for a chat and to catch up with the local gossip, which kept mother fairly happy.

All Hallows Catholic School was unable to take us in, for it was overcrowded. But the headmaster put our names down, as a replacement, if any pupils should happen to leave. But for the time being, we were placed in Brownly Green Comprehensive, being the next school, within walking distance.

One Tuesday morning, in June, I walked through the gates of my new school, and was to make friends with a girl, who to this very day is most dear to me.

Starting my first day at school was an ordeal, to say the least. I was taken nervously to my new classroom, to be introduced to Mr Fisher my form teacher, and then my new classmates.

'Go and sit down, at the empty desk, in the top left hand corner, next to Patricia Scholes and Linda Hicks!' I sat down shyly next to my new schoolchums, and as the pretty blonde haired girl looked across, she smiled and introduced herself.

'I'm Linda, and this is Pat! Would you like to be our friend?' We all giggled, as I happily accepted their friendship, and the three of us were to remain good friends, in my stay of two years in Brownley Green School, until mother got decidedly restless and announced we were moving away, yet again.

Linda and myself became firm friends, while we lived in Peel Hall and her home became my second home, as I stayed over most weekends. She was an only child at home, for her elder brother Dave, had recently married his new wife, Vera.

Her mother, Mrs Hicks, had a stroke in her late thirties, which left her paralysed down one side, so Linda had quite a responsible job, looking after her. Each morning before leaving for school, she'd wash and dress her, and generally making sure she was left quite comfortable, for the rest of the day. Mr Hicks worked shifts, down the coalmines, so often came home late. So if Linda should be late for school, or have leave of absence, it was all taken into consideration, regarding her situation, at home.

Her parents were easy going, and she was allowed to wear the latest fashion, and she also made her own dresses. If any material was left over from one of her newly made dresses, one would soon be made for me, much to my delight.

After tea, I'd rush to her house and change into my new gear, consisting of a black mini skirt and a pair of green 4inch high, stilettos. Black shoe polish was applied to the eyelashes, and gravy browning applied to the legs, which served its purpose, as stockings were unaffordable, but you just prayed it wouldn't rain as the gravy browning would run down your legs-not a pretty sight. Once ready we'd sneak out quickly so her parents couldn't see us, for they wouldn't have approved, of our way of dress and being so heavily made up.

Every few weeks, Linda would bleach her mother's hair. There was always some bleach left over, so we'd experiment by dying the front of our hair, and eventually bleaching it all, which resulted in my having dark roots, and eventually ruining my own natural blonde colour. Father went ballistic, as he was strict with the girls in our family, regarding hair and fashion. I'd leave the house each evening, with a black pleated skirt, plain jumper and brogue shoes, and he'd never have recognised me dressed up, for it was a complete transformation.

The gang would meet up each evening, and hang around the crescent, hoping for a cigarette and a ride on a motorbike. All the girls had a crush on Paul Ryan, for he owned a Triumph Bonnieval.

With his black leather bomber jacket, and wearing his blonde hair slicked back with Brylcreem. He looked forever like the pop idol (Joe Brown) and would take us round the estate in turn, on the back of his bike, bombing up the road at top speed, and the wind would try its best, to blow through my over bleached, sugar sprayed, bouffant hair style, but to no avail.

As the evening passed, we'd make our way back to Linda house. I'd brush my hair straight, and change into my other set of clothes, before returning home, a little like Cinderella.

One evening, things didn't run according to plan. Lights were unlit as we returned to Linda's home, and she hadn't taken her door key, as her mother was usually at home. Panicking and thinking something had happened to her mum, she knocked on her neighbour's front door. The neighbour went on to explain, that her parents had gone out to the cinema, and would be home later and presumed she had taken her door key with her.

Seeing Linda locked out, they invited us in to wait. I had to be home by 9.30pm, so refused the offer politely and made my way home. Feeling for the door key which was tied round my neck, fear was already setting in, for if father was to see me dressed like this all hell would be let loose.

Hurrying home and thinking- I would put the key in the front door ever so quietly and run up stairs. Hoping no one would be in the bathroom, I'd then lock the door and change into one of the old dressing gowns hanging up behind, and wrap my shoes and clothes into a towel, and no one would be any the wiser.

Approaching the well- lit house, I opened and closed the gate very quietly, then put my key in the lock gently ready to make an almighty dash for the stairs, but to my dismay, found it to be locked.

Peeping through the window, another shock was in store, as father was decorating the front room. He always made a point of sending everyone off to bed early out of his way, so the job could be completed by morning, and without us having to listen to him swearing, as well as getting thoroughly angry and frustrated.

What a dilemma - he must have thought I was already home and in bed.

Walking thoughtfully to the cubby- hole at the side of the house, I took off my green stilettos and climbed on top of the bunker, while thinking of a plan. There was no options left, I'd just have to go round the back of the house and throw stones up at our bedroom window, and just hope Anne would look through first and not shout my father to open the front door for me.

So deep in thought, I was unaware of the coal chute beneath me, moving slowly inwards, so moving to the side I pushed it a little more, and not quite believing my luck, that it could still be open, as mother locked it religiously, every night.

126

Looking down, I could see there'd been a delivery of coal, which would mean, a less of a drop, should I decide to go for it and jump inside. The kitchen light could also be seen, seeping through the door at the bottom of the coal- hole, leading through to the kitchen, so that door hadn't been locked either. Being claustrophobic though, put me off, but if father saw me dressed like this, I'd be belted and my whole secret life would be blown apart. I'd never get to ride on Paul Ryan's motor bike again, either, as he wouldn't want to know me, sporting my old long skirt and brogue shoes.

Well! That was it I had no choice, other than to go for it, and being of an impulsive nature, decided to jump. I opened the chute lid, threw in my stilettos and slid down quickly, but the chute closed with a force behind me, and there was only one way out now, as the chute only opened inwards, and only a glimmer of light given, to guide me to the entrance, and there was no option now but to slide down the coal. What I hadn't bargained for, was the large sharp black shiny shards, piercing my cheep plastic skirt and into the warm flesh, of my buttocks. 'Ouch.' I could have screamed out in agony.

Sliding down a little further and making it a bit more comfortable to sit on, I suddenly froze, as fathers whistling could be heard, while making his way to the kitchen, then suddenly pushing the coalhole door ajar, he was more than likely, stoking up the fire as he did most evenings.

I sat as quiet as a mouse, with my heart thumping madly, as well as holding on for dear life to the lumps of coal, and hoping not to slide down, as the shovel moved in closer to my feet, feeling for larger pieces of coal. Shuffling some of the pieces with my foot, I watched with baited breath, as the coal slid further down, along with one of my green stilettos.

'What the fuckin' 'ell, is this doin' 'ere?' He picked it up, throwing it to one side, as he plonked the rest of the coal on top of the laden down shovel, which would obviously suffice until morning,

I was praying he wouldn't lock the coal-hole door otherwise I'd just have to start screaming. He was just about to lock it, when a large piece of coal rolled and wedged in the doorway, he cursed under his breath and walked off, but no doubt he'd be back soon, to lock it securely for the evening.

Seeing my chance and moving rapidly out of the chute, I pictured him putting the coal on the fire. It was performed like a ritual, as the coal was put on methodically, with the larger pieces first, then the smaller pieces and last of all, the slack, It would then keep the home fire burning till morning.

Timing him mentally, I picked up one shoe, deciding to collect the other in a few days, just in case the shoe should come up later in conversation. Taking a clean towel from the clothes maiden, I quickly cleaned each coal footprint, off the kitchen floor, making sure to leave no tell tale signs, behind.

Looking through the slit in the living room door on the way upstairs, father could be seen, throwing the last shovel of coal slack over, his work of art, done to perfection.

Perfectly timed, I happily strode upstairs the bathroom had someone in so I tiptoed gently into our room, trying my best not to disturb our Ann, on hearing me though, the lamp was switched on.

'What are you doing dressed like that? Your filthy, too, so I'm going to shout father and tell him you've just come home!'

'You dare! They'll be murder! Or is that what you want?'

'I don't care! Cos' if he sees you dressed like that, you deserve to be murdered.' She was getting right up my nose, for all I wanted was to wash and get into bed, and the trauma of being in the coal chute. Well... I could have happily, slapped her face.

'Your only jealous Ann, cos' you can't go on the back of Paul Ryan's motor bike.'

'That's it!' She screeched. I'm telling father, right this very minute!'

'Shush, listen you can have one of my new dresses! Or, I'll ask Linda if she'll make you another of your own choice.' Ann looked thoughtful for a moment, and knowing full well, she had me over a barrel.

'Well! You can give me the blue striped dress and I'll say nothing more about tonight.' Not so slow Ann, after all.' I thought.

'What the bleedin' 'ells all that racket up there? Get to sleep the pair of yer, or else!'

We'd disturbed father, and he just might walk upstairs any minute, and I still hadn't had a chance to wash or change.

'Sorry father! Just using the bathroom won't be long!'

'Well hurry up then, and turn off all them, bleedin' lights!'

Staying over at Linda's house at weekends became a regular habit. It was a Saturday morning and I'd returned home to change into some fresh clothes, for we were going on a visit to her Aunt Lilly's for the afternoon.

On entering the hall, the smell of burnt toast wafted from the kitchen and stale cigarette smoke, hung heavy in the air. Wandering into the untidy kitchen, I unlocked the window to let in some fresh air and filled the kettle automatically, to make some fresh tea. My younger siblings could be seen playing happily in the back garden, as it was a beautiful sunny day and our Geoffrey was finishing his breakfast. Mother had her back to me and her head bowed, as she filled the much needed second hand washing machine, father had recently bought her, as she turned to put some soap powder in the machine, I recoiled at the sight of her hair, for she'd hacked it off in all directions., leaving her beautiful tresses, to be seen no more. I studied her for a moment, trying to comprehend, her uncharacteristic action.

'What on earth have you done? Your hair looks absolutely, dreadful!'

'No worse than yours!' She retorted. 'Since you've bleached it, you should grow it back to its natural colour? That's what you should do.'

'No need to be sarcastic! After all, I've haven't hacked mine off.' Turning, she switched on the washing machine.

'I'll trim it evenly for you tonight mother, probably after tea, then maybe father will treat you to the hairdressers, to have it cut professionally. Has he seen it yet? She responded half-heartedly, as I handed her some tea.

'This morning actually, but he's not very pleased, by all accounts.'

Feeling concerned, I carried on making some toast, a used knife still stuck in the margarine tub came in handy to butter it, as I rushed around anxiously, and without recognising any signs, that mother was heading for a nervous breakdown, for cutting off your own hair in clumps, for no apparent reason, seemingly, is one of them.

I felt concerned, since her only friend Joanie, moved away from the area, for she wouldn't make friends with the other women on the estate, obviously, not wanting them to know any of her business. It wasn't doing her any good either, as she was once again, retreating into her shell.

She'd been happy with her friend calling each week, but unforeseen, Joanie was to have a serious accident, on her way home from work one evening.

The old Pauldings Store, situated on the corner of Stretford Road, was being demolished. A serious traffic accident caused the bus, in which she was travelling, to topple over, into the demolished area, resulting in her being seriously injured. She was never to recover, suffering with bad nerves, and unable to work again. Soon after the family moved away, to live in Fleetwood

Joanie wrote several times, asking if mother would like to spend the weekend with them, but of course, she never went.

'Here's a list of groceries to buy, when your in town, and you can pay some money off the furniture bill for me!'

Taking the list, I hurried upstairs to wash and change. Our Geoffrey had gone out to play, but returned just as quickly for he'd been beaten to a pulp, by the local bully, being a few years older. Apparently he' been bullying Geoffrey for weeks, and it was really getting on mothers nerves.

Leaving the house, to meet Linda, mother suddenly brushed past on the doorstep, and walked casually up the avenue, to confront the bully and apparently twice her size.

'Leave my son alone, or else!' By this time, a few had gathered round, as he arrogantly stood before her.

'Why what are you going to do?` Next, to all amazement, she raised her right fist and punched him full force in the face. He fell back in shock, as she went for him again, pulling at his hair and punching him in the side of his head, there was just no stopping her.

'You'll not touch my son again! You bastard! Or next time, I'll fucking, kill you!' Myself, and a neighbour, tried to tear her away, as the bully finally shrank back in fear. His parents were soon on the scene, and seeing the state of their son, called in the police. The police gave mother a warning, but his parents changed their minds, and decided not to prosecute. They knew their son, to be a bully on the estate and probably, like the rest of us, thought he deserved everything he got. Needless to say, he never touched Geoffrey again.

Mother's unstable side of her nature seemed to have reappeared and it was worrying to know just how much she could take, before finally going over the edge.

After an interesting afternoon at Linda's Aunts, I came home early, with the intent of trimming mother's hair into shape.

Placing the change on the mantle-piece from the errands, I noticed a letter behind the clock. The writing looked vaguely familiar so I took a closer look. It was as I thought, Aunt Hilda had written to mother.

'Mother you never mentioned Aunt had written. Did she say when she'd be visiting again? Is she better in herself? I'd really love to see her again. It must be near on three years after all, since I last saw her.' She snatched the letter from behind the clock, and placed it in her apron pocket.

'Mind your own business! It's got nothing to do with you, what Hilda has to write about.'

'It's got everything to do with me!' I snapped. 'She looked after me when I was young, and I feel I've a right to know what's happening in her life! Just tell me, is she still living in Widnes?

131

'Yes! And she's settled down again with Uncle Jim. If she wants to visit us though, she knows where we live. After all, she can afford the travelling expenses, we can't! There's nothing more to be said on the matter, so forget you ever saw the letter and eat your tea it'll be getting cold.'

Joining the rest the family around the table, I ate my tea silently, while feeling a little pensive, and decided I'd see my Aunt sooner than later, especially as I knew where she lived.

Father interrupted my thoughts, as he made his usual drunken appearance, on a late Saturday afternoon. He pointed a finger towards me threateningly, on entering the living room.

'I saw you today, lady! Yer were with Linda Hicks, and both done up to the nines. Yer were wearing loads of make-up, and green stilettos, waitin' for a bus in town, but yer didn't see me.'

Thank god.' I thought   He then staggered over to the table giving me an almighty crack across the head.

'Where'd do get all that bleedin' fancy gear? That's what I'd like to know.'

'Linda lent it to me, if you must know! You never let me wear anything nice. All you'll allow me to wear are long skirts, which are dead old fashioned and them brogue shoes, make me want to puke.'

'That's enough! Yer cheeky little get, and you'll start spending more time 'ere in future, and yer won't be seein' Linda Hicks agen, either. So just watch your step lady. I'm warnin' yer!'   On that last note, he staggered upstairs to bed to hopefully sleep it off, till the following morning.

Mother lit a cigarette casually, while clearing away the dinner plates.

'Don't be looking to me for support! Your father's right for once. You hardly ever spend any time here and I could do with some help with the younger ones, especially at weekends.'   The thoughts of having to stay home every weekend brought my usual placid temper to ahead.

'I did my share of looking after, when John was a baby! Its time one of the others helped out for a change, and anyway, I'm sick of living here! I'll be glad when I'm old enough, to move out!'

Speaking out of turn, must have struck a wrong cord with mother, for the dishes were suddenly thrown into the kitchen sink with a crash, then everything happened so quickly and unexpectedly. My hair was in her grasp in minutes, as she dragged me screaming round the table. I tried loosening her hands, but she held on tight, as Ann ran out of the room for help.

Drunk as father was, he was down stairs in minutes, trying to loosen her grip. I was screaming, she was screaming, as her grip on my hair, was finally released.

'I'm not putting up with her bloody cheek anymore Jimmy! I've just about had enough of her!'

'All right Winnie! Sit down a minute. Ann! Make your mother a cup of sweet tea? And you lady, can piss off upstairs to bed, out of my bleedin' sight. Yer cause more trouble than your worth, these days!'

Ann came to our room later, after it had all quietened down.

'You shouldn't upset mum like you do. You ought to have more consideration for her and help out a bit more, with the household chores. After all, she's not very well these days.' I looked at her in amazement.

'You've got some nerve! You should help out a bit more, as you do very little around the house, come to think of it, you never did.' I started brushing my hair, as large clumps fell to the floor.

'I happen to be working! So I contribute, by helping out financially, if you must know!' She announced proudly.

'That's a poor excuse, if ever I heard one!' She chose to ignore my last comment, as she prepared herself for a night out. Then hurriedly left the bedroom in a temper and slamming the door behind.

Well I'd had enough. I would visit my Aunt Hilda first thing Monday morning, and see if she would allow me stay with her.

Thinking of mother though was a disturbing fact, for I'd been the second person she'd attacked in one day, and as the cheval mirror sprung to mind, it left a chill running down my spine, for it appeared she'd become unstable from that day on, almost three years since. Whatever- I couldn't stand living with my parents any longer, always being on the receiving end of their outbursts of frustration and bad temper.

Later the following Sunday evening, I put the minimal of clothing into a carrier bag and hid it under the bed. I counted my savings of just eleven shillings, hoping it would suffice to pay for my journey to Widnes. I couldn't tell Linda of my plans, even though she was my best friend, for she might possibly mention it to her father. It would undoubtedly be cause for concern and he would notify my parents.

Sleep was hard to come by, having to be awake for 3.3o am. It was also uncomfortable, wearing jeans and a sweater in bed, for dressing early would have disturbed our Ann.

There was a bus due at 4am, for the early workers going to Trafford Park, so all I needed, was Aunt's address from the letter, which was still in mother's apron pocket and folded neatly over her bedroom chair.

Looking at the clock from the light of the moon seeping through the curtains, I could see it was time to go. Slipping on my shoes and socks and taking my packed clothes from under the bed, I sneaked into my parent's room. Father muttered something about 'Whose there?' Whilst in a haze, but fell back into his disturbed sleep, seconds later, I pulled the apron carefully from the chair then managed to take the letter from the pocket, then quietly replaced the apron.

Moving slowly down stairs and trying not to stand on the creaky ones, I opened the letter and read the address, then quickly placed the letter in the kitchen draw. Opening the front door then closing it gently behind, I made my escape, but unknown to me then, had disturbed my father.

Five people stood at the bus stop, and a few glanced in my direction, for a young person being out alone at such an early hour, appeared unusual. The bus arrived on time and we all boarded, while the other passengers went upstairs, presumably to smoke cigarettes. I was left alone downstairs so sat on the long seat.

Just as the young bus conductor rang the bell, I glanced up to see father running after the bus and shaking his fist in anger. The conductor noticed, yet chose to ignore him, on seeing my shocked and startled expression. After father faded out of sight, he seated himself beside me smiling warmly I in turn returned his friendly smile, while offering him my fare.

'Town please?' He then handed me my ticket and change.

'What's this then darling, is it a garden gate?' He ruffled my blonde straight fringe on my forehead, as he slipped his arm around my shoulder.

'So, what's all this about? Running away are we? I seen all that back there yer know, and I could easily 'ave stopped the bus and let him on, but I thought, no I won't, seems the lass is in some kind of bother, like.' He looked thoughtful for a moment, before continuing.

'Should yer be lukin' for somewhere to stay for a few days though! I've got this smashin' little flat in Didsbury, and live there alone, like, but as I say, yer welcome to stay, as I wouldn't see anyone 'omeless! Social worker and bus conductor all rolled into one-that's me!'

'Really, I replied coldly, whilst removing his arm from around my shoulder, h e looked miffed for a few seconds, and then annoyed.

'Excuse me?' He shouted down my ear. 'I've just rescued yer from a nutter, and this is all the thanks I get.' Feeling somewhat intimidated, I started to move to another seat.

'Must be my unlucky day then, seems I've just fallen into the hands of another.' I retorted, icily.

'Right, I'm reporting yer to the police when we reach the bus station, cos' you're a runaway!'

'I'll report you too, you pervey, enticing young girls to your flat.' With my last remark, he angrily moved towards the front of the bus, as other passengers started to board his bus.

Feeling a little safer, I relaxed for the rest of the journey into town, but noticed it was still only 4.40am, on reaching the bus station, and still very few people about. Making my way to Victoria station, I caught a glimpse of my reflection in a shop window, and looked forever like a young boy, wearing jeans and sweater, with my short blonde hair brushed straight.

The train station was practically deserted on purchasing my one-way ticket to Widnes, but didn't have to wait too long, as the train arrived half an hour later.

Seated by a window and feeling more confident, in reaching my destination safely, all thoughts turned to Aunt. I felt nervous yet excited, at the prospects of seeing her again, and wandered how she'd respond to my unexpected visit and at such an early hour.

It was only a short journey, and soon reached Widnes Station, but looking around the town centre, it was still too early to call at Aunts, for it was still only 6.ooam. Counting my money, there was enough to buy some tea and toast in the local café, and there'd be some left over, to pay my bus fare to the council estate on which she lived.

Finally approaching her house, I walked down the garden path then made my way to the back door and looked carefully through the kitchen window, to see if she was up. She was ready and preparing some breakfast, but her back was towards me, and as she buttered some toast, I was shocked at the sight of her shrunken frame. Was this woman, really my Aunt? Obviously, her dark secret from the past had finally taken its toll, for the once beautiful buxom woman with light brown curly hair, was lost forever, and reducing her, to a shadow of her former self. The frail grey haired lady then turned slightly to reveal her once beautiful profile. It was definitely my Aunt.

Feeling choked, I knocked on the door gently, but when Aunt opened it, the shock of disbelief at seeing me was written all over her almost unrecognisable, features.

Jim! Jim! Come 'ere quick? We've got a surprise visitor!' We were both hugging each other tightly, as tears streamed down our faces, but the prepared smile of a welcome, for his unexpected visitor, died on his face in seconds. It spoke volumes.

'Oh hello, what brings you here? And at such an unearthly hour.` Suddenly feeling unwelcome, I looked to the floor.

'I just thought I'd make an early start!'

'Well! You can say that again?' Ever since he'd been on the scene, all those years ago, I had a feeling he was envious of the closeness Aunt and myself had together, or maybe I was just being cynical.

Aunt stepped back to take a better look.

'Well! I never thought I'd see this day, just luk' at her Jim? She's changing, into a lovely young woman!' She wiped a tear from her face.

'Come on, yer can tell me all about it, while I make us some breakfast, yer must be starved

After Aunt had gotten over the initial shock of the earlier events of the morning, she sat down to delve a little further, into my unexpected visit.

'So yer mother doesn't know you've come all this way to see me? Wel,l that can't be right, can it? She's bound to be worried, as to yer whereabouts!'

'She won't mind, really Aunt, as I stay at my friend Linda's house, quite a lot.'

'Its not the point luv'! It's a long way, and it'll only cause trouble, and its trouble I can well do without, these days!' Not giving up easily and trying to win her over, I gave it more thought, while finishing my breakfast.

'I'll write a note to mother to explain and she'll receive it sometime tomorrow, and maybe then, she let me stay here?' Aunt looked a little flustered at this point, and appeared to have given in.

'Okay luv'! If that's what yer want to do, I suppose it'll be okay, for the time being.'

We chatted for the rest of the morning, by catching up on old times then later, she combed her hair, and after putting on a fresh dress and some lipstick, started to look like the Aunt I used to know.

Whilst she was in the kitchen, doing some baking, Jim called me into the lounge.

'Sit down a minute love! I want a word with you. This arrangement isn't going to work out for any of us, as you still need to be looked after, even though you are getting older.' I thought on for a moment, while trying to avoid his fixed gaze.

'Aunt doesn't have too! I can look after myself, and I'll help with the household chores each day!'

'It's not the cleaning aspect of it love, the thing is.' He paused for a second, looking slightly embarrassed. 'Well it's teenagers-specially girls, they can bring problems into the home, and your Aunt isn't strong enough to cope. You can always spend weekends here though, and you'd have your own room, just like before. So what do you say to that? I'm sure your Aunt would be pleased as punch too, to that arrangement!'

Toying with the idea for a few moments, yet feeling pushed out once again. I reluctantly agreed. Aunt walked into the lounge, with her hands full of flour from baking, soon after, unaware of our little discussion.

'Come upstairs, luv!' Our James's old record player is still in use, so yer can play some records while teas getting ready.' It seemed a great idea, and would bring back some fond memories.

While listening to the music, the slamming of a car door could be heard. Looking out of the front bedroom window, I was taken by surprise, for mother could be seen walking up the garden path with two police officers. Rushing down stairs and without a second thought, I ran into the back garden, I hid in some privet's and stayed very quiet, but the thoughts of any insects crawling around, made me want to scream, but the fear of being caught, put paid to that one.

'She was upstairs a while ago!' I could hear the anxious tone of Aunt's voice. 'All I can say is, you must 'ave frightened her away.'

Soon they were all in the back garden, and looking from one side to the other. Poor Aunt looked devastated.

'She posted a letter this morning, saying where she was stayin'. You'd 'ave got it first thing.' Mother appeared to be seething, and her face was flushed, but at least her hair had been cut professionally, after that dreadful attempt at cutting it herself.

'She's coming home with me, so that's an end to it all, and just wait till I get my hands on her! Having me chasing after her, and wasting money on train fares, I can't afford.'

One of the police officers, walked closer to the privet's, and separated each one with his baton, while my small frame was crushed against the garden fence, as well as his size eleven shoe, practically touching my own.

'No! There's no one 'ere! The lass must be making her way back to the village, but we'll soon catch up with her. No need for concern, at this early stage... Mrs Neill!'

Waiting a few moments after the back door shut. I crawled from my hiding place, shuddering and itching, at the very thoughts. Opening the back door, I ran upstairs, having to wash myself down, regardless of being caught, then quickly changed into some other clothing, I'd brought with me.

Aunt closed the front door and stopped at the bottom of the stairs, on hearing the tap water running.

'Is that you, our Veronica?'

'Yes! And you don't have to worry I'm going to the train station to catch up with mother! Sorry to have caused you all this trouble. I really am!' She walked up to the bathroom slowly, looking old and frail once again.

'You can stay over at weekends, whenever yer like, luv'? Just let me know and I'll send on the train fare!' We gave each other a hug tearfully, then making our way to the front-door Jim could be seen looking on, expressionless.

139

Arriving at the train station, my mother didn't look too surprised, as I made my way up the platform, and sat down next to her. On the journey home, we hardly spoke a word until nearing home, when she announced she'd be paying a visit to Linda Hicks's mother, the very next day, to put a stop to my staying over, at weekends.

Father washed his hands of me, from that day on, deciding mother made a better job of keeping me in check.

Following day whilst in school, I mentioned to Linda, of mothers plans, she rushed home at lunchtime, to prepare sandwiches and set the tea tray, for Mrs Hicks was quite looking forward to the visit, and a nice long afternoon chat.

Knowing where mother would be all afternoon, and knowing our house was empty, Linda and myself, played truant from school. With our feet up on the coffee table, drinking endless cups of coffee, and smoking cigarettes, we happily chatted, for the rest of the afternoon.

Hearing the gate slam unexpectedly, we stubbed out our cigarettes quickly, as well as knocking over the dregs of coffee, onto the table, as we dived under the window ledge for cover.

I presumed it was father home from work early, but no key was used, as the visitor persistently knocked on the front door. I presumed wrong for it was the familiar voice of Mr Ormrod, from the school board. We stayed quite still, as he shouted through the letterbox, then the next minute he was looking through the front window.

'I know your both in there! I've just called at your home, Linda Hicks, and by all accounts both your mothers have sent you into school, so you'd better open the door at once, or you'll be in deep trouble. Do you hear me? I want an explanation immediately, or else!'

We were near to hysterics with fright, but also afraid, for we knew we'd been caught out and would have to face the consequences, the next morning. We stayed quiet nonetheless, until the gate finally closed shut, with a hard slam.

Next day in school, we had a lecture from the Headmaster, and were both separated in the classroom, from that day on. Both our parent's apparently blamed each other for the bad influence, felled on their child, by the other. Of course the inevitable happened, and we each found a new school friend, but always keep in touch-regardless.

It was dreadful having to stay home each evening after school, for I resented the endless chores, which had to be done after completing my homework.

Mother sat in her chair smoking endless cigarettes, and hardly ever moving after making the evening meal, but at least we had the television to take away the monotony, which would be watched by all, apart from Ann, who was becoming more independent by the day, because of her work.

One particular evening, while totally involved in watching the new series of Coronation Street, Mother unexpectedly sprang from her chair, and picking up the poker from the fireplace, violently obliterated the television screen, it went up in a puff of smoke, as we all rushed into the hall to escape her madness. Father tried to remove the poker from her grasp, but it was near impossible, as she continued to smash ornaments and such like.

Our neighbour Mrs Wilmot heard the screams and breakage, and immediately called in the police. We just stood in the garden, absolutely petrified, and not understanding that our mother had, had a nervous breakdown. An Ambulance arrived, and took mother to hospital, where she was admitted to a psychiatric ward and so remaining there, for some weeks. But after receiving a course of medication and electric shock treatment, she was eventually allowed home.

While my mother was in hospital, and with the headmaster's permission, I was allowed two weeks off school, to take care of the younger ones. Father took two weeks off from work later, so we managed okay. I felt guilty because of mother's breakdown, and felt we should have pulled our weight a bit more under the circumstances, and been more aware of the obvious changes, regarding her mental state. So I made sure we all helped a little more in the future, and as the atmosphere in the home slowly changed, it acquired a sense of balance, so giving us all the much needed, piece of mind, so lacking in the past.

Chapter Ten.

It was to last for almost a year. I was approaching my fourteenth birthday, when it was announced yet again, we were moving on.

We exchanged our nice three bed roomed house, for an old four bed- roomed terrace, on the corner of Empress street, situated in the Old Trafford area, of Manchester.

I attended my last year in the catholic school nearby, and making some nice friends, both at school, and in my new neighbourhood.

A youth club opened every Tuesday evening, which I frequented most weeks. I kept in touch with Linda too, and sometimes she'd call up, and join us at the club. She'd only stay a couple of hours, as she still lived in Wythenshawe, which required a lengthy journey home.

Almost ready for my regular Tuesday night out, I looked down at my tatty low- heeled shoes. It was a while since my last pair had been bought, and our Ann's new 4inch bronze stilettos sat neatly on the floor, at the side of her bed. Looking once again at my own shoes, I took my chance.

Slipping them on, they fitted nice and snug, and suited my old, yet fashionable drainpipes. Removing the shoes again, I walked across the landing. I'd have to tiptoe downstairs and make a quick exit, out the front door. Just as my foot touched the first stair though, Ann and mother came out of the parlour, chatting cosily together, as they always did, and mother was as usual lighting up another of her Senior Service cigarettes.

'I'm really pleased for you Ann! Paul sounds like a really nice lad, and I hope you both enjoy your night out at the pictures! I'll leave to get ready then, as there's no one in the bathroom, and you might as well take advantage of a nice long soak.'

I stepped back into the bathroom, and looked around. There was no alternative, but to leave through the back yard, I'd have to climb out the bathroom window and down the drainpipe. But having to be quick, for Linda would be waiting at the club soon and it was nearly seven.

Slipping Ann's shoes back on, I opened the window. Looking down below, it seemed a fair drop, should I happen to slip- but needs must.

Clambering down the drainpipe, wearing drainpipes, and 4inch stilettos wasn't easy, by any stretch of the imagination, for I couldn't have thrown the shoes first, as someone would have seen them pass the living room window, and even more so, the heels could have snapped, and then I'd be in real trouble. Just as my feet touched the ground, the dreaded screech could be heard from the kitchen.

'Oh mum! Our Veronica's pinched my new shoes! What the heck am I going to wear tonight? She's gone and ruined my night out!' Mother's voice could be heard, adding to the excitement.

'I'll bloody kill her, when I get my hands on her! Just you see if I don't!'

Taking off the shoes and running like the clappers down the back street. I glanced back only once, to see if there was any sign of mother chasing, but the street was deserted. I pushed the dreaded consequences to the back of my mind, and enjoyed the rest of the evening- Might as well be hung for a sheep as a lamb.' I thought.

Nearing the youth club, Linda could be seen in the doorway, she gave a wave, as I stood for a moment, putting on the shoes, at the same time, making myself feel cool, calm, and collective whilst passing a group of youths. The wolf whistles, held no bounds.

That night, mother gave me a clip round the ears, it stung, as well as my feet killing me. Serve me right, for ruining Ann's first date, and from that night on, her shoes were left next to the television table, under the scrutiny of mother's eye.

Needing some new clothes and shoes to wear for work, as leaving school was imminent. I decided to discuss it with mother, sooner than later.

Middle of the week, we had two unexpected visitors. It was my Aunt and uncle Jim. Aunt looked ever so frail, and was still in a deep depression, having gone under surgery, for an overactive thyroid

144

gland. Showing concern, Jim thought it might help, if she was to visit her family, once again.

We weren't to know then, but it was to be the last time any of us would see her alive. I felt sorry for Jim, as the strain of living with Aunt, must have sapped him of all his energy, for it was a well known fact, living with someone, suffering from depression, tends to drag oneself down, too.

Following Sunday afternoon, Jim visited alone. He was to bring the sad news of Aunt's tragic death, and went on to explain, to myself, and my deeply saddened mother.

Yesterday, it had been a pleasant day, weather wise. Hilda prepared herself for a day out alone. She appeared unusually happy, yet somehow secretive as to where she was going, so he decided not to ask, as she would probably tell him later where she had been.

Before leaving, she strolled through to the kitchen for some tea and toast, but he had to look twice at her transformation, for her hair shone and the Navy Blue suit and cream blouse she wore - looked really smart. She'd also applied the minimal of make-up to cover her pallid skin, which her complexion had taken on in the last few years, caused through her illness, then completed her outfit, with a touch of lavender scent. The overall effect looked stunning, and as he whistled his approval, she added a warm smile, showing her lovely white even teeth, a family trait of the Morton's.

'I'll be late in Jim! So don't prepare any tea for me, as I'm eating out.' She brushed him lightly on the lips then disappeared.

He couldn't believe how she'd gotten over her depression, so quickly. Why? Only yesterday, it was driving her to the brink of suicide, and wanting more than anything to dispel herself from this very planet. Maybe it was a turn for the better, and he hoped she'd be in the same good mood when she returned, but for the time being, he'd keep himself busy in the gardens, and later go down to the pub. After all, it would be a nice for him to have some space, for a change too, but for some unknown reason, nagging doubts were to cloud his mind, until he saw her later that evening. She'd looked so radiant

145

earlier, it had crossed his mind she might be meeting another man, but banished all ridiculous thoughts, as quickly as they came.

When she eventually came home that Saturday night, she still looked radiant, but a little hungry, so they had supper and chatted, but still there was no mention of her whereabouts that day. He didn't push the issue, but came to the conclusion she'd probably visited her mother, who was living for some years, in an old folks home in Preston, which her visits were few and far between, for they were always upsetting.

She kissed him, once comfortable in their bed that night and told him she would always love him. But in the early hours he was disturbed, for she was heard talking in her sleep, seemingly to her son, and saying how pleased she was to see him. Jim presumed her to be dreaming, and went back to sleep.

Unknown to him, she must have been in her final hours, for it has been said, when close to death, some see their loved ones - but its only speculation.

That same evening before retiring to bed, she went to the bathroom and locked the door. She mixed her lethal cocktail of drugs, and with her final decision, slowly downed the concoction, knowing within hours, she would never be part of her husband life again. Although unheard, I'm sure she would have said her goodbyes, to those held, most closely to her heart. When it was time to meet her maker, I'd hoped he would let her through the gates, if only for a moment, to see her beloved son, the very son who's life she abruptly ended, at the tender age of two. If it were possible, I'm sure baby Donald would have found it in his heart long ago, to forgive his mother of the dreadful deed she'd done. Though her tormented soul had ceased to exist, peace of mind blissfully came at last.

Of course Aunt wasn't childless, as I'd been led to believe all those years, for she'd had a beautiful baby son, at the age of seventeen.

But for two years, her husband Bob tormented her, believing him-self, not to be the child's father, for reasons best left unsaid.

On that fatal day, Aunt could no longer take anymore of his torment and accusations, and being of an unbalanced state of mind, took it upon herself, to drown her beloved son, while washing his hair in a bucket of water. Beatrice Charlsworth, a good friend and neighbour, was in a state of shock after her findings, and immediately called in the police.

Aunt was taken away, to spend many years as a patient, in Winick mental hospital, but being a model patient, was allowed home, after just six years. But she was never free of guilt, and paid her debt to society, with her life.

I hope some will feel compassion, and not judge her too harshly, and I do sympathise with her to a certain extent, after all, she was a mentally ill woman, but contrary to the facts, she managed to raise James, and myself to become two happy well- adjusted people, for without her help we would have had no real concept of a good and decent way of life. She will always be remembered, and I will cherish her memory, forever.

Aunt set up home again, with her husband Bob, when she eventually came home from Winick hospital, but no one could understand why they remained together, due to the tragic circumstances of the past.

After two years, my parents allowed her to take care of our James, completely trusting and believing her, to be of a reformed character. Father's side of the family were incensed, at my parent's decision and practically refrained from speaking to either of them again, their feelings of indifference towards the rest of us, over the coming years, was also very apparent.

Unanswered questions were to be answered.
The day I walked into Aunt's bedroom that dismal evening, and told to. ` Get out.' She had been dreadfully upset, for it happened to be her son's birthday. She must have been deeply saddened.

147

I can also recall the day in Wales, when she beat the woman at the stop-tap, always on the defensive, and so giving the chosen few a damned, good hiding. So if women were seen talking amongst themselves, she assumed they were discussing her dreadful secret she'd harboured for years- infanticide, for she was undoubtedly becoming paranoid.

It became apparent over the years, when discovering Beatrice Charlsworth living opposite her, on Langley Estate, for she couldn't believe her past was finally catching up, and so bringing the paranoia to ahead. Father didn't help matters either, for he had both my mother and Aunt over a barrel, for whenever he beat mother, he would shut her up screaming, by threatening to tell all, of her sister's crime. And finally becoming crystal clear, as to why Aunt let me go so readily that dreadful day when my parents came to take me home to Grenham Avenue, for she obviously had no choice in the matter.

The funeral was to take place at Southern cemetery, which turned out a quiet affair, and Aunt's coffin was laid out in the front parlour for family and friends to pay their last respects. Later while everyone chatted quietly in the sitting room, I went in alone, to pay my last respects.

Looking more peaceful than I ever imagined, and dressed in a white silk gown, I said goodbye to my most precious Aunt. My special love for her, I will take to my grave.

When the funeral service was over, we came home for some light refreshments, before the relatives finally left, together with Jim, who appeared positively heartbroken. My mother who was also feeling the loss of her dear sister, stood at the front door looking sombre, as she waved them off goodbye.

On clearing the table, I took the used plates into the kitchen and noticed father sitting alone. He was crying softly to himself, and totally oblivious to my presence. I was quite taken aback, as well as feeling intrusive in his moment of grief, and placed the plates gently on the draining board so as not to disturb him, then quickly left the kitchen. I had a notion as to why he was grieving over his sister in law's death, but ours is not to reason, why.

BOOK TWO
INTO THE FIRE.

Chapter Eleven.

'Hurry up! Will you? It's your job interview, in half an hour and your going to be late.' I responded half-heartedly to mother, while rummaging through Ann's wardrobe.

'It would help if I had something suitable to wear! I've a pair of jeans and a sweater. I can hardly go for an interview wearing those, can I?' Once again, it seemed my statement fell on deaf ears, regarding some much needed, new clothes.

Putting on a black pleated skirt and a cream blouse of Ann's, I looked in the mirror, although they looked smart, they were a little old fashioned. I had to borrow a pair of her stocking too, and held them up with a pair of mother's old garters. Then slipping on my polished shoes, my outfit was completed. I combed my hair, and as a last minute thought, brushed my lips with the minimal, of iced pink lipstick.

A job interview had been rehearsed at school, on several occasions, before leaving, so giving a general idea of the procedure awaiting me. Once making myself known, at the reception desk, in the Photographers, I waited my turn, accompanied by two other girls of similar age, and both dressed to the nines, so leaving my own clothes a lot to be desired, and making me feel a little anxious as to filling the position, as junior in the colour department. The job would have been convenient, as it was only a stones throw away from where I lived, hence the travel. .

After my interview though, I felt more optimistic. Mr Rackham made me feel at ease, and it seemed to go in my favour, living close by. He would let me know by Saturday morning, by post, should the job be available.

Keeping my fingers crossed, I waited hopefully for the Saturday mornings post. Sure enough, the letter arrived, and felt elated as I read on, for I'd passed the interview, and had to report to work, the following Monday, at 8.30am.

A white cotton overall was provided, which solved the problem of what to wear each day, and June the supervisor, introduced me to two other older ladies, whom I would be working, alongside.

My work entailed learning the basics of colour photography, and after six months, if my knowledge of work was to prove, worthwhile, I would be promoted to a more extensive and progressive part of the department, and the prospects of an increase of salary too.

The photographers were a family concern - Mr Rackham, his two sons, two daughters in law and a grandson Philip, who was of similar age to myself and worked with his grandfather. They were all very friendly and helpful, and by lunchtime, I'd started to settle into my new work environment.

June came to see me at lunchtime, and handed me some money, asking if I'd go to the corner shop, for she wanted fourteen cakes. Presuming it must be a form of tradition carried out, when it was someone's birthday, I thought nothing more of the tall order, and went on my way. Mabel, the owner of the corner shop, new me well, for I frequented her shop, most days.

'Ello luv! Tell us what yer first day was like then, with Mr Rackham?' I put Junes order, and told her I was settling in quite well. She looked somewhat confused, as she took my order, but carried on chatting, regardless.

`I've known the Rackams for years there a nice friendly family. So what was it agen'? Fourteen cakes, did yer say? Strange, I'd 'ave thought June would 'ave mentioned the large cake order, last Friday, you'll be lucky if I've got that many cakes in the shop. Eventually, the last cake was put into the fourth cake box, but returning to work was a bit of a struggle, as I could hardly see over the top of the boxes. I eventually pushed open the staff room door and staggered in. Junes face was a picture to say the least though, as she looked on, somewhat bemused.

'What the bloody 'ell 'ave yer got there?' Nonplussed, I put the boxes down onto the table, as she busied herself, having to move mugs and plates to one side, for extra room.

'You asked for fourteen cakes. So here they are!'

`Fourteen cakes, I asked for four teacakes!' Everyone set about laughing, and couldn't remember when they'd laughed so much, especially on a Monday. I felt such a fool not hearing June's errand correctly, and put it down to the noise of the machinery.

Mr Rackham strolled into the staff room on hearing all the commotion, and seeing the funny side, returned Junes money, he then proceeded to share the cakes out, amongst his surprised staff. The mistake certainly went in my favour, for it broke the ice, and as June realised I was as mad as the rest of them, readily accepted me into her fold.

My take home wage was £2-10 shillings a week. Mother kept £2 and I had the remaining 10 shillings, which had to suffice, to pay for stockings, lipstick and the occasional trip to the pictures.

After working for two weeks, and thoroughly enjoying every minute. I soon settled into my new routine.

June's younger daughter Pamela, who worked in the black and white department, came upstairs at lunchtimes and sat in our group. While chatting, she mentioned the works annual trip out to Blackpool, which was to take place the following Saturday, but being a new member of staff, and not contributing money each week to the fund, I didn't think I would be invited, but I was pleasantly surprised, when told I could go, although I would have to go on a few errands, for souvenirs and such like, when we arrived, for the older ones, wanted to spend their time, in the pub.

I felt excited, for I hadn't seen the beach for some years, but all nice thoughts were suddenly clouded, wandering what on earth, I could possibly wear, another reason to ask mother for some new clothes, and I would bring the subject up at the dinner table, that very evening.

Seated around the dinner table, but biding my time for the right moment, I dived in.

'Mother, there's a works annual trip out on Saturday, to Blackpool. I've been invited, but I need some new clothes and shoes. Can you arrange for the clubman to give me a credit note, the same as you did for our Ann, and I'll pay you back, at 2/6 a week?`

Eluding the situation, she moved her dinner plate into the centre of the table, then lighting up a cigarette, inhaled the smoke deep into her lungs. I sat waiting hopefully for an answer, through a haze of smoke and a momentary, uninterrupted silence.

'I've already told you! We'll discuss it in a couple of months, when I've paid half the credit bill. Until then the subject is closed. The £2 you give me each week, doesn't go far either, as the rents just gone up by 3 shillings a week. So that's taken a chunk out of it.'

'That's not my fault! Why don't you ask father to contribute some more of his wages? After all! Most of his are spent in the bookies and the pub.' She stood up abruptly from the table, choosing to ignore me, as she cleared leftovers, onto an empty plate. Feeling disheartened, I pushed the issue further. 'And another thing, you always make sure Ann looks okay, when she goes out on a date, or a works outing, so why is she treated differently, tell me that?' I knew I was being down right petty, but nonetheless, I would get my message over, she suddenly stopped washing up, and took notice for once, while drying her hands, on an old tea towel.

'I'll tell you why? Ann works dammed hard in a factory, working all the hours god sends. She earns good money, £8 a week, including overtime. So with £4 a week to spend, she can well afford clothes, from the clubman. So that's the reason!
Unlike yourself! Working in a photographers, for a meagre wage, and just because your happy there. You make me bloody laugh, with your high and mighty attitude. Just because you think you've got a better job than anyone else in the family, and there might be a promotion in the offing. You think your going places. Well, let me tell you something lady, you are going nowhere, because poverty breed's poverty in this life, and you'd do well to remember that. So I suggest you get off that high horse of yours and start looking for a decent paid job. You've to work hard, to earn good money. All this nonsense of being happy in your work doesn't come into the equation.`

154

Well, that was myself, well and truly told off. I noticed Ann was still seated at the table, looking smug, and as a smirk seemingly spread across her face, I could have happily slapped her.

I had wandered when mother would mention her disapproval, of my new job, and any hopes of staying on in the future, were now dashed. I expect it wouldn't be long, before I'd have to start looking for new employment. But I would cross that bridge when I come to it, for my main concern at present, was having some new clothes to wear. Come rain or come shine, I would have some to wear for Blackpool, if I were to pay dearly for it, later.

There was no alternative, but to take the credit book from the top draw of the sideboard and write a note as if it was from mother, asking for a credit note, to the value of, twenty pounds.

The following morning I had the credit book in my jeans pocket, and went into work, then booked a few hours off for the afternoon. Within hours, I was stood at the reception desk in the department store, with my note in hand.

I was confronted, by a stern looking middle aged woman, with hair tied back severely from her forehead, and sad looking pinched red lips. She acknowledged me through her Margery Proops styled spectacles, in a condescending manner, causing me to go pink from head to toe. She scanned the note quickly.

'I'm sorry! But I don't think this note will suffice within our company policy, with oneself being so young, and being unaccompanied by your mother, that doesn't help matters, either. Just wait there a few moments please, while I contact one of my colleagues.'

At least we were not on the phone, 'I thought, so mother couldn't be of any immediate contact. She returned sharpish, while holding a folder in front of her, and opening it up, with an air of efficiency.

'I just have to ask a couple of personal questions? How long have you lived at your present address? And what is your mother;s maiden name?' They were both easy questions, and on answering them, she handed me a credit note to the value of twenty pounds, while directing me to the departments.

155

'The ladies clothes department is first on your left, and shoes are on the first floor.' She suddenly smiled broadly, which lit up her face, and making her look really attractive, after all.

I couldn't believe my luck at getting through the door and went loopy feckin loops. First call the lingerie department, I wallowed in the feel of the silk against my skin, and chose two sets of underwear, along with some stockings and suspenders. Further down the shop floor was the main clothes section. I settled eventually, for a navy cotton suit, some matching co-ordinates and a cool stone coloured chiffon dress, for Saturday.

Next call, the shoe department, and a pair of low- heeled sandals were essential, to walk the golden mile in Blackpool, and a pair of 4inch stiletto heels in navy, completed my blue outfit. My spending spree soon came to an abrupt ending, by spending £2 over the said amount without even realising, and knew mother would kill me, without a shadow of a doubt.

On leaving the store, I suddenly felt a pang of guilt, but quickly pushed the thought to the back of my mind, confident in my knowing, the 2/6 would be paid each Friday evening, to the clubman.

The front door of our home was always left slightly ajar, for our John and Jane played on the front, and were continuously running in and out. It was now 4.30pm and mother would usually be in the kitchen starting the evening meal. Pushing the door gently and walking into the hall, I listened for signs of life from the front room, but all was quiet, so giving me time to run upstairs and quickly unpack the clothes. The underwear was hidden under the mattress, along with the shoes, and the suit and co-ordinates were put into Ann's wardrobe and covered with a couple of old coats, of which were never worn. Once downstairs and in the front room, I surreptitiously replaced the book in the draw. Hopefully, mother would be none the wiser, until the following week.

Come Friday morning, I took the dress and sandals into work and placed them in my locker, to change into on Saturday morning, for Blackpool. I needn't have wasted time though, ducking and diving, for at six o'clock Friday night, the clubman called. Asking for the usual weekly payment of 4/6 and adding on my 2/6. We were finishing our tea, when mother could be heard arguing her point in the parlour.

'I'm sorry Mr Sloane! I've already told you, you've obviously made a mistake, for I haven't had any credit from you for quite some time.` He suddenly adapted a nervous cough on answering.

'I beg to differ, Mrs Neill! But your daughter came into our store only days ago, with a letter from your good self! She was given a credit note, to the value of twenty pounds, but spent a little over.'

All went quiet around the dinner table, as I suddenly paled.

'Veronica! I want to see you this very minute?' I left the table and reached for my purse off the sideboard, then walking into the parlour, offered the money.

'It's okay mother! Take the 2/6, and I'll be paying the same amount each week, until the clothes are paid for.' Mr Sloane looked decidedly uncomfortable, as he deducted the payment then made a swift exit. Mother closed the front door, and on doing so, slapped me hard across the ears.

'Well! I've never felt so humiliated in all my born days! How dare you show me up in front of Mr Sloane? You've made me look a right fool! Do you realise that?' Just at that moment, father walked downstairs from the bathroom, cleaning the shaving crème from his chin then sticking some tissue paper on his cuts.

'What's all the commotion about? Can't a man 'ave some bleedin' peace and quiet, in his own 'ome.`

'Can you believe it? She's only taken the clothing credit book from the drawer, and spent £22 last Tuesday afternoon, without asking, my permission!`

'I'm going to pay it back each week though!' I chimed, but was awarded yet another crack, as she waved the club book in the air.

'Shut up! Audacious, isn't the word for you! You'll never pay that amount back, not in a million years. You know damned well you won't!' More trouble was ahead - this time from father, when surprisingly, he took my side.

'I'm not condoning what she's done Winnie and she's gone the wrong way about it, but she's working now, and bringing money into the 'ome. She'll want to go out of an evenin' so yer can't expect her to wear the same clothes for work, and for going out at night. Can yer?'

'She still shouldn't have gone behind my back! It's the principle of the matter.' All went quiet, as she lit a thin strip of newspaper from the dying embers, to light up yet another Senior Service. I was half expecting her to return the goods, first thing Monday, which would have caused the argument to flare.

'Well! You might as well show us what you've bought? And as long as you find yourself a higher paid job, which will enable you to pay each week. There'll be no more said about it!'

Saturday morning, I took time preparing for the day out, by soaking in a nice soapy bath, but still went out a little earlier, to change into my dress and sandals, I'd left in work the previous day.

Father surprised me yet again, on the way out, by giving me £2 to spend at the pleasure beach. He'd given the same amount, to the rest of the family and mother £10, having struck lucky on the horses, the previous day. It must have been some win, and probably the reason for him being in a good mood, the day before, and taking my side for once.

Blackpool turned out to be an interesting and adventurous day, and getting to know my colleagues was even better, for some were quite funny and entertaining, especially after a few beers. I tasted my first alcoholic drink, consisting of Sherry and lime (yuk). Pamela had been drinking it all afternoon, and encouraged me to try some. Saying `It was the height of sophistication, to be seen drinking it, opposed to a glass of beer.`

The following Friday evening, Ann spoke of a vacancy for a machinist, which had become available at the factory where she worked. Full training would be given, and there'd be plenty of

158

overtime. The take home pay to start with would be £5-10 shillings a week. This brought music to mother's ears.

'Our Veronica, will apply for that job. So make sure you get an interview arranged, for next week. It's £3 more than she's earning at present.' I sat staring for a moment, dumbfounded. How dare she plan my life? Pushing my unfinished meal, into the middle of the table, I stood my ground, defiantly.

'Excuse me! But I do happen to be sat here you know, you talk as if I'm not in the same room, and for your information, I don't want to work as a machinist, I'm happy where I am, thank you very much, and if you want me to leave my job, to work elsewhere, to earn extra money, to pay off the clothes voucher. Well! You needn't worry, for I'll manage fine on whatever is left each week, from my present wages. She looked across the table towards Ann, who had a smirk on her face, yet again.

'Take no notice Ann! Still arrange that interview for her, like I asked, first thing, Monday morning.`

Mother was adamant. Granted, she needed the extra money, but she should look to father for more financial support. The £2 a week she took out of my wage packet was sufficient, as far as I was concerned, but if I should achieve promotion in the near future, she could happily have the extra board.

Arrangements had been made that evening, to meet Pamela. Her boyfriend Richard worked as a fire fighter and had to work alternate weekends, so she'd take a flask of tea and some sandwiches, in time for his lunch break. I'd accompany her to the fire station, and we'd chat with him and his friends for half an hour in the canteen, then we'd call in our local pub for a drink, on our way home.

Time was passing, but the bathroom was empty, so I was able to have a bath and change into my new navy cotton suit, pale blue bolero top and new shoes, mother caught me on the way out though, and ushered me back into the front room.

'Your fathers here now, so you can tell him what you've just told me. Well hurry up then! Tell him?' Freeing myself from her grasp, I made my way to the front door again.

'I'll tell him later, if you don't mind. I've to meet Pamela, and I'm already late!' She lunged forward gripping my arm again, and ushering me back, into the front room.

'Never mind bloody Pamela, you can explain to your father first.'

He was sat in the chair nearest the fire, and obviously worse for wear. Geoffrey had brought some mugs of tea from the kitchen and placed them nervously on the top of the mantle- piece, but his troubled expression was cause for concern, as he could sense the inevitable. Finally shrugging free from mothers grasp, I straightened up, preparing for the off once again, as she pushed me forward.

'Well go on tell him? Tell him you won't leave the photographers, to work with our Ann. for £3 a week more!' Father picked up his mug of tea, and started to sip it, whilst looking towards me in a drunken stupor.

'You must 'ave a fuckin' slate loose girl! How can yer ignore an opportunity to make more money each week? Yer need your 'ed testin'! Anyway you'll do as I say. If Ann can get an interview arranged, you'll bleedin' go, do yer 'ere me?' At this point I was fuming.

'I'm not leaving my present job, for you or mother.' I screeched. `And if you pressure me anymore, I'm leaving home.' At that moment, mother shocked us all, as she reached for her mug of sweet milky tea.

'You'll do as I bloody well say, cos you'll not threaten me!' Lucky for me, she always drank her tea tepid, for in seconds she'd thrown it over me, and smashed the mug over the top of my head. Our John and Jane could be heard screaming with fright, as father and Geoffrey grabbed a hold of her, she'd obviously lost it, and was about to finish off the violent attack, with a beating.

Both shocked and stunned, I ran from the scene. The sweet milky tea had already gone sticky as it hit the fresh air, and sticking to my lovely new clothes, along with the blood, trickling from the open wound. Oblivious to the stares from onlookers, I continued running, and eventually found myself in Grenham, Avenue, where I once lived, as a child.

160

Stopping for a moment, and feeling disoriented, I looked around. Where could I go? I couldn't very well turn up on Maureen's doorstep, not after all these years, and looking such a mess. So there was no alternative, but to call on Aunt Agnus. Making my way quickly, I was suddenly aware of the shocked stares of people passing, but in a matter of minutes I was inside the front door, for it was always left ajar.

I can recall when I was younger, when mother would ask me to borrow money from Agnus. She must have had at least eight children, running in and out then. So a train station often sprung to mind.

Aunt Agnus was washing up, and a look of total surprise, suddenly spread across her face, not just because of my state, but one of not seeing me for many years.

'God Almighty Our 'arold, come 'ere quick, `ave yer seen the state of our Veronica?' The look of shock on Uncle Harolds face as he walked from the front room, frightened me somewhat, but I must have frightened him, even more so.

'What the 'ecks 'appened to yer luv?'

I blurted out what happened, in minutes, as Agnus handed me a large glass of brandy.

'What did I tell yer about our Winnie, 'arold? I told yer didn't I? Somethin' terrible would 'appen, one day. She's not been a well woman, since her nervous breakdown, in Wythenshawe, and our Jimmy 'asn't 'elped matters either. Knockin' 'er about, over the years, and for Christ sake 'arold, will yer go and flag a taxi down, on City Road? And stop lookin' bleedin' gormless. We'll 'ave to tek' 'er to the Royal Infirmary, as she's going to need some stitches, by all accounts. So be quick!'

I cringed, as dear Aunt Agnus, only doing her best, but never to have won. 'Cleaner, of the year award' suddenly plonked an old tea towel on top of my head, to help reduce the flow of blood, until we arrived at the hospital.

'You'd better change out of those clothes too, or they'll be ruined. Hang on a minute, while I get something of our Dorothy's, for yer to wear, and I'll steep yours overnight. When there dried I'll come 'ome with yer, and 'ave a word with yer mother.'

Although later, Agnus agreed wholeheartedly with mother's decision, and thought I should go for the machinist job, so increasing her board, and saying. 'I shouldn't pick and choose at my age, and should do as I was told.'

Harold quickly returned, though completely out of breath, through rushing around. 'The taxis outside our Agnus, so if your ready, we'll go?' Once inside the taxi, I felt a lot better, but also a little giddy, for the brandy was taking effect. Harold looked towards Agnus, while looking a little coy.

'I could do with a tot of that brandy meself our Agnus, when we reach 'ome? Only I've come over all pukey.' She rolled her eyes and tutted. 'You'll just 'ave to bloody well want, then, cos' that brandy's expensive, and been locked away in the cupboard! It's for special occasions, that is. With her last remark, we all looked to each other and burst out laughing, which helped me enormously, and putting me in a better mood, while in the casualty dept, when receiving four stitches and having a chunk of hair cut away from my scalp, the size of a penny. Seated in the taxi, on the way home, I was suddenly aware, of their kindness and support, and was to remember them in my special wedding guests list, unknown to me then of course, but was to take place, in the very near future. Being married though was to take me down the road, of a living hell, for the next five years of my life.

Agnus took me home the following morning, and father had taken the morning off work, fearing mother might go off her head, when confronting me again, but she appeared quite calm and even more so, when I agreed to meet her halfway. I'd give up my present job, once I'd found something else, which was suitable.

While having three days off sick, I scanned the Evening News for vacancies, but decided to broaden my horizons and work further out into the city. Two jobs were of interest, one at Affleck and Browns, as a shop assistant, and the other at Sharrocks on Oldham Street, as a ledger clerk. Both were in the centre of Piccadilly, and full training would be given. Just as well, for I'd no experience in either field. Interviews were arranged by phone, for the following morning.

Agnus saved my best clothes from being ruined, through the bloodstains, by steeping them overnight, so I was able to wear them again for my two interviews. Back combing my hair, then clipping it down, solved the problem of covering the stitches. So no one, was any the wiser.

Being offered both jobs, as the interviews went successfully, I chose Sharrocks, for it was an increase of salary, by twelve shillings a week. Mr Stevens the manager, appeared pleasant and friendly and asked if I would start work the following Monday.

Mr Rackham and his staff were surprised, when handing in my notice, and I was really upset, for I really didn't want to leave, but had no choice, under the circumstances. I'd enjoyed working with them all immensely, but it was now time to move on.

Chapter Twelve.

Mena, the office junior at Sharrock's, until my arrival, was happy to hand over the tedious duties, of the 'Office Goffa,' now it was my turn. We were both younger than the other ladies in our office, and soon became good friends, for she was friendly, outgoing, and proved lots of fun to be around. We were to remain good friends, for some years later.

Mena checked her watch, for it was nearly lunchtime.

'Get your jacket! I'll take you to the sandwich store then you'll know in future, where it is!' She suddenly started to giggle.

'We'll be passing Lloyds furniture store on our way! There's a salesman working in there, called Terry. He has an eye for a pretty girl, so be warned, and take no notice of his flirtatious ways, for he thinks he's gods gift! He's also courting Margaret from the bridal shop next door, and they'll be announcing their engagement, in the near future'

Just about to pass the store, Terry walked out, seating himself comfortably, on the side of the electrical appliances.

I was taken aback, by the tall extremely good- looking Irishman, with thick light brown wavy hair, and dressed very smart. He smiled broadly, while showing beautiful white even teeth.

'Who's this then? The new office junior.` Mena turned a deep plum colour, on answering, and keep your eyes off, cos' I've already warned her.' He proceeded to rifle his pockets, for some small change.

'Mena! Get us the usual sarny will yer luv'? There's a good girl, and tell her not to put too much beetroot on as it gives me indigestion, and don't forget to buy your own, out of the change!' She snatched the money from his hand, in a jovial manner.

'I don't know? I must be barmy, running errands after you every day!'

For the next few months while going for the lunches, Terry would be stood outside waiting, and of course I carried on from where Mena left off, and went for his sandwiches. He'd buy mine too, which helped, for there was very little money left over out of my weekly spends, after bus-fares were deducted.

At the age of seventeen, life became a regular routine. My social life was fairly quiet, spending most evenings, listening to music, in Pamela house, and the weekends with Mena,where we'd go to the pictures in town, or for a drink in the Shambles. I was also settled into my work, and was eventually promoted, to make way for the new office junior.

A new project was being built, on the opposite side of the road, to our office, and at lunchtime the builders would sit on the wall, they'd shout friendly banter across to the office, for we'd have the windows open, it being the middle of summer. The office staff enjoyed the friendly banter, and some of the women went out on the occasional dates, the odd affair was struck up too, causing the office to buzz, and so adding a little excitement, to our boring little lives.

After work, one particular evening, Paul the youngest builder, and similar age to myself, was waiting outside. He asked if I'd like to go for a drink, I hesitated for a moment but then told him I would have to think it about it, and would let him know, the following day.

Going into work, the following morning, Terry could be seen moving an appliance into a delivery van, and called me over.

'Do yer fancy going for a Chinese meal, tonight?'

'Not really!' I replied, while trying to hide my utter shock of disbelief. 'Your already spoken for! Or so I'm led to believe.'

'Not anymore, I'm not! I packed Margaret in, cos' she was borin'! So what do yer say then? Still in utter shock, I tried to act, cool calm and collective.

'I don't know? I'll have to think about it!'

'Well don't leave it too long, cos' someone else, might snatch me up!'

'Two dates in two days! You lucky girl! And Terry's absolutely gorgeous. Well which one is it to be then?' Asked Mena, becoming a little flustered, on my behalf. Paul was really nice, and had a great personality, but he wasn't good looking, when your young and foolish, good looks account for everything.

What a dilemma! Terry, or Paul? Paul, or Terry? In the end, I chose the latter.

Terry was waiting outside work that same evening. 'Hi! are yer coming out with me, tonight, or not?' I suddenly felt a pang of guilt, having turned Paul down, for he seemed rather disappointed.

'Yes, although I'll have to go home, and freshen up first.'

He looked me over and winked. 'You look just fine the way yer are kid, so we might as well go out from 'ere, and we'll go to a great Chinese restaurant, I frequently go to.`

A restaurant, I hope it's not too posh' I thought, for the nearest I'd got to dining out, was the local café at lunchtime, with Mena, so I'd just have to play it by ear. We crossed the busy street, and were making our way towards China town, when he suddenly stopped outside the Kings Head pub.

'Let's just call in 'ere first, for a pint, I need to quench me thirst! Moving kitchen appliances all day, makes thirsty work!'

That one -pint, developed into four, within an hour, while I was still sipping, the same gin and tonic, strange really, for it didn't appear to effect or alter his personality in anyway. Father crossed my mind for a moment, remembering, how he was affected and became aggressive, after drinking just a couple of pints. But the fleeting thought faded, as quickly as it came.

Later that evening, we went for a Chinese meal and somehow I managed to master the art of eating with chopsticks, which was just as well, for we were to frequent his favourite restaurant often, while courting.

I'd been going out with Terry for some months, and as well as finding him to be a kind, generous and compassionate man, he also proved to be a positive energy person, to be around. We'd go shopping on countless occasions, where he'd buy expensive jewellery and clothes, and was eventually to have a wardrobe containing suits and dresses, I could only ever have imagined.

166

Walking into the office one Monday morning, with yet another new outfit, the meows got louder, which made me feel, quite smug, after all, I was a very, very, lucky girl.

Going into the Kings Head after work, and Terry downing pints of bitter like they were going out of fashion, became a regular habit, but by this time, I'd fallen for him hook line and sinker. Every now and then doubts would creep into my mind, remembering father's ill treatment of mother, after heavy bouts of drinking, but I'd whisk them away, as quickly as they came. After all, Terry wasn't of a violent nature, and what harm was he doing anyway. He worked hard, so deserving some relaxation and socialising, after work.

One particular Monday morning, while passing Terry's place of work, his manager Solly, was stood at the other end of the showroom, and beckoned me inside.

'I want a quite word with you, if you can spare it! Terry's just phoned in sick, and I'm afraid I've had to sack him! So he can collect his cards at the end of the week.' He paused for a moment before continuing, and looked decidedly uncomfortable. 'I know it's none of my business, and you can tell me to shut up, if you wish! But I think you'd be wise to pack him in. He's going nowhere in life, and he's on the road to becoming an alcoholic! I've just found out, would you believe? On my day off from work, he shuts up shop and goes in the kings Head. Well I won't tolerate drinking in working hours, so that's the reason I've had to sack him! It's a pity really, because he's a good salesman, but it's the same reason why Margaret, packed him in. She suddenly came to her senses -no danger!' Seething at his insinuations, and not believing a word, I turned on him vehemently.

'How dare you? Have the audacity to talk of Terry in that disrespectful way! He's been a dammed good worker for you, so at the end of the day, it'll be your loss not his, for sacking him, and as for accusing him of becoming an alcoholic. Well! It's just blackening his character, as far as I'm concerned, and he won't be too pleased to hear about that one. I can assure you!' I stormed out of the store, but his last few words regarding Margaret, were not lost on me.

That same evening Terry was waiting outside Sharrocks. It was unexpected and I was surprised to see him, but even more so, as he appeared unperturbed, regarding the loss of his job.

'I've just spoken to Solly! He can stick is job, where the sun don't shine, and I'm not that concerned anyway, cos' I'm confident I'll find another job, in the next few days. So cheer up, I'm tekin' yer to meet me ma, she's 'erd so much about yer and is dyin' to meet yer!'

He lived off Wilmslow Road, in the Rusholme area, and as we stepped out of the taxi, noticed it was very Cosmopolitan and friendly. With its added hustle and bustle of nightlife, and the universities being a stone's throw away, it obviously attracted a home ground, for the students.

He ushered me down a side street. 'I forgot to mention! Me ma owns a pub, and this is it, just around 'ere. It's called the 'Albert', and she'll be in there now, 'avin' her usual glass of guiness. You'd never believe it was our pub though, cos' she's always on the customers side of the bar. But that's me ma, for yer! Another thing I forgot to mention, were stayin' just across the road, in a two bedroomed terrace. It's just somewhere to stay, until our four bedroomed house, situated in Bramhall, has had its renovation, completed!'

I started to relax, and even more so, in his mothers jovial company. She was a tall, dark, striking looking Irish woman, with a good bone structure and beautiful thick dark short wavy hair. She was in her mid forties, and at a glance, you'd be reminded of the late. 'Jackie Kennedy.'

She went along with Terry's fantasies, and found it quite amusing, just how gullible I really was. But fantasies didn't exist in my world, being a realist, so not realising, Terry's life was a charade, for he was already an, habitual liar and his life unmanageable, without alcohol. He portrayed a picture of honesty, inner strength and happiness, so lulling me, into a false sense of security.

Later that evening, they invited me into their home. But it was in stark contrast, to the well- dressed Terry, I knew of.

'Coffee…Tea?' She asked, while throwing her expensive camel coat, onto the back of an old comfortable, but cluttered armchair.

'Tea please, White with one sugar.' I added, while at the same time, noticing Terry had opened a bottle of Whisky and downed half a tumbler, within seconds. Josie sat down, making herself, comfortable alongside me, after handing out cups of tea and cigarettes, then chatted on about one thing and another, and before the evening was over, I was to learn a little more about herself and Terry's dad - Nicholas.

It was sometime before I was to see Josie again, and it was to let her know of our wedding plans, for the following June. Terry still lived in Coburg place too, which was surprising, as I assumed they might have moved. But no mention of uprooting to live in Bramhall was ever mentioned. I was later to find, Coburg Place was his permanent home, and his parents had no intentions of moving to a middle class area, and surprise, surprise, the pub wasn't his parent's, either.

The whole situation soon became relatively obscure, and coupled with the idea, he could even suppose, I wouldn't go out with him, because of where he lived - baffled me. It really didn't matter one iota, for it was him who was important in my life, and everything else, just paled into insignificance, so why all the pretence? After all, he hadn't visited my home and ours was a humble abode, but I certainly wasn't ashamed, and he could have called, whenever.

We'd been courting for over a year, when he asked me to marry him, and in all that time he'd never met my parents, always reluctant, and making excuses, of one kind or another.

Well he was cornered this particular evening, for I'd made arrangements to have dinner with my parents then make a social evening of it, by going into father's local.

169

I was still working in Sharrocks, and Terry was working as a salesman, in a furniture store in Deansgate, so we met later that same evening, in his favourite haunt. Surprisingly, he'd had very little to drink, and probably wanting to create a good impression, but I hadn't the heart to mention, father had been an alcoholic for years, and to have introduced Terry, a little worse for wear, would have pleased him immensely - a man after his own heart, and a future son in law, at that.

When introducing Terry, as my future husband, mother disliked him immediately, and showed her disapproval. Father had a different view and shook hands with Terry, in a friendly gesture, the feeling appeared mutual.

After dinner, we made our way to the pub, and once inside, made ourselves comfortable for the next couple of hours. Mother and myself not being drinkers, held our same glass all evening, while Terry frequented the bar every fifteen minutes or so, and accompanied by my father, who was obviously taking advantage of his generosity, and calling Terry –son, before the evening was over. Mother hadn't missed a trick and was seething, but bit her tongue until we arrived home. Once in the kitchen to make some tea though, she lit up a cigarette and had her say.

'Are you blind or something? Sit down and listen carefully! If you've any sense, you'll get rid of Terry, he's no good! There like peas in a pod, can't you see that? Terry drinks more than your father too, which is patently obvious, but one thing about your father, he never went out with other women…not to my knowledge, anyway. But Terry! Well… He's got an eye for the women, mark my words he's trouble. There's no two ways about it, so get rid, while the goings good!'

How dare she, I thought. He's my knight in shining armour. Someone at last to take me away from this miserable, depressing, place, supposedly called home.

'I'm marrying him! No matter what you say! He's kind and considerate and will make a good husband. He's just a little nervous

170

tonight, that's all - and no wonder, giving him sour looks all evening, it's enough to turn any man to drink.'

'You cheeky sod! You don't deserve any sound advice, carrying on like you do. I'm your mother and you should show a little more respect.'

Father wavered into the kitchen at hearing the row, with his usual purple coloured face after drinking. 'What's all the noise about? And where's that bleedin' tea? We've been waitin' ages.'

'Never mind the tea! Call that Terry in here. I want a word!' Terry walked in, on hearing the commotion, as she pointed to a chair.

'Sit down and listen carefully? And this goes for you too, our Veronica. I shan't beat about the bush Terry, I don't like you, and if you decide to marry my daughter, I won't stand in your way, but I'm not attending the wedding, that's final!' Father got up from his chair, looking decidedly uncomfortable, regarding mother's tactlessness.

'Aye Winnie! There's no need to speak to the lad like that! I think he'll make Veronica a fine husband and he's generous to a fault!' She stopped drinking her tea, and turned on him, vehemently.

'You would! After all, you've just supped half a brewery, at his expense, haven't you? So your bound to be bias!' Terry stood up to leave and obviously annoyed at being treated as such.

'It's been nice meetin' yer both, and I'm sorry the meetin' turned out the way it did, but yer suit yerself Mrs Neill, the weddin' will tek place without yer, so it'll be your loss, at the end of the day!' He shook hands with father then made his way to the front door. I was really upset the way the evening had turned out, and thought Terry would have done a runner, there and then.

'Don't worry! It'll all blow over before the weddin' and your mother is bound to come round to the idea, before then! But that father of yours, well... He's a different kettle of fish, altogether. He's one cheeky get! He never once, put his hand in his pocket all evening, and he was on whisky chasers too. I'll know different next time though, just yer see if I don't, once bitten twice shy.'

171

I watched till he disappeared out of sight, and knew I would marry him, for there was no doubt in my mind, and thought him the best thing, since chocolate biscuits. So regardless of mother's disapproval, it would be her loss not mine, if she decided not to accept him as her son- in- law, and I'd prove to her once and for all, what a poor judge of character, she really was.

Chapter Thirteen.

The wedding took place as planned, on a beautiful warm June morning, and father gave me away. Linda had made my dress out of satin brocade. It looked stunning. I will never forget how dedicated she was into making it just so, along with the bride maids dresses in Salmon pink. The dress was my wedding gift, from her and Tommy, and it was to be treasured, for many years.

Our wedding day went superbly, and everything went as planned, but still couldn't believe, I was actually Mrs Taylor. My mother never attended the church, which didn't surprise me, although she did turn up at the reception later that evening, and looking very smart, in a pale cream suit and navy accessories. She didn't apologise for not attending the wedding, but I forgave her anyway, and put it down to her frequent bouts of depression. Besides, nothing or anyone was going to mar our special day.

Earlier in the year, Josie, had spoken to her landlord and asked if any of the houses in Coburg Place, should became vacant, could we have first refusal. While courting Terry, I'd spent some time in the area and found it quite a nice friendly neighbourhood, and decided I could live there for a year or so, as the rent would be reasonably cheap, and would enable us to save, for a deposit on our own home.

We were pleased, when a terraced house became vacant, at the end of Josies street. It seemed really strange having a home of our own, and immediately set about, painting and decorating, and was eventually completed, just before the wedding. It was tastefully furnished with expensive leather and oak furnishings, which he'd managed to buy much cheaper, being in the furniture trade. With the subdued lighting on the walls, the overall effect was stunning, and looked like a palace.

After the wedding, our gifts were taken to our new home to be opened. We couldn't afford a honeymoon, as we'd both saved for the wedding ourselves, so moved into our new home the same day.

My grandmother, from my father's side, stayed overnight after the wedding, at Josies house. The next morning before returning home, she called to our new home, to nosey round a little, like families usually do, then she offered to help unwrap some of our wedding gifts.

'I'm sure you'll appreciate what I chose for you both.' She said, while looking round. 'For it's just what you'll need, especially for the winter!' We continued opening all the gifts, but still couldn't find grandmothers, as she looked on somewhat puzzled.

'It's strange that is, for it's really bulky, and I might as well tell you, it's a Bedding Bale, but it's definitely not here!'

Visiting her some weeks later, I was to find she'd given my father, the wedding gift, to give to us, rather than struggle with it herself in a taxi, on our wedding day, but he had taken it upon himself, to call into the nearest pawnshop and pawn the bedding bale for £8, then call in the bookies and put it on a horse. The horse lost, and our wedding gift was never redeemed. Grandmother thought it a diabolical liberty to take, and didn't speak to her son, for many months after.

Chapter Fourteen.

We were happy in our first year of marriage, and now had a beautiful baby son -Warren Mark Nicholas. We also counted ourselves lucky, for we had no financial worry and no debts, for Terry received a decent salary. I eventually made some new friends of similar age, in the neighbourhood, for they were also young mothers, with babies and toddlers. We'd spend our afternoons, walking round the lake in Platt Fields, and feeding the ducks, or when it rained we'd go shopping, my life at that time, generally being a happy one.

I fell pregnant again some months later, and a noticeable change in our marriage, became apparent. Terry started working late, and countless teas were ruined in the oven, as well as the occasional night, spent away from home. His excuse being, he'd called in the pub on the way home from work with some of his colleagues then carry on to the casino for a game of cards, and inevitably lose track of time. I bought this excuse, for some time.

Josie proved to be a good mother in law, and appeared to be on my side, for she'd have her say, if he should stay out at night, even though he would tell her, to keep her nose out. I had noticed she appeared a little afraid of him sometimes too, but put it down to imagination, on my part.

First insight, to Terry's unstable side of his nature surfacing, went unnoticed. Preparing himself for work one morning, he politely mentioned, he'd invited his boss David and his wife Bella, for a meal for the following Tuesday night. I was excited, for it would give me a chance to use our new dinner service, we'd had bought, for a wedding present.

That following Tuesday soon came around, and on the way out to work, Terry gave me some extra money, to buy some expensive bottles of wine. He wanted everything to be just so, as promotion for an area manager was in the offing. So I spent the late afternoon, preparing the special meal, of salmon steaks, cauliflower cheese, new potatoes, and a side salad. It was one of Terry's favourite dishes, so thought it ideal for our guests.

Warren was a good boy, and went to bed at a set time each evening, and once tucked in, I was able to freshen up. With the table set and dinner in the oven, everything seemed timed to perfection. All I needed was the guests to arrive. So I sat, waiting and waiting and waiting, until I was frantic with worry. It was 9pm and still no sign of anyone, of course we didn't have a phone, so there was no immediate contact and we didn't own a car either, but his boss did. They could have had an accident…anything. I turned off the cooker, and opened a bottle of wine, then sipping a glass slowly, while feeling positively useless, and fearing the worse.

Holding the same glass of wine, seemingly forever, Terry walked in, a little worse for wear and leaving his language a lot to be desired. I started to feel afraid for the first time since we'd married, as he staggered about different parts of the furniture.

'Bastard, that's what that David is, a funkin' wanker! Well, he can stick his job up his fuckin' arse. I don't need it! I don't need anyone in this fuckin' life! Do yer 'ere me, yer stupid bitch?' He fell against the dinner table while taking off his jacket, and knocking the wine bottle and glasses to the floor.

'What's all this about then? Spendin' all me money, on fuckin' fancy dinner parties! Yer must think I'm made of the fuckin stuff.'

The tablecloth was suddenly pulled from under the dinner- set, and all crashed to the floor, while I stood rooted to the spot and at the same time, hoping Warren wouldn't be disturbed and start to cry. Terry just threw his coat over a chair then strolled upstairs to bed, still muttering and cursing, to himself.

After cleaning up the dreadful mess, in a somewhat state of shock and confusion, I sat downstairs for the rest of the night. Not able to comprehend such an outrages and despicable act on his part, for it was completely out of character. Anger suddenly took over, thinking of all the time and effort spent in the kitchen, and only to be called a 'stupid bitch' at the end of it all. Well, I would certainly clock that one up for future reference, no two ways about it.

Next morning, he came down stairs, as sober as a judge, I tore into him and gave him what for, as I didn't feel intimidated when he was in his right frame of mind, and could have my say. He apologised profusely and wanted to make it up, and suggested an evening out at our favourite restaurant. I was bought yet again.

Josie came round that evening, to baby- sit and I wouldn't have dreamed of mentioning Terry's uncharacteristic outburst, the previous evening, but I'm sure she could sense, the tense atmosphere, nonetheless.

Terry had been upset the previous day, for David had offered the area managers job to another member of staff, and so the dinner was cancelled. I argued that he still could have come home and let me know, and it would have saved all that time and effort. He was sorry, and promised it would never happen again, and certainly wouldn't be so presumptuous in the future, regarding any hint of promotion at work.

Terry was in his fifth job, since we'd married. Apparently, it was always someone else's fault, when he'd been given the sack, and of course, I'd always taken his side, but had pondered over the last sacking. Maybe it was related to his increasing drinking habit, especially, as he went straight from work to the pub and stayed out more frequently, until the early hours. He always dressed immaculate though, and would be ready for work on time, regardless.

A clean white shirt was always worn, with a starched detached collar, for each working day. A batch of five would be taken to the dry cleaners and another batch, would be ready for collection. If he needed a collar to wear for over the weekend, he would turn the cleanest of the five over, and that would suffice. His two best suits were also taken to the dry cleaners, for sponge and pressing, and collected every Friday morning.

His new job included attending courses, he'd mentioned it earlier in the week, as one was taking place, the following Monday, so I should have his suits back from the cleaners for Friday lunch, for an early conference was taking place in a hotel, the following morning.

I called to the cleaners Friday morning, only to find they'd closed, and gone away for the weekend, and a notice was put in the window apologising to the customer for such a short notice, but would be reopening again, at 8.am, Monday morning.

Returning home, without any real concern, I opened the front door. Terry was ironing some clothes and a suitcase was open on the chair.

'The dry cleaners are closed, until Monday.' I was just about to say I'd sponge and press his other suits, when his fist hit me full force in the face, sending me crashing down against the front door.

'Yer useless cow, you've fuckin' ruined, my weekend! Don't yer ever read a notice on a shop door, 'cos I'm sure they would have mentioned to their customers, they'd be goin' away? Yer fuckin' stupid, that's all yer are! I'll 'ave to use my old suits and there nowhere near as smart as the other two.'

I stood up slowly and made my way to the sofa, both stunned and shocked at his violent attack, as Warren started to cry, not quite understanding his father's sudden change of behaviour. I picked him up from his trolley, and tried to calm him. Next thing the front door was slammed shut. Terry was gone, and not a word as to when he'd be returning.

The familiar face of my mother, reflected in the mirror, as I examined my purpley black swollen eye. Memories of the violence, she'd suffered at the hands of my father, were first and foremost in my mind and it seemed like, history was to repeat itself.

Terry had never used violence before, and I'm sure he would never use it again, so why was I feeling intimidated in his company, and always wanting everything to be just so. It seemed he was on a short fuse these days, and things were going from bad to worse.

Well, I wouldn't make the same mistake again. I'd always check if the dry cleaners were going to close early, in future, as I couldn't afford a repeat performance of today, being five months pregnant.

Sunday morning he returned home, full of apologies, while handing me a large box of chocolates and some flowers.

'Sorry luv'! I never meant that to happen. It's just the new job I'm in, it means such a lot and I want to earn enough money to get us out of this place.'

My eye was looking better by Monday and was less noticeable, and especially covered with eye makeup. We were going out to our favourite Chinese restaurant again that evening and Josie was babysitting, she'd also noticed my swollen eye, but decided not to comment - very wise.

Chapter Fifteen.

Life seemed quiet for some months after, and Terry was contented in a job he'd strived for, as area manager. Moving to a new home, in a different area was also imminent, as we'd saved enough for our first deposit.

A month after Christmas, another beautiful son, was added to our family unit... Lee Anthony Philip. It was two months after Lee was born, that an argument broke out, concerning his future godparent's. I'd chosen Linda to be godmother, and Terry didn't want her to be, so chose his mother. I told him it was a ludicrous idea, as his mother was already Lee's grandmother, and I wanted someone special outside of the family circle. I stayed adamant about my decision, and decided on, Linda and Brian. I presumed that would be the end of it, but was to presume wrong.

He stormed out to the pub, but later returned in a drunken stupor. Warren was asleep in his bed, and I was feeding Lee, in the armchair. He took Lee from my arms and placed him in his crib, then dragging me from the chair, punched me violently in the face and body. Blood oozed from my nose profusely, as I tried to escape the blows, but to no avail. His mother was going to be godmother, and that was final. Another word and I'd be beaten again. He stormed off to bed, leaving me to face whoever the next day, with yet another black eye, and the worry of facing family and friends, at the Christening the following weekend.

Mary, a friend who lived in our street, called as usual to go shopping. She was the only person apart from his mother, who new of Terry's ill treatment, and couldn't believe it, for he seemed such a kind, considerate person, on the outside. So until I was looking more presentable, she helped with the shopping and such like and would take Warren to the park, which was a tremendous help.

Mary was the only friend he made welcome in our home, and made it quite obvious to Linda and Mena, that he didn't like either of them. So in the future, I had to make arrangements to meet them in town, for a coffee and a chat, for whenever any of them visited, he would sulk, upset the home and accuse me of talking about him behind his back. Of course the accusations were ludicrous to say the least, for I didn't want anyone knowing our marriage was heading for the rocks, but as his paranoia set in, the more absurd the situation became.

The day of the christening came and went without any qualms, for Terry had won the fight.

My family attended that day, and were to learn nothing, regarding the violence in my marriage, for I'd managed to cover up quite well, both mentally and physically and could have won an Oscar, for the fact, I'd hidden the truth from everyone, including myself, for so long, that I'd married a man the replica of my father. Well, I'd made my bed of roses, and would have to lie on it... or would I.

To endure a life of violence, like my mother's, would be intolerable to say the least, so something positive would have to be done, and soon.

As usual, life quietened down for a while. It started to fall into a familiar pattern, of a beating for something so trivial, as bordering on the ridiculous, then falling peaceful and calm for a time, but that time was up, and could feel it in my bones, as the atmosphere in the home started to turn sour.

Terry had yet another course to attend, and asked for his suits to be collected from the dry cleaners. It was early Friday lunch and I'd called to the cleaners, only to find them closed for the weekend once again, yet I could have sworn they hadn't left a note in the window, to let the customer know.

Well, it was too late, and panic started to well up inside. There'd be murder, no two ways about it, and could almost taste the fear, while making my way home. Sweat started to trickle down my spine and my hands became clammy, knowing what lay ahead, for I'd just gotten over the last hiding, and didn't want to face another, but there was nowhere else to go.

Nearing home, I called on Mary. It would be best if Warren and Lee were left with her, and I'd face the consequences, alone.

When explaining about the cleaners, she put her thinking cap on.

'Go home and try to explain!' It brought a sudden smile to my face, as she really didn't have a clue. 'I'll call a minute or two later, and if he's causing you any trouble, it'll have to stop. He's hardly going to hit you with me around…is he?'

Her husband Bill walked in from the kitchen at that moment and caught the tail end of our conversation. He wasn't much good to Mary and I didn't like him, for he'd leave her short of money, was uncouth and often swore, in front of his young family. But she wasn't afraid of him and he wasn't violent towards her ever, even in drink.

'What the 'ell's goin' on then? Trouble agen`? Mary went on to explain about the cleaners, as he looked on thoughtfully, while straightened his pencil thin moustache.

'Well! Why can't he sponge and press his own feckin' suits? After all, it won't feckin' kill him, will it? So if yer need me to go in with yer? I will! I'm not frightened of him, as big as he is!'

I perished at the thoughts of involving Bill or anyone else for that matter and quickly made my way to the door.

'I'd better be on my way and thanks all the same, and if you can call soon… Mary?'

'Of course I will!'

I put Mary's plan into action, and walked the few doors up. Putting my key in the front door, I braced myself for the first punch, but was shocked to see Terry doubled up on the sofa, and sweating profusely.

'Get me a doctor and quick? Tell him it's my appendix, I think they've bursts!'

I ran to the nearest phone box, and it wasn't long when the doctor arrived, and on examining Terry, phoned for an emergency ambulance. He was rushed to hospital with a diagnosed peritonitis, and was to remain there for several days. He had complained of a grumbling appendix, for some time, but chose to ignore it until it finally came to ahead, apparently just at the right moment too, and saving me from a fate, worse than death.

Mary, a staunch catholic, believed that god worked in mysterious ways. 'I'm only saying, god was watching over you today and Terry definitely got his comeuppance!'

Come Monday, I collected his suits, but I was to find out something that day, which was to be a turning point in my life.

Mrs Nosey Parker - her nickname by all and sundry, stopped for a chat, and stood as always, with her somewhat, irritating arrogance.

'Are yer still livin with yer hubby then?' I was quite taken aback, as to why she should enquire.

'Of course, why on earth, should you think any different?' She appeared unperturbed at my somewhat look of dismay, and continued.

'Well! Tell me to mind me own business if yer like? I was at Bellvue dogs, a few weeks ago and yer hubby was there, at first I thought he was with you, but as they approached, I could see the woman accompanying him, was a few years older and very glamorous... I might add!'

I could see Mrs Nosey Parker was enjoying herself and was waiting for a surprised reaction, which she happily witnessed when all colour drained.

'Well thanks for that bit of information! It's done me a power of good!' I replied sarcastically. Then wishing I hadn't, for I'd obviously made it known to her. Her so- called good deed, for the day, had been done.

Why didn't I see it coming, the weekends spent away on his so called courses, it was all there in plain black and white, it didn't have to jump up and slap me in the face-but it did, and it was Terry being intimate with another woman- that cut the deepest.

After I'd put the children to bed, I sat on the sofa, thinking, as it seemed for hours and turning over in my mind, every little detail. He'd started to change, long before Lee was born, so I assumed the affair must have started at least a year since.

Maybe, that's what triggered off his violent tempers? Maybe it was just plain guilt on his part? So why didn't he just up and go and leave us in peace, I could have picked up the pieces and started again. Actually, I felt a tinge of relief, for I knew when confronting him over his affair, he'd have to admit to it, and probably leave-anyway. I should have visited him in hospital that evening, but being wrapped up in thought, forgot all about it. Just as well, for I knew I would lose my usually placid temper, on seeing him. Better to have given him a wide birth.

Mary called, once her children were tucked up in bed. It was a kind of escapism from Bill, and doing her some good, to have a drink and a chat.

'Why didn't you visit Terry at the hospital this evening? I'd have had the children, as you well know!' My mind was in turmoil, as I poured two glasses of wine.

'It's okay! He can manage without me for one night, as with most other night- lately!' She sensed the animosity in my voice and decided to coax me a little further.

'It's a real problem at the moment, isn't it? Especially as he's turned violent towards you! Even his mother seems a little afraid of him lately! Have you noticed that?' I switched off the television and moved an ashtray into the centre of the coffee table, before fetching in the wine and making myself comfortable, alongside her.

'Strange you should say that! I put it down to my imagination, for I've noticed it for some time!'

As the topic of conversation leaned towards Terry, I decided to tell her of my findings that day, from Mrs Nosey Parker. Mary suddenly turned a deep purple and appeared uncomfortable, under my fixed gaze.

'Come on Mary, you must know something? It's written all over your face!' She quickly lit up a cigarette, as if to find something to do, to hide her obvious embarrassment.

'Well... I can only elaborate on what you've just said. But it's common knowledge around these parts, that he's been seen on countless occasions, with another woman! I didn't want to say, as you've enough problems as it is. But you do have the right to know, so there- I've said it!' She looked somewhat relieved to have it out in the open, while I was left, feeling devastated.

'Why didn't you say something earlier? You're supposed to be my friend!' She stubbed out her cigarette end in the ashtray, nervously and paced the floor.

'It's easier said than done! And anyway, I thought the affair might peter out and you'd know, no different!'

There's that word again - affair' I thought. It seemed to scream out from all directions, and in the future, it was a word to be used in my day, today vocabulary, while awaiting my divorce.

'Well! It hasn't petered out, has it? And it's very true what they say- the wife's always the last to know! So when did you find out Mary? And you don't have to spare my feelings... just get on with it!'

'It was Bill, if you must know? He used to frequent the Oceans Eleven Club, on a Friday night! Well, Terry went in there, with his fancy woman, and you'll be shocked to know, Josie and Nicholas knew too! They went in for a drink one night, and when Nicholas discovered them together, a terrible row broke out, and ending outside the club. Mind you that was well over a year since! That's why Josie appears scared around her son. She thinks it will eventually come out in the open, which has happened anyway, and thinks you'll file for divorce! Well! Her being a staunch catholic and all, it's a bit like going against the grain, so to speak!'

It was my turn to pace the floor while listening, and could never have envisaged such a conversation, taking place in my very own front room.

Mary paused for breath... 'I'm really sorry love! But if there's anything I can do to help? I will! I'll look after the children anytime, should you need to go anywhere important as well, for it's the least I can do, under the circumstances! Anyway, I'd better be going or he'll start moaning, indoors, so I'll call tomorrow, and we'll go shopping, as usual.' So preoccupied with my thoughts, her words went in one ear and out the other.

185

'Are you sure you'll be okay now? As I know you've had a terrible shock, finding out! But someone had to tell you, and it was better coming from me. I'm on your side too, should you decide to divorce him, even though I am catholic, and wouldn't normally agree! But as he's turned violent, you can't be expected to stay under the same roof!'

I appreciated all she'd told me and we said goodnight. I needed sometime to mull over what had been said, and now was a good a time as any, while he was still in hospital.

Closing the door, I glimpsed at our new silver metallic Ford Capri, parked outside- it was Terry's dream car. He'd recently passed his driving test, and put a down payment on it, with all the travelling involved in his new job, it was a necessity. We went shopping together in it, and spent the occasional night out, but that was it. The rest of the time, he went out alone- apart from Sundays, when he'd take Warren out. What was it Warren used to say when he returned home? Being two years old, he could speak quite plain.

'The nice lady gave me orange juice and biscuits!'

I asked Terry out of shear curiosity, and his answer seemed feasible at the time. He had mentioned going into a pub, owned by a friend and the landlady allowed Warren to play with her young children, in her own living quarters. So why should that suddenly spring to mind. I can remember having a flaming row, as I didn't like Warren being taken into a pub-let alone Terry, drinking and driving. Of course it all started to fall into place and realising, he'd been taking Warren, to his lady friend's house and not a pub-after all.

Following day I went to visit my mother. It had been some months, and thought it would be a nice change to get away from the area for a while, and blow away the cobwebs.

Little had changed and she had nothing much to report, except father was working, so that was something at least. But she did comment about the £2 I'd been sending her each week. It was okay if I couldn't afford it anymore, and anyway I had a family of my own to take care of, and it didn't seem fair.

186

But I had been sending the money, and with a letter. Being fairly well off in comparison to her, I'd carried on sending her some money, knowing full well she missed the extra income coming into the home, after I'd married. She showed the last letter to me, and I recognised the writing of my father, immediately. He'd obviously been up to his old tricks again. He'd steamed opened the letter when it arrived, usually by early post on a Monday. He'd rewrite a letter, as if from myself, to say. I was sorry there was no money, as Terry was out of work.

We had to laugh at the audacity of the man, for it didn't look like he was ever going to change, but nonetheless, I would still treat mother in the future, and make sure father never benefited from it again. But not at the present, until I'd sorted out my own finances at home, which were becoming complicated, to say the least.

I left mothers home that day and never mentioned the trouble I was enduring at home with Terry, for I'd hate to have to here her say. 'I told you so' and would only land on her doorstep, if absolutely desperate for somewhere to stay.

Terry was discharged from hospital the next day, but couldn't walk very well, as he was still sore through having stitches.

'I'm tekin' a week off work till I recover, and I can't drive the car anyway, as it's far too uncomfortable until the stitches 'ave been removed.' He looked thoughtful, while carrying on his one sided conversation, for I'd switched off, long since.

'Anyway, where were yer, the last couple of nights? You could 'ave at least called. I felt left out in the ward with all the other wives visiting their husbands!'

I was being facetious on answering and was past caring.

'Maybe all the other wives husbands are not having affairs, like you. He stopped dead in his tracks and paled slightly.

'You know somethin' woman? You're a comedienne!'

'Really! First I'm a stupid bitch, and now a comedienne and you still haven't answered my question?' He laughed scornfully, which was quite irritating, for it was me who was supposed to have him, over a barrel.

'Do yer know what's wrong with yer woman? Yer tek things too seriously, yer need to relax and unwind a little then maybe you'll be a bit more fun to be around!'

We were quiet on our way home in the taxi, but had a strange feeling I might have provoked another attack and wasn't far wrong, for as soon as we were behind closed doors, it went off.

'Well! Who told yer? Hurry up, 'cos I want to know!' He slammed his fist down hard on top of the sideboard, and as he was cold sober, he seemed all the more frightening, but I stood my ground, nonetheless.

'Does it really matter? Because, I'm inclined to believe her.` He threw his coat and suitcase, onto a nearby chair.

'It fuckin does, if yer must know, `cos whoever it is, is tryin' to cause trouble between us. So if yer don't tell me, I'll smash the fuckin' 'ome up!' Warren and Lee would be home soon, and the thoughts of them walking into more trouble, was unthinkable.

'It was the local gossip, if you must know. She just happened to see you, and this other woman, at Bellvue races!' His hand violently swept across the sideboard and clearing it of its treasured family photo's and ornaments.

'Yer surprise me by the minute! I can't believe you'd listen to such rubbish! She a fuckin' lyin' witch and I'll tell her, next time I see her!' I knew he wouldn't of course, for she had three grownup sons, each one a fruit and nut case, and often in and out of prison. So he wouldn't have wanted anyone of those landing on his front doorstep.

Mary conveniently interrupted, by calling with the children, while Terry surprisingly, fetched the brush and shovel and swept up the debris, then settled in his comfortable armchair, to watch the football, but even so, appeared to be deep in thought, for the rest of the evening.

The home stayed unbelievably quite, the week he was off work, apart from the children playing, and there was mention of a couple of days out with them, when he felt comfortable enough to drive. I decided to stay quiet and bide my time, to see what further developments would occur, regarding his affair.

The washing machine was to break down. It doesn't rain but it pours. Terry would buy a new one soon, but in the meantime I'd have to use the laundrette, and was to call in three times, that week.

While in the laundrette, and waiting for a clothes drier, Warren pointed to the window for it was Terry- so I beckoned him in. He just happened to have called in the newsagents, for a paper, but he stayed anyway, and helped carry the shopping home, which was a first.

On the third call to the launderette that same week, Terry passed the window again, but I thought nothing of it. A queue was waiting for the drier, so I left the washing with the assistant, who would put it in the next available drier, whilst I did the rest of the shopping. I'd been gone about two hours before arriving home, and Terry was seething.

'Where've yer been all this time?' I ignored him for a moment as Warren started routing through the shopping for a biscuit. It was something new he'd started to do, and would turn it into a little game, while looking through each carrier bag.

'You know full well! You passed the launderette earlier, and could see I was up to my eyes in it!'

'But it doesn't tek two fuckin' hours, and I've been waitin' ages 'cos I've decided to take the car and go for a drive. And do yer know somethin' else? I think you've got another bloke!' I couldn't help but laugh, at such a ludicrous accusation.

'Oh yes! Of course I have! I'm having a mad passionate affair, between the Butchers, Redman's and the Launderette!'

'Don't be flippant with me! Give us yer handbag?' He snatched the bag and scattered the contents onto the floor, then opening the make-up bag, took items of make-up and spread them onto the carpet.

'Warren! Come 'ere son and watch this brand new game? Yer put yer foot over the top of yer mother's make-up and look- it squirts out, all over the carpet!' Warren looked on, but started to cry, obviously sensing the sudden tension in the atmosphere. I ushered him into the kitchen and closed the door, as he started to cry louder, while I quickly removed my handbag from the floor and tried to salvage what was left in the make-up bag.

'Your sick in the head! Do you know that? You should have seen a psychiatrist while you were in hospital, and you know something? I don't think they'd have let you out!'

He ignored me and continued squashing the foundation into the carpet, along with lipstick and eyes-shadow. Soon the carpet was an array of thick coloured wax and such like, which I new wouldn't come out, not ever in a month of Sundays, and by this time, Warren was hysterical in the kitchen.

'Yer can shut that Warren up-as well!' He bellowed, as the empty make-up tubes were kicked around the carpet.

'Well! That's the end of yer wearing anymore of that shit, and it'll be interestin' to see, who'll want to look at yer, without!'

He wasn't jealous, not by any stretch of the imagination, just damned right nasty, through having to stay at home. So with no other interest than gambling to keep him occupied, thought he'd amuse himself and have his bit of fun. He laughed again, that ridiculous irritating laugh, before taking his car keys and slamming the front door, followed by the car engine revving up and zooming down the street, at some ridiculous speed. I knew where he was going and really didn't care, for the sooner he was out of our lives for good-the better.

I'd have to make an appointment to see a solicitor, but having the guts to carry it out, was a different matter, but persevering for the sake of the children, and keeping a roof over our heads, was all well and good, but the situation couldn't go on much longer and there would have to be some radical changes. But it was a big world out there, and didn't relish the thoughts of us becoming homeless, which could happen if Terry became awkward. I also new part of the marriage problem was my fault, for I'd been far too wrapped up in the children, and maybe if I'd changed my attitude towards the affair, I might have handled things differently. But recently he'd become

190

volatile in his behaviour, so his violence towards me through his own guilt -was unforgiving in itself.

He came home that same evening a little worse for wear, and with his drink driving a regular habit, would soon be a menace on the roads. He'd brought in a fish supper and went to the kitchen to butter some bread, but I wasn't hungry and made my way upstairs. But refusing the supper and not wanting to spend any time with him triggered off his violent temper.

I was dragged down stairs and pushed onto a nearby kitchen chair, as the supper was put on the table and pushed in front me. His lips became a tight thin line and his eyes scary, a sign I was getting used too, when he was about to go off his head. He continued his intimidating behaviour, by saying.' I'd have to eat the food, or else he'd obliterate the kitchen, there and then. He opened a new bottle of tomato sauce and poured some over his supper, and knowing full well I detested the stuff, poured the rest over the top of mine. Feeling incarcerated in my own home, as well as the threat hanging over, I started to eat. It was a case of trying to keep the peace, for being bullied by my father over the years, and then Terry, I was easily crushed, and tended to back down. But the sauce burnt into my tongue, causing me to jump up, open the back door, and throw up onto the backyard steps. This caused the situation to exacerbate, so the frenzied attack on the kitchen began.

Cabinet doors were flung open, as flour, sugar, baby, powdered milk, cornflakes and barley, were tipped out and strewn across the floor. Eggs, bottles of milk and Orange juice, were thrown against the walls, and our best crystal glasses, a precious wedding gift, from a member of my family, were smashed one by one, into the kitchen sink. The only glass left untouched, was the kitchen window and was surprised, when it was left intact. I attacked him a couple of times, trying to stop his destruction, only to be flung against the wall, as the rampage continued – it was mayhem.

Draws were opened and cutlery and such like were tipped onto the floor, plates cups and saucers were smashed, and to top it all. The children's two pet goldfish were tipped out onto the floor and the

191

goldfish bowl, smashed against the wall. Poor Peter and Paul, gasping for breath, were mercilessly crushed, beneath his size ten shoe.

Warren, waking up and walking down stairs, to witness the pandemonium, was my worst fear, but miraculously, he slept through it all. Terry's face was ashen and his eyes a blank glazed expression, as he finally went upstairs to bed, leaving a path of destruction behind.

The fear I was experiencing was like no other, but having to come to terms with the fact, I was living under the same roof as an alcoholic maniac - was far worse. The thoughts of my mother and her very words-'I told you so` echoed in my mind, and suddenly living with her again, became appealing, in comparison to this appalling state of existence.

Fraught and angry, I looked around my once beautiful kitchen, while taking in the full reality of the last terrifying half- hour. It was all unwarranted, and was surprised I came out of it unscathed.

It was early hours, when I finally cleaned every inch of the floor, making sure there wasn't a splinter of crockery left, in case Warren awoke, and came down stairs. There was more food on the walls than in the cupboards, so decided to dress the children first thing and take them to Josie, until the shops opened. She wouldn't be very pleased, to hear of her sons latest antics either, but I would have to tell her, for there was no one else to turn too.

Exhausted, I found solace in sleep on the couch, but was disturbed by Terry going out early, for it was only 6am. He must have assumed the sink was still full of glass, so was making an early start, to wash and change, elsewhere.

He was to disappear, for five days, leaving me without any money for the second week. My savings were dwindling rapidly, and on top of food and rent, new kitchen utensils and such like, had to be replaced. My neighbour Rose, called in on her way to work that same morning, apparently not to pleased, at having her sleep disturbed, through my chopping wood in the cellar, the previous night. She really didn't have a clue, and as I couldn't begin to explain what the noise really was, just apologised and assured her it wouldn't happen again.

The kitchen had taken on a sad look, with the cupboards, hanging from their hinges, and seemed to reflect all the bad times that were suddenly occurring in our daily lives. That evening when the children were asleep, I set about cleaning the walls, trying to make the place look a bit more presentable, should Josie or Mary call, and for Warren and Lee's sake. A white lie had been told, after they'd asked after their two pet goldfish, and promised them a replacement, next time the rag- bone man came around.

I'd stopped sleeping upstairs and would stay downstairs, fully dressed and always prepared, for the inevitable. I'd sit in the chair next to the window in the front room, with the light off, for living on the end of a row of terraced houses, gave a well- lit view, to the top of the street. It was Terry's fifth night away from home, and half expecting him to stay out again, as it was nearly eleven. I'd fallen into a light sleep, when the familiar sound of his car stopped at the top of the street. A neighbour had recently been parking his car in our usual parking space, as Terry was hardly ever at home. I sat up quickly, as he locked the car door, and braced myself for more trouble.

He could be seen kicking an overcoat, towards our house, panic had started to well up inside, as he kicked the coat nearer the window, so I switch on the light. On opening the front door, I could hear a whimpering, and was shocked to discover, it wasn't an overcoat he'd been kicking, but his mother. He could be heard cursing as he continued kicking her, and injuries looked horrific. But to think I'd watched from afar, the countless kicking she'd endured, without even knowing, made me want to vomit.

Trying to protect her from any more physical abuse, I ran outside and tried to pull him away, but the impact of his shoe as it hit my stomach, caused me to collapse in a heap beside her. Attempting to get up, he suddenly punched me several times in the face and body, causing me to fall to the ground yet again. I looked up in a daze, and as if seeing him for the first time, could feel the badness emanating

193

from his very being. Turning the most handsome man I had ever seen into one of the most -ugliest.

Everything started to go blurred then, as voices could be heard in the distance, it was two of our shocked neighbours, quickly helping us back to Josie's House. Josie's face was bathed and we were given a large brandy, which was well appreciated. They wanted us to make a formal complaint to the police and send for an ambulance, but Josie wouldn't here of it, and I was more worried knowing the children were asleep in bed, and hoping he wouldn't disturb them.

A neighbour took a look later and found the lights to be out and all was peaceful, so giving me some time to sleep on Josie's sofa, for a few hours. She managed to climb the stairs, and go to bed that night, but was bruised badly for two weeks after, and unable to go into work. Apparently, she'd been drinking in the same pub as Terry that evening, and had threatened to tell me of his affair, not realising, I already knew, so the kicking he metered out to her, was his revenge. It was a dastardly act on his part, and as bad as my father could be with his own family, he would never have hurt his own mother.

Maureen, a neighbour living opposite, called in at Josie's at 5.30am that morning. She was on her way to her cleaning job, and saw Terry leave with his suitcase, but she was worried as the children were by themselves. Josie had a spare key, so I was able to return home quickly, and thankfully they were still asleep, at such an early hour.

Looking in the wardrobe and draws, I was relieved to find he'd taken all his clothes. Maybe he'd left for good, through the added embarrassment of what he'd done to his mother, and once sober couldn't possibly face her, let alone - his father.

Nicholas my father in law was of a quite, placid, nature. He was a good husband to Josie and a good grandfather too. He worked regular nights and always made sure Josie had her wages every week and was very comfortable. When he arrived home that morning, and discovered what his son had done to his own mother, he went berserk, and in no time at all, had left the house, looking for Terry, with promises of murdering him, on sight.

Chapter Sixteen.

Through my marital problems, I'd lost a considerable amount of weight- two stone in all, and was barely six stone. Being only five foot, I looked ready to disappear. Terry though, had put on weight through excessive drinking, and being six foot tall, looked a giant in comparison. I'd just finished dressing and captured a glimpse of myself in the full- length mirror. The reflection was of mother in her earlier years, for I was nursing yet another black eye and added bruises to my arms and legs, from the last beating.

Warren was counting his coloured bricks on the bedroom floor and looked fairly contented, considering the violent environment, of which he now lived. He left his scattered bricks once I was ready then happily followed Lee and myself downstairs, for some breakfast and then a bath. How peaceful life would be with just the three of us. It was a Sunday morning, Terry hadn't been seen for days, and assumed he was staying with his new woman. Lee had fallen asleep after his bath, and Warren was building his bricks again. It was all milky warmth, with its added peace and tranquillity, when I suddenly couldn't bear the thoughts of Terry walking through the door to spoil it all, and started to harbour murderous thoughts against him.

I could poison his beans on toast, and watch as he ate each mouthful. The poison would slowly take over and cause him to fall to the ground, in excruciating pain, he would cry out for help, but of course none would come. Soon he'd be eliminated from our lives forever and the fear would evaporate from every bone in my body.

Nice thought, but I couldn't really hurt him, for it wasn't in my nature, and looking to my children. How could I possibly be parted from them, but it wasn't fair to subject them any longer, to live their lives with domestic violence. Mother was brave enough to separate from father at one stage in her life, but was plain stupid, to take him back. Well, I'd made a decision to see a solicitor, and would go through a legal separation and then divorce, and make sure Terry never lived with his children again. Catholic or no catholic, and it went against all my beliefs, but no one was helping me out there. I'd have to go it alone and leave my beautiful home and all our possessions. But material things were suddenly unimportant, and the safety of my children coupled with piece of mind, were first and foremost in my mind.

All murderous thoughts quickly banished, through an urgent rapping on the front door and on opening it, was confronted by two police officers.

'Mrs Veronica Taylor?'... 'Yes!' The older of the officers who spoke, flinched, on seeing my state.

'I'm afraid we have some bad news for you! Your husband Terrance Taylor, is in the Royal Infirmary, he's suffered serious injuries and is asking to see you? If you go to the reception area, they will give you all the necessary information... and what's happened, walked into a door, have you? Best get yourself checked out as well, while your at the hospital.'

I thanked them quickly then closed the door, but suddenly felt excited, while putting on the children's coats. Maybe, just maybe, and if I kept my fingers crossed, he might just not- survive.

I took the children to Josie's home to be cared for, before going to the hospital, and on seeing her, tried to show concern over Terry, for she was beside herself with worry, on hearing the bad news.

Oh my beloved son, and all that rubbish, and after the terrible beating, she'd recently endured off him, too.

I called into the reception area, on arriving at the hospital and spoke to the fraught looking receptionist.

'Its Mrs Taylor... The police have informed me that Terrance Taylor- my husband, has been admitted and I'd like to see him!' The receptionist looked a little puzzled.

'I'm sorry! But Mrs Taylor is already with him and arrived a while since.'

'Well I'm sorry too! But there must be some mistake, I'm Mrs Taylor, and would like to see my husband?' More people started to arrive in the casualty department, causing her to become even more fraught.

'Very well, I'll leave you to sort it out with the nurse on duty. He's in ward four, along the corridor then second on your left!'

My mind was in turmoil as I walked towards the ward, and wandered what on earth was happening. Maybe he'd married again, which wouldn't have surprised me, and would make him a bigamist. It was feasible I suppose, as he'd been disappearing for days on end, and if it were the case. I'd well and truly- drop him in it.

Approaching the ward I looked for a nurse, but none was available, so I walked into the ward regardless and braced myself, on coming face to face, with the other woman in his life. I remained cool calm and collective as she sat on the side of the bed, looking bold as brass, which matched her heavily made-up face and lacquered hair. Terry looked ill, and was totally surprised on seeing me, as I threw his toiletry bag and dressing gown onto the bed, and without bothering to ask how he was, either.

'So this is who you've been spending your time with, when supposedly on one of your courses?' He had the grace to look down and suddenly look embarrassed, as I glanced again, in her direction.

'Your welcome to him, and good luck! Because your going to need it...believe me!' She was staring really hard at this stage, but never spoke a word, and her transfixed gaze along with her well made up face- never faltered.

Leaving the ward, I continued to ignore him, as he called out my name, for I was feeling elated at my findings and felt free for the first time in months. It wasn't too long either, when I discovered the reason why he lay injured in hospital. Apparently, he'd ended the affair and wanted to salvage what was left of our marriage and hopefully make a fresh start. She obviously didn't want it to end, so stabbed him in the back, with the tail end of a steel comb.

What I knew of the situation, he never pressed charges against her, and she'd obviously pretended to be Mrs Taylor, to be allowed into the ward to see him. When he returned home from hospital, I was certain he was still seeing her, but he still had the audacity to

198

bring his suitcase home and stay put. Saying it was for the sake of the children, and if I wasn't happy with the situation- then it was just too bad.

It was only a matter of days, when Nicholas and Terry's paths crossed. There was a terrible row and a fight broke out, and in the middle of the street, of all places. Nicholas didn't care if Terry had stitches or not from his recent injury, and battered his son mercilessly. It seemed we were becoming a source of entertainment for our neighbours too, as they came out onto the street in full force, and being of a placid nature, I desperately wanted out. But Terry got the hiding he deserved, which inevitably caused a rift between them, and causing his father not to speak to him, for quite some months after.

It was more difficult than I'd expected, filing for a divorce, but the solicitor was very helpful and went on to explain. Without something tangible to go on, regarding infidelity, I'd have to wait two years, or even longer for a divorce, should the case happen to be adjourned, in the meantime.

Firstly, I needed to name the 'other woman' to site her in my divorce. Proof of a love child, would be of a tremendous help, or even photos of them together, would suffice, but there was nothing. A legal separation could go ahead, but there could be problems, if Terry decided not to leave, the marital home. After all, it was his name in the rent book, so more than likely I'd have to leave with the children, and even then, he might not let me take them. I felt so dispirited, and almost considered staying put, until the children grew older. But the fear of what could happen anytime, while he was under the influence of drink- spurred me on. After all, it couldn't get any worse, and if it came to the crunch, maybe mother would take us in, until alternative accommodation, could be found.

Mary seemed apprehensive, as I told her of my plan, regarding the other woman, in Terry's life.

199

'You've got more nerve than me! I'll give you that much, and what if he discovers you in the back of the car? He'll more than likely- batter you!'

'Well! Needs must! He's hardly going to give me her name and address if I ask. Is he?' So I've no alternative!'

'Just as long as you know what your doing that's all, and I'll see you about 8.0`clock then, when you bring the children round!' I returned home and made the tea, but couldn't admit to Mary, I did have butterflies in my stomach, with the thoughts of what might be discovered, in the hours ahead.

Terry's jacket hung over the back of the armchair. It was nearly 8.0`clock and time. to spring my plan into action. He was sat listening to the results of the horse racing on the television, and the sound was turned up quite loud, so giving me the chance to surreptitiously take the car keys, from his jacket pocket.

'Won't be long, I'm just calling to see your mother, so watch the children for me?' His gaze never left the screen, on answering.

'Well don't be too long, will yer? I'm going out with Brian, for a game of darts, at 8.30!' Liar' I thought.

It was getting a little dark outside, as I made my way to his parked car. Unlocking the door, I looked inside pretending to look for something, then left the door unlocked, before quickly returning. Terry was talking to Warren in the kitchen while shaving, which gave me the chance to replace the car keys. Having to make my next move, I put on the children's coats over their pyjamas.

'Your mother didn't answer the door, Terry, so I presume she must be taking a nap! I'm going to Mary's for a coffee, anyway, so make sure you lock up after you!'

Ushering the children into Mary's, she gave me a hug. 'I'll be keeping my fingers crossed for you, so good Luck!'

Looking around, all was peaceful and not a soul in sight as I opened the car door and slid in the back. Being of a slight frame, it was easy to hide on the floor between the seats, but hoped he wouldn't adjust the position of the drivers seat, or I'd be crushed. My heart was thumping loudly, on suddenly remembering, I hadn't locked the doors from the inside, and his whistling could be heard at that precise moment, so it was too late. As he opened the car door, he could be heard, muttering to himself.

'Strange! I could 'ave sworn I locked the door? I must be losin' it? It's through her in doors- she's sending me round the fuckin' twist!' He turned the music up, which I was grateful for, and could relax, and breath, more easily. But as he whistled happily alongside his favourite music, and seemingly without a care in the world- I could have happily throttled him.

Knowing the area fairly well, I knew he'd turned left into Dickinson Road. As he drove to the top of the road, he turned the left indicator on, just as the lights signalled for him to stop. At this stage of the journey, he wound the window down.

'Hi darlin! Yer lookin' gorgeous tonight! Do yer fancy goin' somewhere nice for the evenin'?' Some choice words were shouted in response to his offer, as he slowly wound up the window.

'Fuckin' charmin'! Women! They are all the same, every last one of them! I can't think why I fuckin' bother!'

I suddenly thought of something, which I hadn't given any thought to earlier. What if they were going out, she would get into the car and they could drive off, anywhere, it could be miles, and I only had a few pounds for a taxi to get home. Money was tight, as he'd reduced my housekeeping by half, and probably spending the other half on nights out, with her.

He turned right again and drove up Kirkmanshulme lane, then turned right, which brought us into the Gorton area, and with a sharp right turn, the car came to a halt, he then got out and locked the door. Getting up carefully, I could see the front door being opened by her, once he was inside the house, I was able to abandon the car and take note of the name of the street, and the house number.

A cab conveniently came into sight, as I made my way to the main road, and I gratefully got in. But as I started to relax, a familiar silver Capri drew up alongside, as the lights changed to stop. So they were going out after all, and lucky for me, she wasn't quite ready, at that precise moment.

Mary opened the door excitedly.

'Look, what you've made me do? I've bitten my beautiful nails right down! Well, hurry up then, tell me all about it?' After I told her of the hair- raising experience, she came up with a brilliant idea, as to finding out, the other woman's name.

'I did some part-time work last year. It involved knocking on doors and asking if they wanted to sign up for the latest catalogue. Well, I still have the clipper board, and some old forms, so I could call to her house and sign her up - should she be interested.
If not, I'll easily obtain her name from a neighbour, but we'll cross that bridge, when we come to it!'

I thought it a good idea, and the next day we caught the bus, to Gorton. I stayed with the children in the next street, while Mary knocked on her door, but was disappointed, as she got no reply, so called next door, to her neighbour.

'Hello! Would you be interested in signing up for are new catalogue.' The untidy looking woman took Mary up on the offer and signed, as Mary continued to enquire about her neighbour.

'Could you tell me when your neighbour will be home? As I can't get any answer!'

'Pauline works part time at the local café, but she'll be in this afternoon!'

'I see! Well, do you think she'll be interested? Otherwise it'll be a waste of time calling back!'

'Pauline loves her clothes, so I know she'll be interested! Anyway, I'll tell her you'll be calling back then – ta-ra luv'.'

Mary hesitated… 'Oh by the way, what was her full name again?' The woman paused… 'Pauline Slater!'

Mary excitedly told of her conversation with the woman, word for word, but felt a little guilty, as she'd be waiting forever, for her new catalogue. Talk about detective work, we'd have made a great Cagney and Lacey team.

At last, I had something tangible to go on, and had grounds for divorce. Although in those days, there was still a stigma attached to getting divorced, but all the same, citing Pauline Slater, as the other woman, enabled the proceedings, to go ahead. In the meantime I wanted a legal separation but realised, I'd probably have to move out of the marital home, with the children.

I told Terry that same evening, of my decision to end our marriage, and thought it best if he moved out and went to live with her- after all, he spent most of his time there. He appeared unperturbed and thought the whole situation hilarious, adding the fact, that I didn't have the guts to go to a solicitor, in the first place. He was still highly amused as he reached for his car keys and closed the front door behind. There was no reasoning with him, and new he wouldn't leave, until it suited him, he also had the upper hand, for he had money and was able to pay the rent and the household bills. I'd spent my savings, in the weeks he'd given me no wages, so as young as the children were, I had no choice but to get a job. But it was finding someone to look after them, for putting them in a nursery would be phenomenal and would swallow up most of my wages, but would cross that bridge, when I come to it.

Terry came home earlier than expected that evening and surprisingly, with very little drink on him.

'I've been thinkin'! If you've been to see a solicitor, I'll agree to a divorce, but I'll fight for custody of my children!'

I thought as much, he'd been to see her and they'd had a tete-a tete, but expect, she would no more want to take care of my children, than the man in the moon.

Listening to his absurd plans and realising just how immature he really was, I decided not to argue my point and go ahead regardless- with my own.

He never left us, to move in with her, and started giving me some wages. There was a method in his madness of course, for he knew I'd pay the rent, so keeping a roof over his head, should his affair end.

That same weekend, he took Warren and Lee out in the car, saying he was going to the park and they'd only be a couple of hours. It made a change, and was nice to have a break from them all, but they never returned at teatime. I waited for hours but still no sign, and decided he must have taken them to Pauline's for the night. He was obviously giving me an insight to the power he had over them, and how easily it was to take them from under my very nose. I spent the night sat up waiting, and by early morning, was frantic with worry, so decided to call at Pauline's home, to see if they were there. It was the last place I'd ever want to go, but new the children would undoubtedly, be fretting.

Waiting at the bus stop, the familiar Capri could be seen in the distance, and as it approached, Terry stopped. I got in and was relieved to see the children sitting happily on the back seat, eating a chocolate bar, and seemingly unperturbed by the whole incident. We drove home and once indoors, a terrible row broke out. It was the first time I'd ever attacked him, and clawed into his face like a woman possessed, leaving his face scratched and bleeding. Lucky for me, he didn't retaliate, but threatened to take the children whenever, and I wouldn't be able to do a thing about it. He stormed out, holding a hanky to his bloody face, and leaving me with dreaded thoughts of what he might do when returning later, in one of his drunken stupors.

I started sleeping downstairs in the chair, in fear of yet another, abduction. Warren would sleep on the couch and Lee in his pram. I'd wait for Terry's car to drive down the street, which could be early hours or not at all, but never the less, couldn't take any chances. He'd become unpredictable again in his mood swings, and had become obsessed with the divorce, but the thoughts of him trying to take the children away and especially, while under the influence of drink, didn't bare thinking about.

Once the car could be heard, I'd quickly put on our coats. Warrens also had Wellingtons to slip into and Lee would be wrapped

204

up in his blanket. We'd escape by the back door, I'd take the key then we'd stand outside in the ginnel. Warren could be whimpering having his sleep disturbed then suddenly finding himself outside, and in all weathers too. But we'd have to wait until the lights were switched off, and after ten minutes or so, I knew Terry would be a sleep. We'd then go in, for I knew a bomb wouldn't waken him, as he was a heavy sleeper, and of course having no conscience, as to where his children might be.

Warren would take his Wellingtons off at the backdoor, for god knows what he might have stood in, then thankfully return to his sleep on the couch, but he'd be disturbed again at 5.30am, when we'd go to Josie's. Having a key, we were able to stay in her home, until Terry had left for work, then return home, to live peacefully for the rest of the day. It couldn't go, but until there was somewhere suitable for us to live, I had no option. Josie was on my side, and thought it the next best thing, for she couldn't envisage, her grandchildren living with her alcoholic son, let alone- another woman.

Chapter Seventeen.

It was normal on a Sunday in the majority of homes, for the wife to spend her time in the kitchen, cooking the lunch, while her other half spent time in his local. Terry would come home after closing time, have his dinner then fall asleep until early evening, then get spruced up and spend the rest of his time, in the pub.

Mary had called earlier and suggested we all go to the park, for it was a lovely warm sunny afternoon. It was always good to escape for a few hours and hopefully by the time we came back, Terry would have washed and changed and left the house again, for the evening. Little did I know at that moment in time, it would be the last day, we would ever spend in our home.

After washing the dishes, we made our way to Platt Fields, but one of Mary's children took ill, so the afternoon was short lived and we returned home. Just about to put the key in the latch, Jacki one of the hardened prostitutes, living on Walmer Street, situated at the back of where we lived- stopped for a chat.

'I've 'erd all about the way your Terry treats yer, I think it's bloody terrible! Just listen to some sound advice luv', yer want to leave and get out, while the going's, good!' I felt rather embarrassed, to find my private life had eventually reached the ears, of Walmer Street, and told her we were managing okay- regardless. At this stage she proceeded to ruffle Warren's hair, in a friendly gesture.

'Luvly' kid, are'nt yer luv'! I'll be on my way then, as I only nipped out to the shops for some bread and ham, for their teas. Anyway luv' be careful, do yer 'ere me?' She suddenly lifted her hand towards her own hair.

'Bleedin' 'ell! It's started rainin' and I've got all me washin' out on the line, and none of them bleedin' lazy gets, will fetch it in... that's for sure!' But it seemed the rain was only on her and as she looked up, Terry could be seen, urinating out of the bedroom window and in broad daylight- too. She quickly moved away in disgust.

'Well yer dirty bastard! You've just pissed on me fuckin' 'ed!'

The floor could have opened and swallowed me up, for I'd never felt so embarrassed. He'd recently, been urinating more frequently in the early hours as well, and in the wardrobes, of all places. I'd moved our clothes into the wardrobe in the spare room, but the house had taken on an unkempt smell and all the cleaning and air-fresheners, couldn't remove it.

Terry looked down, and on seeing Jacki, started shouting abuse.

'Fuck off yer hoar! Get back on the streets, where yer fuckin,' belong. It could easily have turned to fisty cuffs, as Jacki clenched her fists, ready for action.

'Get down 'ere? I'll knock seven bells out of yer! I'm not fuckin' frightened of yer...come on yer bastard!'

Terry closed the window, leaving Jacki seething and drenched in urine.

'I'm tellin' yer luvvy! Piss him off, he's no good, and if he touches yer again, I'll come round and sort him- good and proper!'

It was all very nice, her taking my side but at the end of the day, she didn't have to face him when he was drunk, and it was me who had to live with him. With all the commotion and Terry upsetting Jacki -of all people, it brought the neighbours out in force, so I shamefully ushered us into the house and closed the front door, behind.

I left Lee in his pram and put him near the window, while I gave Warren a biscuit and then started the tea. Terry came down stairs and seated himself in his favourite chair. I took a glimpse of him from the kitchen, and could see by his expression, he was spoiling for a fight, but sat down in the chair opposite with Lee on my knee, regardless. Still not a word was spoken, so adding to the already tense atmosphere

Warren moved towards his toy box and just as well, for in the next instance, Terry picked up a large glass ashtray at his side, and threw it in my direction. Within seconds, I'd seen it coming, covered Lee's head and ducked, as it made a huge dent in the wall, before smashing to the floor in smithereens. Poor Warren stood rooted to the spot in fear, as Terry got up from his chair, picked up his car keys and at the same time threatened to kill me, later that evening.

It was the straw that broke the camels back, for he really didn't care if the children got hurt in his violent attacks, and suddenly felt lucky I'd had quick reflexes, for god only knows what could have happened.

I put Lee in his pram and carried Warren upstairs, while I packed a case. Any personal belongings went into a carrier bag then jackets were put on. Lee was put in his trolley along with his feeding and changing equipment, and I closed the front door behind, and was only ever to return once, to sort out some furniture. I didn't call at their grandmothers to say goodbye, for his car was still in the street and he might have called in to see her, which would have only provoked more trouble.

We stood at the bus stop on Wilmslow Road and boarded the first bus into town. Warren sat near the window, still traumatised, and wandering where we were going next. I gave him some chocolate, and reassured him we'd be fine from now on. Lee was a good baby and slept through it all. Staring through the window, still dazed, and trying to take in the reality of the last hour, I couldn't believe I'd actually left the marital home, for good.

We eventually reached the town centre and alighted, the bus. Time was passing and it was now 4.pm. I stood in the centre of Piccadilly bus station, with suitcase in hand, two children by my side and nowhere to live. Strange, but I was feeling really happy, happy in my knowing, I would never have to go home to face his bullying tactics again. That thought alone, gave me an inner strength, to cope with any crisis that should come my way, for the nightmare was over and there'd just be the three of us. I'd be in charge of our lives from now on, and wherever we slept that night, knew we'd sleep peacefully, for the first time in months.

There was a crisis looming that very moment, where could we stay? There was our James, but there wasn't much room in their small maisonette. I couldn't go to mother for I still had my pride and besides, Terry would probably follow us there and cause her trouble and she'd had enough of that, in her own lifetime. Well I could only think of Linda and Tommy, I was sure they would put us up for at least a night, so we boarded the bus to Wythenshawe. The children were happy to be going, for they and loved their aunt and uncle and still do... to this very day.

When we arrived on their doorstep, they were surprised but not shocked on seeing us, for they could see it coming and new the marriage was heading for the rocks.

They made us very comfortable and we stayed for a week. Linda wouldn't hear of us paying any board for staying, but any money I had was dwindling. Having to look for new accommodation each day swallowed up most of it, and it looked like we might have had to stay on another week, when I decided to visit the Social Security and explain my predicament.

While waiting to be interviewed, I got chatting to a lady sitting nearby.

'So your looking for somewhere to live then? Only I know of somewhere, if you need accommodating immediately! It's my mother's house in the Chorlton area. I'm waiting for it to be sold, but in the meantime its remains unoccupied and has been, for about a year. Your welcome to live there and it would help me too, for its becoming cold and damp. It needs that lived in feeling, and would appear more homely, should a potential buyer want to look round!'

Being desperate for somewhere to live, I readily accepted and took her name, phone number and made arrangements to meet her the following day. Linda thought it all sounded okay and it wasn't too far from where she lived.

Marion picked us up in her car the following day, to view the house, and it turned out to be a neat three bed-roomed semi, situated on a quiet road. It was nicely decorated inside and fully furnished, but its musty smell combined with another strange smell, couldn't be placed, at that moment in time.

We moved in the following day, but had to be said. It was like living in paradise in comparison to Coburg Place and at last, we were able to sleep peacefully, at night. Warren loved the house and ran riot each day, from room to room, never being used to so much space, and sensed I was happy too, which reflected in his daily life.

Marion arranged to collect the rent each Tuesday morning, but as she was about to leave after her first call, she asked an unusual request. If warren should be playing like children do, and happen to find anything unusual, for instance- money, would I phone her immediately, for she assumed her late mother had hidden money in various places around the home, and she had little success in finding any of it, after she'd died.

Windows were opened in every room, and air freshener sprayed, but still the unkempt smell remained. We'd been living there for a month and hadn't seen any neighbours to talk too, when Warren went out into the back garden to play football, and accidentally kicked the ball, into next doors garden. The neighbour came out immediately to have a word, after seeing it roll into her beautiful flowerbeds, but was quite nice about it, all the same, as I apologized for any damaged caused. We soon got chatting about one thing and another, when she happened to comment on the length of time we'd lived in the house, for many people had moved on, in previous months, but their stay was always short lived. Intrigued, I delved a little further, and was to be told the interesting story of her friend and neighbour, of the past thirty years.

'Else Storman, had brought her son and daughter up more or less on her own, as Mr Storman died of a heart attack, in his early thirties. They weren't a particularly close family, and when the children were old enough they moved out, leaving Else to live alone, but she became lonely, as they very rarely visited.

Some years later, after retiring, she became ill through lack of a healthy diet, for it consisted only of oranges and packets of crisps. Apparently some years earlier, she'd bought a potato pie and while eating it, discovered a large rusty nail, of which put her off food, apart from crisps, because they were out of a packet, and oranges, which provided her with vitamin c. I'd invited her for many a meal, hoping to coax her into eating healthy again- but to no avail.

I went on holiday for ten days and on returning, called on Else, but there was no reply, I kept a spare door key, so let myself in. That first sight will haunt me forever... and that smell. Apparently, she'd fallen downstairs, it was a bad fall and she'd lost a considerable amount of blood, which had spattered the walls, banister and carpet. She didn't die quickly either, and was to lie there unaided for a few days, before eventually dying.

She wasn't neighbourly with anyone- apart from myself, so no one particularly missed her. I phoned her daughter Marion immediately and the police, then the badly decomposed body was removed.

That same night Marion returned with her family, they switched on every light then turned the house over, from top to bottom, supposedly looking for money. They searched every nook and cranny and even taking up floorboards, but nothing was found- except for a few pounds in her purse. When they eventually looked under her bed, they discovered a suitcase, but were disappointed to find, it was crammed with empty crisp packets and green mouldy orange peel. It was some weeks later, when they returned to clean the bloodstains off the walls, but try as they may, it wouldn't come off, so they ended up having to redecorate the landing. Marion was keen to sell the house, which was left to her and her brother, for it was the only possession left to them in their mother's will. They were shocked to discover, she'd left the rest of her money to a-cattery, probably on purpose, for the way they'd treated her, while she was alive. Potential buyers had viewed the house in previous months, much to Marion's delight, but it was the smell- that was off putting!'

I must have taken on an insipid look as all colour, drained and by all accounts hadn't gone unnoticed.

'I hope I haven't unnerved you dear, for there's nothing to be afraid of! As our poor Else, wouldn't hurt a fly!' I stood listening, while absolutely stunned, but at the same time feeling uneasy. Warren was pulling at my skirt, to let me know his brother was

211

crying, but I hadn't heard him, so left my somewhat interesting yet scary neighbour, to quickly rush indoors.

We stayed on for a couple of months after hearing the tragic story, for it was still a hundred times better, than living with Terry, but never felt happy or comfortable again, after my findings, and to top it all. Each time Marion called for her rent, she'd ask if Warren had found any money, and when the answer was still the same, she would look on, suspiciously. I mentioned this, on one of our visits to mother, so she suggested if we weren't happy, we could move in with her until after Christmas, which was only a matter of weeks away. Terry had long since given up, calling round to mothers house and was convinced we weren't living there, so he'd be none the wiser as to our whereabouts, so undoubtedly there'd be no trouble, and decided take her up, on her generous offer.

Our Catherine had turned the parlour into a bed-sit, so were able to share her room, and all managed to live quite comfortably for the time being. I'd left the front door key on the kitchen table, alongside a note for Marion, before leaving, and thanked her for helping us out, when most needed.

Two weeks into the new-year and it was time to move on. The situation at mothers was far from idyllic, with its lack of space and the odd bit of tetchiness creeping in. Warren had contacted German, Measles, which had caused more work for her, as she helped nurse him until he recovered. Once up and about though. Warren, thought it great fun to pull the toilet chain, at every opportune moment, which drove her to distraction.

It was Sunday afternoon, so after lunch, I wrapped Warren and myself up nice and warm then went out to look for some new accommodation. We boarded a bus, which took us to Stockport Road, Longsight. It was a good a place as any to browse, for there were newsagent's dotted around on every street, and countless adverts in their shop windows. Just about to look in the first window, I stopped to adjust Warren's scarf, and happened to glance up at a bus going in the opposite direction, to the Gorton area. A chill ran down my spine, as Terry could be seen seated on the top deck. Thankfully he was reading a paper, so hadn't noticed, for there was no doubt, he'd have come after us and there'd have been ructions, especially has he hadn't seen Warren and Lee for over five months. But he didn't deserve such a privilege, not after the last despicable act, regarding the glass ashtray, so he just wasn't safe to be around the children, in my eyes. It was unusual though, to see him using public transport, maybe he'd been banned from driving, which was no bad thing.   Seeing him again, made me realize just how lucky we really were, and were now far happier, without him.

Scanning the adverts in the second newsagent's window, one caught my eye of a considerable interest.

'Housekeeper required to live in! Children welcome!' I jotted down the name and address, and remembered seeing the street name a little earlier, so thought I'd call there and then, and find out what it all entailed.

I knocked at the door of the large terraced house, as a pleasant looking dark haired man answered, presumably in his late forties, and smiled in a lascivious manner. I enquired as to the job advertised, and if it was still available. He nodded and invited us inside the nicely decorated hallway, as he was about to introduce himself, two young girls of about eleven years old, skipped passed, down the hallway.

He held out his hand in a friendly gesture.

'I'm Sam Turner and the girl with the dark hair, who just passed- is my only daughter, Jeanette!' As he continued to show us round, I explained our present situation. He then considered for a moment.

'If you decide you like the place! I can't think why you can't move in immediately?' That brought music to my ears, as we continued into the lounge, of which was clean, spacious, and comfortable. The bedroom was light and airy too, and had a cot, situated next to the double bed, which would be ideal for our Lee.

We continued into the kitchen, but were surprised to see a jam tart, thrown up against the sidewall. He smiled on seeing my puzzled expression then went on to explain.

'That was our Jeanette! She threw it at me last night! Well… It can stay there as far as I'm concerned, because I'm not cleaning it up!' He suddenly looked a little embarrassed. 'Sorry! I hope that's not put you off, wanting to live here?'

I saw the funny side of it, and decided there and then to accept the job, and was about to tell Mr Turner of my decision, when I unexpectedly slid across the floor, on a slice of Jeanette's crushed jam tart, and suddenly wished there was another jam tart on hand, that I too, could throw up against Mr Turner's kitchen wall. For at that moment in time, it would have done me the power of good.

He went onto explain, he worked down the pit and didn't arrive home till late in the evening, so needed someone to take care of Jeanette, when she came home from school. A cooked meal each evening and a warm homely atmosphere, had been lacking, since her mother left some years ago-to live with another man, so the idea was put to him by a work colleague, to advertise for a housekeeper.

The children gradually settled into a regular routine at Sam's and Jeanette was really good with them. So in all, it was working out quite well.

There was still the furniture to sort out in my old home and thought it a good a time as any to call, while Terry was out at work. Most of the time he lived at Pauline's, so there was a good chance the coast was clear. I took the children along, to see their grandparent's and later called in to see Mary. She had mentioned previously, when discussing my furniture, that it would be okay to store some in her spare room. I wasn't taking much anyway, just the sideboard, couch, pictures and the dining table and chairs. Terry was welcome to the rest.

While talking with Josie, her friend Edna happened to call in, just as we were talking of leaving the furniture for another time, for Nicholas wasn't home and I needed him to help move the furniture out. Edna's husband Paul was home though, and she suggested it would be no trouble for him to help, and I could store the furniture in their home, as they had more space than Mary.

I took the key off Josie, and walked up to my old home. On opening the door, the stale smell of cigarette smoke was overpowering and noticed the smashed ashtray was still on the floor, after all those months. Next to it, was our wedding album, he'd torn it into shreds, and expect it was just one of his cynical ways, of letting me know- should I happen to return, that our marriage, was well and truly over.

I wheeled Lee's pram out first, just as Edna and Paul walked over to help. They in turn helped carry the dining suite and sideboard over to their own house, along with the couch. I was really grateful for their help and told them, I'd probably collect the furniture in about six months. Hopefully by that time, we'd have found a home of our own.

We were happy at Sam's and the children took to him, he'd read them stories and on the odd occasion, he'd take us for a day out, to Bellvue Zoo, or the cinema. We'd been there for some months, when one evening, when the children were in bed, and we were watching television, Sam had a word regarding our situation. Had it not come to my notice for instance, that he'd grown fond of me and wanted the relationship to flourish and become that of a couple. I was quite taken aback and recoiled at the very thought. But apart from everything else, I had regarded him- as a father figure.

My answer was a definite. 'No!' But he didn't seem too surprised at the time, and we carried on as normal, but I could tell by the tense atmosphere, that he'd had time to dwell on it and was none too pleased. So eventually he asked us to leave, whenever suitable accommodation could be found.

Next day I packed our cases, and ended back on mother's doorstep. She was none too pleased either, as she herself was having problems with my father again, and this would only add to it. So we could only stay for a few days, in our Catherine's room.

I did stress the fact, if Sam should call, to say I wasn't there, as I was getting pretty fed up, with everything.

215

Early hours the next morning- we were disturbed, by someone knocking impatiently on the front door, my father had gone to work and we were still in bed. Mother opened the door, after faffing about for ten minutes or more, to find Sam on the doorstep, looking very distraught.

'Hello Mrs Neill! I'm sorry to disturb you, but is your Veronica at home? Only I want a word!' I'd got out of bed and peeped through the lace, but on seeing Sam, jumped back under the bedclothes.

'I'm sorry Mr Turner, but I haven't seen her for some time!'

'Well, if you should see her, will you tell her she's welcome to come back? I won't push the issue, any further- she'll know what I'm talking about, and the last thing I ever wanted to do, was upset her!'

Listening to mother, having to lie through her teeth, and knowing she would be really cross, once he'd gone. Set Catherine and myself off laughing and by the time she came into our room, we were near to hysterics, under the bedclothes. Once the front door closed, she was in our room in seconds and not being in a good temper at the best of times- let alone first thing in the morning, went berserk.

'Well really! Having to lie to such a nice, decent man, I felt awful! You could do a lot worst in life, than live with Sam... believe me! Well, I'm bloody sick of the lot of you! What with you, your kids and now your bloody father! I've just about had enough, so you'd better start looking for somewhere else to live...today. Do you hear me?'

'Yes I heard? But if you think I'm going to live with Sam, as a couple, just to keep a roof over our heads-your very much mistaken! So I'll start looking elsewhere, after breakfast.'

Catherine looked after the children, while I made yet another trek, having to scan various newsagents, windows. One advert caught my attention, it wasn't too far away, in the Moss side area, and children were welcome. I boarded the next bus, and it wasn't

216

long before I was discussing with my new landlady, when we could move in.

It was a cramped room, consisting of a double bed, a wardrobe and a table and two chairs. A gas meter stood in the corner, and a two-shilling piece had to be used for a couple of days gas, but by the end of the week, I knew someone had been in our room, while we were out, and emptying the meter. We had to share the kitchen and bathroom with the other tenants, and when we needed to use the bathroom, I'd take along a bottle of bleach, to make sure the toilet was clean, for the children to use- it was a total nightmare.

The children were very unhappy, being pushed from pillow to post and my unhappiness, obviously reflected theirs, which didn't help matters any. We'd be up earlier each morning and out by nine, and always remembering to put any personal belongings, in the back pocket of Lee's trolley. I'd then spend most of the day looking in shop windows at adverts, looking for somewhere else, to live.

Strange really! Living in Moss side, for it was my birthplace, and one day we took a walk to the house where I was born. It didn't compare of course with the photos I'd remembered, but that was quite some time ago. I can remember mother telling us, the house was owned by a doctor, apart from his family we were the only other family living there. But through her marital problems spilling over into their household, they were happy when she'd found a new home in Wythenshawe.

After a tiring day, we made our way back to our room. Being out all day caused the children to be tired, so after tea, they were ready for their bed. We didn't have a television or a radio, so I'd read a book, with the side lamp on, until ready for retiring myself. The odd time though, I would be distracted.

Our room was back to back with some private dwellings and looking from our window gave a view into their lounges. It reminded me of the film. Room with a view. The family opposite would sit around in the evenings in front of a blazing fire, watching television, and all appeared nice and cosy. On a Sunday morning, they could be seen putting on their best hats and coats in front of the mirror, probably going to a church service. It appeared to be two daughters and their parents. In all- it seemed a nice happy family unit, and making me long even more, for us to be in their position, at sometime in our lives.

On this particular morning, I happened to look, down into the back yard. I hadn't taken much notice before, but for some days I'd heard dogs whining. The landlady was hanging out her washing, I stretched a little further and she caught my eye and waved. I was about to move away, when two dogs could be seen, they'd obviously moved from another position. They were chained up, and to my horror could see they were emaciated, then one being so weak, fell to the ground and started whimpering.

I reached for our coats immediately, and in on time, had phoned the R.S.P.C.A. They reacted to my call quickly, as I couldn't stress enough, how urgent it was, to rescue those poor pathetic animals. The dogs were eventually taken to a vet, and onto a dog's home.

The landlady new I'd reported her and was none to pleased, she was upstairs in minutes, hammering on my door and telling me to leave the flat by weekend, for she didn't want a spy living in her household. As far as I can remember, in those days, tenants didn't have the same rights, as they have today. So if you were asked to leave, there was nothing more you could do over the matter.

Fate must have played a part in our lives that day, for after reporting those poor pathetic dogs, which inevitably lead to our eviction of the flat, I made a quick decision to change our plans for the morning, by taking a different path. It was to define our lives forever, and lead us to a place, where I would happily bring up my children, and still live to this day. I have sometimes wandered what would have happened to our lives-otherwise.

Chapter Eighteen.

It was a warm spring morning, and as we made our way to the shops, I didn't relish the thoughts of yet another tedious day, looking for somewhere else to live. The misery was etched on Warrens face, as he had to walk the same distance as myself, so on the spur of the moment, I decided on a change of scenery.

Taking a sharp right towards Platt Fields, I purchased some sandwiches, fruit and orange juice, from the nearest grocery store, and told Warren we were having a picnic in the park. It made his face light up and made me feel a whole lot better, too. We turned into another side street, when suddenly a car drew up alongside. As the driver wound down his window, he called out my name.

'Hello, Mrs Taylor! It's been along time, since I last saw you?' I turned, and was confronted by my old landlord from Coburg Place. He'd always been interested in the children, having grandchildren of his own, and smiled at Warren and Lee, as he continued to chat.

'I only found out recently from your mother in law, that you'd moved away, so where are you living now?'

Not wanting to go into any great detail of the past months, I went on to explain. I was looking for some new accommodation and a change of scenery, for it was really cramped and not very pleasant where we were living at present. He paused for a moment.

'If your really desperate for somewhere to live, I know of a two bed-roomed terrace, its one in a block of terraced houses I used to own, in the Bellvue area. Apparently the area is due for demolition, in the coming months, but you can look it over, if you wish!'

My mind was reeling and it must have shown.

'You don't have to look so worried dear! It's not going to fall down around your ears. Although I have to add you wouldn't be paying rent, so you'd be classed as a squatter, for the house has recently been taken over by the council. But it would be your own front door for a week or two, and giving you time, to find somewhere else to live!' He started rummaging through his briefcase.

'In fact, I'm sure I still have a set of keys!' He eventually handed them to me and wished us luck in the future, before finally driving away. I was never to see him again.

We spent the afternoon in the park and the children enjoyed their picnic. It was quiet, so giving me time to mull over the last few hours, as everything seemed to have happened so quickly, but then doubts, started to cloud my thoughts. The consequences to face, for living in a house due for demolition and not paying rent, was alone terrifying, but the added thoughts of nowhere to live by weekend, spurred me into action.

Clearing up after our picnic, I then freshened up the children in the ladies toilets. They were both very tired, so I managed to fit them both comfortably in the trolley, it was still early afternoon, and as we walked out of the park gates, I could feel the keys given to me, by my old landlord, jangling in my jacket pocket. Without a second thought, I decided to take a look at the house, and boarded the next bus to Bellvue.

It was quite a long street and number107 was situated at the very end. Its grubby lace hanging from the dusty windows, stood out, in comparison to the rest of the resident's shiny windows. Putting the key in door and opening it, we found ourselves in the lounge, and on trying the light switch, found the electricity hadn't been turned off. A large sofa stood against the back wall, but the rest of the room was void of any furnishings. The kitchen was large, but again, no appliances. But looking out into the back yard, two bags of coal could be seen, so at least a fire could be made and there'd be no problem cooking a meal. Looking in the cupboards, I found some clean crockery, alongside some pans, and decided there and then, this would be a good a place as any to live for the time being, and it would be private too. Upstairs were two bright spacious bedrooms. We hadn't any beds, but would manage sleeping downstairs on the sofa for the time being, and would collect our furniture from Edna's house and buy two beds, on a weekly credit system, the following day.

On our way back to the flat, we called to see Josie. It was late afternoon, but I knew Terry would still be at work, so found it safe to be in Coburg place. She had some bad news for us though, for Edna and Paul had moved away from the street, that very morning, along with my furniture. Josie was out at work, so hadn't a clue where they could have moved too. They'd obviously bided their time, and waited till the coast was clear, so they could take my furniture, along with their own.

So we had no furniture, and would have to start from scratch. Josie was concerned we had no beds, so took us to the nearest furniture store and purchased two singles, along with a dining table and chairs. Her kindness will always be remembered.

Money was needed to buy towels bedding and curtains, so I sold my wedding and engagement ring and without any qualms, for I was happy to see the back of them. We moved into our new home the next day, and later were sat in front of a blazing fire, which I'd managed to light by using spells- as my mother used to call them, for they always worked for her. Wrapping plenty of sheets of newspapers up tightly then tying them in a knot, gave sufficient heat beneath the coal, to set it alight.

We snuggled up happily that night on the large sofa, with Warren and Lee at one end, and myself at the other- then all fell into a much needed, sleep. I hadn't bought a clock, but Lee always awoke early, so it didn't really matter, but somehow, all managed to sleep through till late. A concerned neighbour, disturbed us with her knocking on the side window, and on opening the door, she introduced herself.

'Hello! I'm Dawn from next door! Is everything okay? Only it's ever so quiet and its past ten. It's just that I noticed you have two children and you know how rowdy children can be- first thing. I've got two lads of my own and their up by six every morning! Anyway! When you've got time, call in for a coffee and a chat, and the kids can play together and can get to know one another!' I thanked her and decided to take her up on her offer, later that day, for it was nice to see a friendly face.

We called in later, and Dawn was to enlighten me, as to what was happening in the near future, regarding the area in which we lived. She was looking forward to moving to a new house with a garden back and front, but more than likely it wouldn't be for a year. For the council were really slow, as they most often were- regarding a new project. If they said six months you could guarantee another six months would be added on. Secretly, the news made me feel a little more secure and would give me more time, to find a new home.

Our furniture was to be delivered the following weekend, but in the meantime, we slept on the sofa. After a couple of days though, the children started scratching their heads, and so did I. I looked through their hair and to my horror, found they had head lice. But we'd caught something else too, which was of a much greater concern. I had a word with Dawn and she took us to her local G.P. We were able to register with him, and on examining us, he diagnosed, Scabies. He went on to explain, it was due to having dirt in the home, which caused the complaint. I was quite offended by his remark, and assured him I was very clean and hygienic, but had recently moved into some old property and had been sleeping on a sofa, left behind by the last occupants. He advised me to throw it out immediately and disinfect and bleach every room. Evidently germs and such like, can live in furniture for quite some time.

Dawn was very good and helped to clean the house from top to bottom and allowed us to stay in her home, until it dried out. That same day, nit lotion was applied to our head, but using the lotion on the children's bodies for scabies, proved to be a nightmare, as it burned their skin for several minutes, causing them to scream out in pain. I'm sure the neighbours thought they were being murdered, for by the end of the week, I'd be lucky to catch either of them, as they hid under the table for dear life, but the dreaded lotion had to be applied-nonetheless.

Once the furniture was in our home, it started to look more comfortable, although floors remained bare, apart from a fireside rug, Dawn had given to us. She remained a good friend while we lived in the street, and her kindness, will always be remembered.

222

Finishing some household chores, before treating the children to day out at their Aunty Lynes, I had unexpected visitors, Josie and Terry- of all people. Josie assured me there would be no trouble, as Terry pushed passed and made a beeline for his children. Fear welled up inside as I watched him excitingly pick them up as he very pleased to see them. I had warned him previous to this visit, I didn't want any infringement in our new life, but he just smiled and asked if it was possible to make arrangements to see them again, in a couple of weeks. Terry assured me he wouldn't do anything stupid again by taking them away over night without my permission-,either. I couldn't believe Josie could be so stupid as to let Terry know where we were living, and knew once again we would have to find somewhere else to live in the near future. We would never have any peace of mind, otherwise.

Terry had mentioned he was going away on a business trip for a couple of weeks but on returning would contact me to make arrangements to see the children. The children then gave their grandma and dad a hug then warren ran outside to play with his friends, Josie and Terry left soon after in a taxi. On the surface Terry seemed okay, but I knew he was secretly in his eliment at finding out where we were living, and would once again stir up trouble when it suited him.

The divorce was months away and there was still nothing tangible to go on, apart from the other womans name and address. As far as I knew Terry was still living in Coburg Place, so they werent living together, as such. Two weeks went by and Terry never called to see the children. It was a Bank Holiday Monday, and Dawn suggested we go out for the day, maybe Bell-Vue. Her husband worked away frequently and so she was on her own with her children. We ended up having a great day out and the children really enjoyed themselves, having fun rides, and eating Candy Floss. The children were happy but exhausted so we decided to call it a day, the evening was drawing in and we just wanted to relax and watch some telly. Dawn said goodbye as she put her key in the door, as I was approaching our front door and use my key, I noticed something was wrong. The front door was ajar and I could have sworn I'd shut the door when we left for our day out. Dawn could see from her door that something was wrong and quickly made her way to ours. We both gingerly entered the house, then the lounge, and were shocked to find, I'd been broken into. It wasn't long before I put two and two together and realising the culprit was Terry. He'd put a brick through the back window and climbed through, then venting out his anger and smashing the kitchen to pieces-similar to his outburst at Coburg Place. Dawn took the children into her home to stay over for the night, while I called in the police. As I waited, I took in the distruction before me. Debris was every-where, food was thrown around the floor, and he'd torn up our wedding album, and cut up pictures, including treasured photos of my children. The draws were turned out and my family allowance book had been taken. All the money I had left to see me through the rest of the week had gone, and there was nothing left in my purse after treating the children to a day out at Bell-Vue. The police, they couldn't do much either, unless Terry physically harmed me, but advised me to take an injunction out against him, immediately, nonetheless.

So I was back to square one, enduring sleepless nights and whenever venturing out, wandering what fresh hell awaited me on returning home.

When I think back I should have given Store Street a wide-birth, for Pauline Slater only lived streets away. I hadn't given it much thought though, being desperate for somewhere to live with the children, for they were first and foremost in my mind.

The following day after the break in, I went to the local post-office to report the theft of my Family Allowance book but so engrossed at the time explaining the unusual circumstances surrounding the theft, I didn't take much notice of Warren trying to attract my attention, and pointing to a lady in the queue. It was only when we leaving did I take note and was shocked to see, it was Pauline Slater and very heavily pregnant too. She hadn't noticed Warren or myself, but once outside, my mind started to reel. At last I had some -thing tangible to go on regarding my divorce, although it couldn't be proven as yet that Terry was actually the father of her child, but would certainly find out in the not so distant future. I had an appointment with my solicitor that same week and explained to him my findings. It's feasible he assured me, but I would have to wait till the baby was born and registered and hopefully in Terry's surname, and would have to visit Sunlight house with a letter from my solicitor, for a copy of the birth certificate and only then could I proceed with our divorce, and file for adultery.

I'd taken Dawn into my confidence over the months I'd been living in Store Street, so she knew a fair bit about my marital problems .It was Dawn that kindly lent me some money till my money was sorted out too. When telling her of my seeing Pauline Slater, surprisingly she knew of her. This particular morning Dawn called in for a coffee. "Do you want to hear a bit of local gossip?" I smiled and nodded interestingly. "Go on then, lets here a bit of scandal." She could hardly contain herself as she chatted on. "You'll never guess who I saw this morning, and pushing a pram." I couldn't think properly through her over all excitement " Pauline Slater, that's who!" Our Sarah went over to take a look at the baby, and apparently, it's a girl, and only two weeks old. So it looks like at last, you have your evidence for continuing your divorce"

It was like music to my ears, and just couldn't believe my luck, for it seemed the last piece of the jig-saw had finally fallen into place.

On the next visit to my solicitor and explaining the possibility that Pauline Slater could have given birth to Terry's child in the last couple of weeks, I was handed a letter to take to Sunlight House to obtain a copy of the birth certificate. Should Terry's name be confirmed on it of course, well thereon, I would have my divorce through earlier. Mary accompanied me the next day and Dawn looked after the children. We went into the reception area and handed over the solicitor's letter, then waited nervously for her return. Within moments she returned with the copy of the child's Birth Certificate. Sure enough Terry's surname name was on it .They named her Emily Louise Taylor.

225

The necessary information was returned to my solicitor, and within weeks a date was set to attend court.

When the long awaited day finally arrived, I wore my one and only grey suit and black stillhettoe shoes, then applied my make-up carefully, which made me feel better and give myself a bit of confidence, which was so lacking.

Arriving at court, I seated myself next to half a dozen other fraught up women, while their husbands sat opposite. It was an emotional time to say the least for most of us, and you could have cut the atmosphere with a knife, as couples looked to each other with obvious feelings of contempt. Terry turned up late as usual, with only a little time left before proceeding into the court room. He was in a fowl mood to say the least, which didn't help any. Surprisingly he didn't seat himself next to the other husbands, and so sat next to me.

Once comfortable he whispered threats in my ear, about beating me up outside the court room, later, which absolutely terrified me. As one of the clerks to the justice passed by, terry cursed him quietly. I hate all bastard judges, as well.

We were all called to the courtroom together. Once seated we all had to listen to each other's case in turn. Some were far worse than I'd ever encountered, while living under the same roof as Terry. Eventually it was my turn to take the stand, I felt really nervous as I had to take an oath on the bible. One of the first questioned asked of me was

."Did your husband ever swear in front of you, while living in the marital home?"

"on many occasions"

"When was the last time you heard your husband swear?" I hesitated at first, with thoughts of should I or shouldn't, which in the past had always caused me problems one way or another, for I could never make my mind up which would be the best way out.

"Actually, It was not long since outside in the corridor" I answered. The judge looked towards me thoughtfully.

"What were his very words, and I might add you must be truthful, as your under oath"

"My husband said" "I hate those bastard judges!" The courtroom was in uproar, as I looked across at Terry, with his head bowed down and hands covering his face. The judge was looking none too pleased either and looked on a little po-faced, while ordering everyone to be quite immediately, before continuing his questioning regarding other aspects of the irretrievable breakdown of our marriage.

I left the courtroom soon afterwards, relieved it was all finally over, and secretly pleased I'd dropped Terry in it. Serve him right, I thought, for breaking into my home and destroying everything. Maybe it would teach him a lesson in the future, to leave well alone.

That same evening,there was an urgent knocking on the frontdoor, I'd just finished bathing the children and was putting on their pygamas, ready for bed. It was a terrible cold night and lashing down with rain outside. A dreadful feeling of apprehension came over me. Could it be Terry wanting his revenge, after all? I looked through the lace curtain gingerly and to my surprise, it was Pauline Slater. I quickly opened the door and beconed her in as she held her new baby in her arms. By her side were two other young children drenched through with the rain.

"I know you must be shocked, me turning up like this, and I won't stay long, it just I have nowhere else to go, till Terry goes out, but I just want some advice " She was obviously traumatised and upset and I noticed she was nursing a black eye.

I took the coats off the two children to dry out on the fireguard in front of the fire, then made a hot drink of chocolate for them and gave them a biscuit. I did notice at one stage and wandered how the children all got on so well as they sat together watching televsion, when it suddenly dawned on me, they already knew each other well through obvious reason, relating to the past few years. I made some coffee then, for the two of us, my mind in a quandry, as to what my next reaction to her turning up so unexpectedly on my doorstep, might incur. Warren and Lee were then put to bed, and once settled I sat down on the opposite chair to Pauline, as she continued giving her baby her undivided attention. I was focusing hard before carrying on the conversation, where I'd left off, but instead, let her explain her awful situation, first. She was shivering and for a fleeting moment I felt sorry for her and the predicament she was in, when I suddenly corrected my feelings, and realising why my children and myself were living like were today, and in absolute fear. All because of Terry and this woman before me, and their total selfishness, yet I couldn't send the children home straight away on such a filthy night, after all it was not their faults.

"Its Terry you see, I'm terrified of him,even the children have to be careful what they say or do in front of him. Last night he threw a glass of whisky in my face, I couldn't see for several minutes, as it stung badly, but I had our Emily on my knee" I noticed she had the grace to look away for a second, on saying . "Our Emily" " Terry then took her from my arms and put her down in her cot, he then beat me sensless. Our David and Ruth ran outside absolutly terrified. Terry seems to have changed since I had the baby and for the worse, I might add." Tell me about it ,I thought.

While she nursed the baby for a while, I couldn't help but think he'd treated us both the same, and beat his own mother too. Using his bullying tactics,and leaving a trail of broken women, and children behind. After tending to her baby she carried on from where she left off.

" I want to know how you managed to get rid of him out of your life? If I can't get rid, I'm going to Blackpool to live with my mother, because I now fear for all our lives"

"So what advise do you want from me" I asked frostily.

"Well, you don't have any trouble from him now, do you" I looked at her for some moments in utter amazement. Could it really be the same woman before me, who with the help of my husband, had between them wrecked my marriage and caused so much devastation and heartbreak for my family. How desperate was she now, to have the gall to ask my advice on how to get rid of that very same man. On answering I couldn't help but let a bit of bitchiness creep in.

"Let's hope he eventually meets a woman similar to your- self because it didn't matter to you when you started the affair that he was a married man with two children, to take care of. Well I really can't help you, except to suggest, you move away-maybe. Not that it will help much, because he will only find you, like he always finds us. Even though were now divorced and I have a court order out against him, I don't feel safe and can never answer the door, without feeling both fear, and apprehension." She removed the children's coats from the fire- guard and put them on, then made her way to the front door.

" I should never have called here as you have been through a great deal of hardship as well as heartbreak, and I do understand why you are so bitter. I will take you up on your advice though and move away to Blackpool. It will be a new start for the children and be a lot safer. Maybe you should do the same!" I will stay with a friend tonight as I don't relish the thoughts of staying under the same roof as Terry another night, and the children will be safer." The children waved goodbye and looked a little happy knowing they were going to live with their grandma. But what the future held for us all-god only knew. I did hear some days later that Pauline Slater had moved on, but as far as they new Terry was still living in her house which somehow left a churning in my stomach ,when realising I was living to near him and maybe it was are turn to move on too, and quickly.

We were never to see or hear from Terry for over a year, seemingly he'd moved in a new woman and was getting on with his life –thank god.

We'd been living in Store Street for just over a year, when a letter arrived which I'd been dreading. It was about us squatting at the property and had to leave immediatly. Well, I did want to leave immediatly if that was possible,as I'd been to the Town Hall when first arriving in Store Street and explaining my situation and offering to pay rent, even though it was unfit for human habitation. I stressed the fact I'd had my name down on the housing list for some time now, and wanted to move away a soon as possible in the interest of my children, and move away from my ex-husband. "Someone wouil be in touch in the very near future to discuss my case, but no one ever called. We was'nt eligible for a new house now , anyway so it looked like I was back to square one.

For the first time of being on our own, I started to feel panic set in. It was my own fault, for I'd lapsed into a comfortable mode, after Dawn mentioning the fact, that we might have some extra time to stay in the area. Well, there was no alternative left, but to call in at the town hall and take it from there.

We sat in the housing office alongside other would be hopefuls and their unruly children. It was almost lunchtime and Warren and Lee were getting restless, although they were under control, not like some children, who were running around wild and totally out of control. Eventually my name was called out, and soon found myself seated in front of a stern matronly looking housing assistant.

Mrs Cullen was not happy at the fact I'd moved into the house in the first place and made it patently obvious I had been in the wrong to do so- even though I had offered to pay rent. At this stage, the children were getting tetchy, and I in turn, felt the panic rising, for the second time that day, so without a second thought, sat the children on her desk.

'Here you can look after them! I've just about had enough of the lot of it!' With those last words, I rushed from the office and away from the shocked stares of the onlookers, as I made my way quickly, downstairs.

'Mrs Taylor! Haven't you forgotten something?' I was immediately stopped at the main entrance by a member of staff, but knowing I would have returned for the children, once I'd calmed down, I followed him back up to the office.

Lee always had a marred look about him as a baby, and looked even more so, as I walked in the room. 'Oh mummy, don't leave me! Oh mummy, don't leave me!' Taking them both off the desktop, Lee was soon made comfortable in his trolley and Warren sat on my knee, as Mrs Cullen took a sudden keen interest in my case.

'Well! What was all that about? If you want to leave your children, by all means please do, but not on my desktop!' She continued to take two sets of keys from her draw.

'I'd already reviewed your case earlier in the week, but because of your impulsive act just now, left me little chance, to explain!' She went on to hand me the two sets of keys.

'The addresses are on the tags, so chose which house you want, then return the key, which will not be required!'

I accepted the keys gratefully, and the following day viewed the first house. It was situated in the knutsford area, which was quite a journey on the train, and seemed miles away from anywhere, but that same afternoon we took a look at the house in Denton- it was perfect. A two bed-roomed terrace, decorated throughout and close to all amenities.

Next day the spare key was handed in to Mrs Cullen, and that same week we moved in to our new home. The children's names were registered in the nearest junior school, something I'd been concerned about for some time, and Warren was able to start immediately. It was our first real home and happily settled into the neighbourhood, and remained for some years.

I am a much stronger person today, and know I would never be attracted to a man like Terry again, and have a feeling of confidence, which I never had before. Our divorce finally came through and he had access to the children. But most importantly, we had piece of mind and a sense of freedom. Safe in the knowledge, we could look to the future- tentatively maybe? But at last a fresh new start.

Family Update.

James my eldest brother is happily married and has two grown-daughters and is also a granddad.

My younger brother now lives in Australia, and is happily married, they have no children.

My sisters, Anne and Jane, sadly passed away, and my youngest brother John, also passed away.

My youngest sister Catherine, is married and has a grown-up daughter, and is now a grandmother.

Acknowledgements.

To Barry- my inspiration.

To my children Warren, Lee, and Hayley.
To my precious grandsons, Phillip and Jay and also to family and friends.

<u>Veronica Neill.</u>

Printed in Great Britain
by Amazon